WITHDRAWN

WordPress® Web Design

FOR

DUMMIES®

A Wiley Brand

2nd Edition

by Lisa Sabin-Wilson

FOR
DUMMIES®
A Wiley Brand

WordPress® Web Design For Dummies®, 2nd Edition

Published by: **John Wiley & Sons, Inc.**, 111 River Street, Hoboken, NJ 07030-5774, www.wiley.com

Copyright © 2013 by John Wiley & Sons, Inc., Hoboken, New Jersey

Published simultaneously in Canada

For general information on our other products and services, please contact our Customer Care Department within the U.S. at 877-762-2974, outside the U.S. at 317-572-3993, or fax 317-572-4002. For technical support, please visit www.wiley.com/techsupport.

Wiley publishes in a variety of print and electronic formats and by print-on-demand. Some material included with standard print versions of this book may not be included in e-books or in print-on-demand. If this book refers to media such as a CD or DVD that is not included in the version you purchased, you may download this material at http://booksupport.wiley.com. For more information about Wiley products, visit www.wiley.com.

Library of Congress Control Number: 2013942776

ISBN 978-1-118-54661-1 (pbk); ISBN 978-1-118-54637-6 (ebk); ISBN 978-1-118-54663-5 (ebk); ISBN 978-1-118-54654-3 (ebk)

Manufactured in the United States of America

10 9 8 7 6 5 4 3 2 1

Table of Contents

Part II: Choosing the Right Tools 65

Introduction

*W*ordPress is the most popular content management system (CMS) on the web. Users of the WordPress platform can easily publish their content on the Internet because of its intuitive user interface. A large segment of the WordPress user community wants to delve a bit deeper into the platform so that they can not only publish content but also make their websites look fantastic by designing, customizing, and manipulating their WordPress themes. In fact, as a WordPress designer and consultant myself, two of the most frequent questions I hear from my clients are "How can I design my own theme for WordPress?" and "How can I design and build my entire website with WordPress?"

WordPress Web Design For Dummies, 2nd Edition, answers those questions and unlocks the mysteries of designing websites with the WordPress content management system. If you have ever tried to tweak an existing WordPress theme file, or even design your own WordPress theme from scratch, and have found it to be intimidating or too difficult to understand, this book breaks it down for you in a friendly and easy-to-understand manner.

About This Book

This book starts by walking you through the basics of understanding and setting up WordPress so that you can

- ✔ Understand the fundamental difference between a blog and a website.
- ✔ Define what a content management system (CMS) is.
- ✔ Explore different ways that websites use WordPress.
- ✔ Get to know WordPress basic requirements.
- ✔ Explore web- hosting recommendations.
- ✔ Install WordPress on your web server.
- ✔ Discover ways to publish and manage your content.

In this book, you also discover the right tools to use for publishing and designing with WordPress, including tools that help you

- ✔ Write and edit code.
- ✔ Transfer files from your computer to your web server.
- ✔ Create, edit, and design graphics.
- ✔ Choose colors schemes and fonts.
- ✔ Plan your design strategy.

WordPress Web Design For Dummies, 2nd Edition, also addresses issues related to web design by walking you through some basic design skills, such as understanding and designing with Cascading Style Sheets (CSS) and HyperText Markup Language (HTML). You also explore basic design concepts, such as color, typography, and layouts.

Finally, this book wouldn't be complete without in-depth information on using the WordPress technology to create dynamic websites. I introduce templates and themes and explain how to use WordPress template tags to create great features. I show how to use WordPress to build all sorts of websites, such as small business sites, e-commerce sites, photo galleries and portfolios, real-estate sites, social communities and discussion forums, and more.

Foolish Assumptions

I made a few small assumptions, and one very large one, about you while I wrote this book. I want to get the large one out of the way immediately: You already know how to use WordPress.

Yes, that's right — this book doesn't show you how to use the WordPress software to publish posts, create categories, or use the Dashboard, for example. I assume you have that knowledge already and you've been working with WordPress for at least a few weeks. My other book, *WordPress For Dummies,* is a fantastic companion to this one because it takes you, starting with step 1, through all the steps you need to know to use WordPress. If you feel you may need a review or a solid introduction to the WordPress software, pick up a copy of that book too.

I also assume you use the self-hosted version of WordPress that you down-loaded from the official WordPress website at http://wordpress.org. The other version of WordPress, the hosted service at http://wordpress.com, is *not* compatible with the extensive theme customizations and plugin usage and installations discussed in this book. In fact, the hosted service that WordPress offers at http://wordpress.com is *not* covered in this book.

Other assumptions I make about you include these:

- ✔ You're interested in finding out how to tweak and/or build a WordPress theme. This includes aspects of graphic design, CSS, and HTML.
- ✔ You have a domain name and a hosting account, or you will set them up very soon, as described in Chapter 2. (You can't use the hosted WordPress.com service to accomplish everything I present in this book.)
- ✔ You're a savvy Internet user, and you can use the Internet to search for information, download files, and browse websites and blogs.
- ✔ You have a basic understanding of what blogs are and how people use them to communicate their thoughts and content on the web.

Icons Used in This Book

Icons are those little pictures in the margins of this book that emphasize information that I think you may find helpful, that may be a danger to be aware of, that's aimed for techies, or that's a point to remember. Those points are illustrated as follows:

Tips are little bits of information that you may find useful — procedures that aren't necessarily obvious to the casual user or beginner.

When your mother warned you, "Don't touch that pan — it's hot!" but you touched it anyway, you discovered the meaning of the word *"Ouch!"* I use this icon for situations like that.

You don't need to possess a PhD in computer programming to understand how to build websites using WordPress; however, occasionally the information presented in this book can inch a little more into the geeky side. That's when I use this icon.

This icon is self-explanatory — I use it next to information I want you to remember and possibly come back to later.

Beyond the Book

To supplement the content in this book, you can find extra content online. Go online to find the following items:

- **Cheat Sheet:** At www.dummies.com/cheatsheet/wordpressweb design, you'll discover WordPress tools and resources, how to use HTML and CSS to customize your theme, how to select image-editing programs for your web design projects, and how to find several resources for WordPress themes.

- **Dummies.com online articles:** At www.dummies.com/extras/wordpresswebdesign, you'll discover great add-on web design tools for the popular Firefox browser, explore the commercial WordPress theme offerings available on the web today, learn how to optimize your WordPress website for search engines, and discover ten great free themes that you can start using on your WordPress website today!

- **Updates:** Occasionally, Wiley's technology books are updated. If this book has technical updates, they'll be posted at www.dummies.com/extras/wordpresswebdesign.

Part I

Establishing a WordPress Foundation

In this part . . .

✔ Get an overview of the concepts of WordPress web design, including the basic requirements needed to design with WordPress.

✔ Discover how to install WordPress on your web server.

✔ Explore the different types of content that can be published with WordPress.

✔ Build a solid starting point for designing your website with WordPress.

1

Exploring Web Design
with WordPress

In This Chapter

▷ Comparing blogs and websites

▷ Introducing WordPress as a content management system (CMS)

▷ Understanding ways to publish content with WordPress

▷ Discovering WordPress free and premium theme options

*W*hen you discover that you can build and design more than just a blog with WordPress, you begin to realize the potential of the software and how you can apply it to your website-building efforts. For me, the light bulb went off in 2005 when my clients came to me wanting more than a blog on their sites. Many of them ran small businesses and needed to add other features to their websites, aside from the chronological display of the blog posts they'd been publishing.

This chapter introduces you to the concept of using WordPress as a content management system (CMS). You find out what CMS really means and see how you can apply it to your own website-designing efforts. You also discover what types of content you can publish with WordPress software and how you can leverage that content to build dynamic websites.

Additionally, this chapter introduces you to the world of WordPress themes — what's currently available for you to use right away, what you can tweak to your own liking, and what you can research and dig through to discover more about WordPress design and theme building. You find out which themes are free for the taking and which themes cost you money to use. (*Hint:* The free ones are the best ones to practice with because there's no cost to you!)

This book deals *only* with the *self-hosted* version of WordPress that you download from the official WordPress website (http://wordpress.org). You can't fully customize and use WordPress as a CMS, as described throughout this book, if you use the *hosted* service at WordPress.com (http://wordpress.com). The names (and domains) are so close that it's easy to confuse them, so the basic rule of thumb is this: If you did *not* install the software on a web-hosting account for your own domain, you're using the incorrect version of WordPress.

Delving Into the Differences between Blogs and Websites

If you read the introduction to this book, you know that I assume you already know how to use WordPress to publish content on the web. Therefore, you're likely already aware of what a blog is and can recognize one when you encounter it on the Internet.

But just in case, a *blog* is typically a chronological listing of blog posts (or articles) that you (as a blogger) have published on the web. Often, having only a blog on a domain suits many people just fine — these people are referred to as bloggers, because they blog; that is pretty much all they do on their domain.

Figure 1-1 shows you what a typical blog looks like with the display of blog posts in one column and navigation links and menu items in a smaller column to either the left or the right side.

Blogs have predictable features that you can assume exist, including

- A chronological listing of blog posts
- Blog posts archived by date, category, author, and *tags* (microcategories)
- A commenting feature that invites readers to leave comments on blog posts
- RSS (really simple syndication) feeds for posts and comments that get syndicated in RSS feed readers like Feedly (`http://feedly.com`) or Bloglines Reader (`www.bloglines.com`).

You can build a website with WordPress as well; however, it encompasses so much more than just having a blog on your domain. Many websites built with WordPress, such as business or corporate sites, don't even have a blog. Other websites have blogs, but they're not the main focus of the site. Several types of sites, such as business sites, have more content and features than just blog posts to offer visitors, and WordPress allows you to have both a blog and a full-blown website.

Figure 1-1: My personal blog at `http://lisasabin-wilson.com/`.

 When designing a website, you need to sit down and map out which of the many WordPress features you're going to use, as well as decide how and where you're going to use them on the site. Chapter 8 takes you through planning your design strategy — don't miss it!

My business website, WebDevStudios (`http://webdevstudios.com`), is a good example of using WordPress as a content management system (CMS) to design and create a small business website. For instance, in Figure 1-2, you see that the front page of my business website doesn't look anything like a traditional blog; however, if you look near the top, you see a link to the blog.

You can manage and maintain several sections of your website through the use of one installation of the WordPress software on your web-hosting account, and create the visual look and design/layout of the site through manipulation of the WordPress theme templates. (I introduce themes later in this chapter.)

Figure 1-2: My business website is powered by WordPress.

I have a blog on my business website, but it's secondary to the other content I display there, including

- A front-page portal that displays content from several sections of my internal website pages
- A design portfolio of work (http://webdevstudios.com/work-portfolio)
- Frequently asked questions that readers can browse to get more information on my design services
- A page of client testimonials
- Specific pages that outline the company's services, terms, and privacy statements
- An e-mail contact form that allows readers to get in touch
- An order form that gives visitors the chance to submit a request for services

The chapters in Part III of this book give you the information you need to work with and create WordPress theme templates, and Part IV provides solid information about design concepts like CSS and HTML that help you put your entire WordPress theme together for your own unique website design.

My business site, shown in Figure 1-2, is just one example of a type of website that can be built with the WordPress software, with or without a blog. Figures 1-1 and 1-2 illustrate some basic differences between a blog and a website. This book concentrates on website design overall, not just blog design (although all concepts presented in the chapters in this book can be applied to both).

Using WordPress as a Content Management System

A term that you'll hear regularly in the WordPress community is the term *CMS*, which stands for *content management system.* Whether you run a blog, a website, or both, you use WordPress to manage your content by publishing and editing it regularly.

When WordPress was first released in 2003, it became well known, worldwide, as the most popular blogging platform available on the web. That is still the case; however, as WordPress development has evolved over the years, it has grown from a blogging platform into a full-featured content management system that allows you to publish all sorts of content types to the web with very little technical ability or skill. Because you install WordPress on your web server, and you access the back-end controls — the *Dashboard* — via a web address, it's considered a web-based content management system.

You may be asking yourself how a blogging platform, which allows you to publish content on the web, differs from a web-based content management system. The two seem to be interchangeable, and some say it's just a matter of semantics. You'll find that in the WordPress community, *content management system* refers to the ability to easily publish different types of content using one installation of WordPress. More than just a blog, you can build and design a website that includes different content types, including (but not limited to)

✔ **E-commerce:** Host a store, or marketplace, to sell your products and services directly on your website. Figure 1-3 shows a website called IconDock (`http://icondock.com`), which is a great example of WordPress being used as an e-commerce online store.

Figure 1-3: IconDock is a website that uses WordPress to power its online storefront.

- ✔ **Photo gallery or portfolio:** Create and publish photo galleries or an online portfolio of design work, creative pieces, or photography, for example.

- ✔ **Discussion forum:** Host a forum on your website where visitors can create new and respond to existing threads of conversation with other site visitors, based around topics of shared interest.

- ✔ **Social community:** Create an integrated social community on your WordPress site that allows visitors to create profiles, groups, and forums, enabling them to interact with other visitors on your domain.

- ✔ **Small business:** Create an entire website for your business that includes *static pages* for content that doesn't change all that often (FAQ pages, terms of service, and sales pages, for example). You can decide to have a blog on your business site, or no blog at all — WordPress lets you do both.

- ✔ **Forms:** Create and include forms on your website to allow your visitors to get in touch with you directly from the pages on your domain. You can use forms as e-mail communication tools or sales tools, or to conduct surveys to gather feedback from your readers and/or clients.

- ✔ **Social media integration:** Gather the content that you publish on other networks like Facebook or Twitter and integrate it into your website using different techniques and plugins available for WordPress.

Open source and the GPL

WordPress is an open-source software project (OSS); therefore, the base code that powers the WordPress software is open and available to the public for you to view, read, learn from, and maybe even apply to your own projects. Additionally, WordPress is licensed by the GPLv2 license from the Free Software Foundation (http://www.fsf.org/). A copy of the license is included in every installation of the WordPress software, if you care to read it. Basically, the GPL license gives anyone the ability to view, copy, and re-release or redistribute the code without any legal consequence. This concept applies to themes and plugins, as well. That makes them an accessible tool to learn from, and because the software is free, it makes your education free (and priceless). Understand that any theme you create using WordPress must also be released under the GPL license; because they use the WordPress core code as a foundation, your theme projects automatically inherit the GPL license.

The preceding list is just a sampling of the different types of content that you can publish and manage using WordPress as a CMS rather than as a blogging platform only. Be sure to check out Chapter 18 for some other real-life examples of websites that use WordPress as a CMS.

To include these different content types on your website, in some cases — such as with e-commerce and social communities — you need to install special *plugins,* or scripts, that extend the feature set of the WordPress software. And in certain cases like discussion forums and photo galleries, you need to account for these different content types in your WordPress theme design as well, through the use of template tags, CSS, and HTML. Part III of this book (Chapters 9 through 13) takes you through what you need to know for creating WordPress themes and templates, and Chapters 15 and 16 give you some great ideas for techniques and plugins you can use to create different features and content types on your WordPress-powered website.

Discovering the World of WordPress Themes

WordPress *themes* are simply a group of files, called *templates,* which determine the look and basic function of your site. Literally thousands upon thousands of free WordPress themes are available for you to choose from. WordPress has an official Themes Directory on its website at http://wordpress.org/extend/themes (shown in Figure 1-4).

Additionally, you can browse, download, and install free WordPress themes from the comfort of your own WordPress Dashboard. All the themes that you find in the official Free Themes Directory are also accessible within your Dashboard by choosing Appearance⟡Themes and then clicking the Install Themes tab, as shown in Figure 1-5. (See Chapter 9 for the lowdown on installing themes.)

Figure 1-4: The official WordPress Themes Directory.

Figure 1-5: Browse thousands of free WordPress themes from your Dashboard.

WordPress themes that appear in the official directory are fully checked out, vetted, and approved for listing by WordPress. With this theme review, you can feel comfortable knowing that the theme you're using meets the guidelines that WordPress has put in place for quality control.

It's possible that you'll find exactly what you're looking for in a theme using one from the Free Themes Directory; however, you and I haven't even met, but I know something about you based on the fact that you're reading this book. You want to learn how to tweak, customize, and create your own WordPress theme by learning and applying the skills necessary to do that. Free WordPress themes are a great place to start, especially themes from the official WordPress Free Theme Directory. The free themes from the directory contain all the standard features that users expect from themes, so they make an excellent starting point in your learning process. That's right, I said it! Open up one of those themes from the free directory and start reading, learning, and applying the code you find there to themes that you create for yourself, your friends, or your clients.

Typically, it would be a big no-no to tell you to copy work from another person; however, that is *exactly* the spirit of the WordPress community, and the spirit of open source and the GPL (General Public License) that WordPress (and its themes and plugins) is released under (see the "Open source and the GPL" sidebar). In fact, Chapters 10 and 11 take you through the steps of doing just that; Chapter 10 walks you through the (free) default WordPress theme called Twenty Thirteen, and Chapter 11 dissects the template files. Chapters 12 and 14 take you through template tags, and how to customize their look and design with CSS and HTML coding.

Checking Out Premium WordPress Themes and Frameworks

Not all WordPress themes are created equal; that is to say, not every WordPress theme you encounter is free. GPL-licensed software, like WordPress and related plugins and themes, is not always free, as in price. Several years ago, a premium theme market emerged within the WordPress community by developers and designers who offer high-quality themes and provide ongoing support for the use of those themes for a price that ranges anywhere from $50–$300 each, depending on which theme you use.

Many of the premium-theme providers offer special themes that they've termed *frameworks.* Frameworks are essentially WordPress themes with all the built-in features and functionality and are optimized and coded to act as a parent theme, making WordPress theme development quicker and allowing you to use it to create an unlimited number of child themes. I cover parent and child themes in depth in Chapter 13; you can head there now to read more about those topics, or file the terms "parent/child themes" in the back of your mind, knowing that you revisit those concepts later in this book.

Premium themes and frameworks offer you an easy way to help yourself, your friends, and your clients design a nice-looking website quickly using WordPress for a lower cost than it would take to hire someone to design and build a custom theme for you. Premium themes have their limitations, as well, however; because someone else built the theme, you are limited to the features and functions that the developer/designer of the theme included. If you want to add additional features, it may mean digging into the code of the template files and making some adjustments. (Later in the book, you find information on how to tweak existing themes.)

Sometimes it's better to code your own theme from scratch, simply because it's easier for you to know your own code than it is to get to know someone else's way of doing things. After you become comfortable designing your own theme, the choice is yours to make.

You can find a very nice selection of premium themes on the WordPress website, listed at `http://wordpress.org/extend/themes/commercial`. Here are some popular theme frameworks on the market today:

- **iThemes Builder:** `http://ithemes.com/purchase/builder-theme`
- **StartBox:** `www.wpstartbox.com`
- **Hybrid:** `http://wordpress.org/extend/themes/hybrid`

Getting Your Site Up and Running

Before you can even think about building themes and designing with WordPress, you have to lay the foundation. Doing so doesn't take very long, but it involves setting up the right environment and gathering some essential tools to get the job done right. Setting up WordPress correctly the first time is important because having to set it up all over again after you've already begun using it is quite a hassle. In the first part of this book, you'll find the steps to get WordPress up and running, including:

- Registering a domain (see Chapter 2)
- Obtaining a web host (see Chapter 2)
- Installing WordPress on your web server (see Chapter 3)

Then after you're up and running, be sure to check out Chapter 4 for the low-down on managing content and Chapter 5 for more about FTP and different web browsers.

2

Understanding WordPress Requirements

In This Chapter

▶ Registering a domain name

▶ Exploring web-hosting environments

▶ Understanding bandwidth and hard drive–space needs

*T*his chapter introduces you to the basic requirements that need to be in place before you can install WordPress on a web server (as described in Chapter 3). I take you through the mechanics of registering a domain name, exploring web-hosting environments, and determining a plan for different WordPress projects in terms of bandwidth needs and hard drive–space options.

If you design WordPress websites for several clients, each client has unique needs for web hosting, depending on the type, scope, and breadth of the website it runs. This chapter helps you take all those factors into consideration to determine the type of hosting environment needed for the job.

Establishing Your Domain

You've read the hype. You've heard the rumors. You've seen the flashy websites powered by WordPress. But where do you start?

The first steps toward installing and setting up a WordPress website are making a decision about a domain name and then purchasing the registration of that name through a *domain registrar,* a company that sells and administers domain names. A *domain name* is the *unique* web address that you type in a web browser's address bar to visit a website — for example, wordpress.org and google.com.

Domain names: Do you own or rent?

In reality, when you "buy" a domain name, you don't really own it. Rather, you purchase the right to use that domain name for the period of time specified in your order. You can register a domain name for one to ten years. Be aware, however, that if you don't renew the domain name when your registration period ends, you lose it — and most often, you lose it right away to someone who preys on abandoned or expired domain names. Some people keep a close watch on expiring domain names, and as soon as the buying window opens, they snap up the names and use them for their own websites, hoping to take advantage of the popularity that the previous owners worked so hard to attain for those domains.

I emphasize *unique* because no two domain names can be the same. If someone else has registered the domain name you want, you can't have it. With that in mind, you may need to take a bit of time to find a domain that isn't already in use.

Understanding domain name extensions

When registering a domain name, consider the extension that you want. The .com, .net, .org, .info, .tv (for video), .fm (for audio), .co, or .biz extension that you see tagged on to the end of any domain name is the *top-level domain (TLD)* extension. A top-level domain is the main domain name of a website, whereas a second level is a subdomain, or subdirectory, within the main domain. For example the main, top-level domain for Wiley is wiley.com; whereas Wiley's Online Library is located on a second-level domain: onlinelibrary.wiley.com. When you register your domain name, you also choose the extension you want for your domain (as long as it's available, that is).

A word to the wise here: Just because you register your domain as a .com doesn't mean that someone else doesn't, or can't, own the very same domain name with a .net. So if you register MyDogHasFleas.com and it becomes a hugely popular site among readers with dogs that have fleas, someone else can come along and register MyDogHasFleas.net — and run a similar site in the hope of riding the coattails of your website's popularity and readership.

You can register your domain name with all available extensions if you want to avert this problem. My personal website, for example, has the domain name http://lisasabin-wilson.com; however, I also own http://lisasabin-wilson.net.

Considering the cost of a domain name

Registering a domain costs you anywhere from $10 to $30 per year, depending on what service you use for a registrar and what options (such as privacy options and search-engine submission services) you apply to your domain name during the registration process.

After you pay the initial domain registration fee, you need to pay another fee when the renewal date comes up again in a year, or two, or five — however many years you choose to register your domain name for. (The length of time you register your domain is up to you, but if it's a domain you're planning to use for a long time, most registrars will give you a slight discount on the price if you register it for more than one year.) Most registrars let you sign up for an auto-renew service to automatically renew your domain name and bill the charges to the credit card you have set up on that account. The registrar sends you a reminder a few months in advance telling you it's time to renew. If you don't have auto renew set up, you need to log in to your registrar account before it expires and manually renew your domain name.

Registering your domain name

Domain registrars are certified and approved by the Internet Corporation for Assigned Names and Numbers (ICANN). Although hundreds of domain registrars exist, the ones in the following list are popular because of their longevity in the industry, competitive pricing, and variety of services they offer in addition to domain name registration (such as web hosting and website traffic builders):

- **GoDaddy.com:** `http://godaddy.com`
- **Register.com:** `http://register.com`
- **Network Solutions:** `http://networksolutions.com`
- **NamesDirect.com/Dotster:** `http://namesdirect.com`

At this time, GoDaddy.com, shown in Figure 2-1, is probably the easiest and most cost-efficient way to register a domain name. At the time of this writing, GoDaddy.com currently has domain name registration starting at $9.99 per year.

Enter domain name to check availability.

Figure 2-1: GoDaddy.com provides an easy, low-cost way to register a domain name.

No matter where you choose to register your domain name, here are the general steps to do so:

1. **Decide on a domain name.**

   Doing a little planning here is necessary. Many people think of a domain name as a *brand* — a way to identify their websites or blogs. Think of potential names for your site; then you can proceed with your plan.

2. **Verify the domain name's availability.**

   In your web browser, enter the URL of the domain registrar of your choice. Look for the section on the registrar's website that lets you enter the domain name (typically, a short text field; refer to Figure 2-1) to see whether it's available. If the domain name isn't available as a `.com`, try `.net` or `.info`.

3. **Purchase the domain name.**

Follow the domain registrar's steps to purchase the name using your credit card. After you complete the checkout process, you receive an e-mail confirming your purchase, so be sure to use a valid e-mail address during the registration process.

After completing these steps, you need to obtain a hosting account, which I cover in the next section.

Some of the domain registrars have hosting services that you can sign up for, but you don't have to use those services. Often, you can find hosting services for a lower cost than most domain registrars offer; it just takes a little research. Check out some of the web-hosting providers I list in the "Finding a host that provides WordPress features" section, later in this chapter.

Finding a Home for Your Website

After you register your domain, you need to find a place for it to live — a *web host* — before you begin working with WordPress.

In the following sections, I cover the different features that web-hosting providers usually offer with a basic hosting account, as well as some recommendations on hosts that include support for the WordPress platform. Additionally, I provide you with some suggestions on how you can determine how much hard drive space and bandwidth you may need for your website.

Examining what services web hosts offer

A *web host* is a business, group, or individual that provides website owners with web-server space and bandwidth for file transfers. Usually, web-hosting services charge a monthly or annual fee — unless you're fortunate enough to know someone who's willing to give you server space and bandwidth for free. The cost varies from host to host, but you can obtain quality web-hosting services from $3 to $10 per month to start. (See the next section of this chapter for a list of some recommended hosts that specialize in WordPress.)

Think of your web host as a garage that you pay to park your car in. The garage gives you the place to store your car *(hard-drive space)*. The host even gives you a driveway so that you, and others, can get to and from your car *(bandwidth)*. The garage owner won't, however, fix your rockin' stereo system (*WordPress or any other third-party software application*) that you've installed — unless you're willing to pay a few extra bucks for that service.

Hosting services generally provide (at least) these services with your account:

- **Hard drive space:** This is nothing more complicated than the hard drive on your own computer. Each hard drive has the capacity, or space, for a certain amount of files. An 80GB (gigabyte) hard drive can hold 80GB of data — and no more. Your hosting account provides you with a limited amount of hard drive space, and the same concept applies. If your web host provides you with 10GB of hard drive space, that's the limit on the file size that you're allowed to have. If you want more hard drive space, you need to upgrade your space limitations. Most web hosts have a mechanism in place for you to upgrade your allotment.

  For a new self-hosted WordPress website, you don't need much hard drive space at all. A good starting point is 3–5GB of storage space. If you find that you need additional space in the future, you can contact your hosting provider for a space upgrade.

  Websites that run large files — such as video, audio, or photo files — generally benefit from more hard drive space compared with sites that don't involve large files. Keep this point in mind when you sign up for your hosting account. Planning now will save you a few headaches down the road.

- **Bandwidth (transfer):** Bandwidth is the amount of data that's carried from point A to point B within a specific period (usually only a second or two). To break it down: I live in the country — pretty much in the middle of nowhere. The water that comes to my house is provided by a private well that lies buried in the backyard somewhere. Between my house and the well are pipes that bring the water to my house. The pipes provide a free flow of water to my home so that everyone can enjoy their long, hot showers while I labor over dishes and laundry, all at the same time. Lucky me!

  The very same concept applies to the bandwidth available with your hosting account. Every web-hosting provider offers a variety of bandwidth limits on the accounts it offers. When you want to view my website in your browser window, the bandwidth is essentially the pipe that lets the data flow from my well to your computer and appear on your monitor. The bandwidth limit is kind of like the pipe connected to my well: It can hold only a certain amount of water before it reaches maximum capacity and won't bring the water from the well any longer.

  Your bandwidth pipe size is determined by how much bandwidth your web host allows for your account — the larger the number, the bigger the pipe. A 50MB bandwidth limit makes for a smaller pipe than a 100MB limit.

Web hosts are pretty generous with the amount of bandwidth they provide in their packages. Like hard drive space, bandwidth is measured in gigabytes. A bandwidth provision of 10–50GB is generally a respectable amount to run a website with a blog.

- **Domain e-mail with web mail access:** The host allows you to have an e-mail address that has your own, unique domain name.

- **File Transfer Protocol (FTP) access:** FTP gives you the ability to transfer files from your computer to your web-hosting account, and vice versa. (See Chapter 5 for the lowdown on FTP.)

- **Comprehensive website statistics:** View detailed information on the traffic that your website receives on a daily, weekly, monthly, and annual basis.

- **MySQL database(s):** This is the database system that WordPress uses to store your data. (See Chapter 3 for information on installing WordPress and using a MySQL database.)

- **PHP:** PHP is the programming language that WordPress is built on.

Because you intend to run WordPress on your web server, you need to look for a host that provides the current recommended, minimum requirements needed to run the WordPress software on your hosting account, which are

- PHP version 5.2.4 (or greater)
- MySQL version 5.0 (or greater)

The easiest way to find out whether a host meets the minimum requirements is to check the FAQ section of the host's website, if it has one. If not, find the contact information for the hosting company and fire off an e-mail requesting information on what exactly it supports.

Finding a host that provides WordPress features

Web hosts consider WordPress a *third-party application;* therefore, the host typically won't provide technical support for WordPress (or any other software application) because it isn't included in your hosting package. However, several web-hosting providers have WordPress-related services available for additional fees.

The popularity of WordPress has given birth to services on the web that emphasize its use. These services include WordPress designers, WordPress consultants, and — yes — web hosts that specialize in using WordPress. Many of these hosts offer a full array of WordPress features, such as an automatic WordPress installation included with your account, a library of

WordPress themes, and a staff of support technicians who are experienced in using WordPress.

Here's a list of some of those providers, each with their own packages, pricing models, and features:

- **Page.ly:** `http://page.ly`
- **WPEngine:** `http://wpengine.com`
- **ZippyKid:** `http://zippykid.com`

To find out whether your chosen host supports WordPress, always ask. As a WordPress user, you can find WordPress support in the official forums at `http://wordpress.org/support`.

A few web-hosting providers offer free domain name registration when you sign up for hosting services. Research the way a hosting provider handles domain registration and read its terms of service because that free domain name may come with conditions. Many of my clients have gone this route only to find out a few months later that the web-hosting provider has full control of the domain name and they aren't allowed to move that domain off the host's servers, either for a set period (usually a year or two) or for infinity. It's always best to have the control in *your* hands, not someone else's, so try and stick with an independent domain registrar, such as Network Solutions.

Planning for future needs

When it comes to bandwidth and hard drive space for website hosting, take into consideration what type of website you're building. Whether for yourself or a client, do everyone a favor and plan ahead to avoid potential problems down the road.

Different types of websites use more bandwidth, hard drive space, and server resources than others. You need to consider the type of traffic the website gets now as well as how much you expect it to get over the course of the next several months. When you think about building additional features on your site, consider the amount of hard drive space (storage) you'll need to store the files and data, and the amount of traffic (bandwidth) required to manage it. For example, a photo gallery or portfolio will require storage for large image files and a good amount of bandwidth to handle the transfer of the large image files from your web server to your visitor's browser; therefore, consider that when calculating hard drive storage space and bandwidth.

If you want to build a social community (see Chapter 16 for information on building/designing a social community with the BuddyPress plugin), there are several other factors to consider because the traffic of your community members will be much more regular. And if you set up the community to allow members to share photos and videos and participate in discussion forums, the hard drive space needed to do that will increase by quite a lot.

Know your site and develop a plan to make sure you have the hosting requirements accounted for and in place — this will save you many headaches down the road.

Being cautious about offers of unlimited space and bandwidth

A lot of hosting providers are out there, and it's an extremely competitive market — trust me. I want to caution you about those hosting providers that offer unlimited packages, though. Basically, for a certain cost per month, you get unlimited bandwidth transfer and unlimited hard drive space (along with unlimited domains, databases . . . pretty much unlimited everything!). This isn't to say that the hosts that do this aren't good ones. But, a popular school of thought says that there's no such thing as unlimited. What you need to do when you encounter these offers is to read the hosting provider's terms of service. Pay particular attention to what they have to say about server resources, or more specifically, CPU (central processing unit that executes the web server) resource usage.

Although these hosting providers may offer unlimited transfer and hard drive space, if your website gets a traffic spike, the CPU resource usage goes up, and many hosts will throttle your site if your account uses a certain amount of the overall server CPU resource. By *throttle,* I mean they'll turn off your website temporarily until the CPU resource use goes down — which generally means that you lose all that traffic that probably caused the rise in CPU resource usage to begin with.

If you see an unlimited offer that looks good to you, pursue it. Just be sure to investigate a bit and ask the right questions, such as "What are the CPU limitations for my account, and what happens if I exceed them?"

Forewarned is forearmed.

3

Installing WordPress on Your Web Server

*W*hen delving in to the world of WordPress web design, you need to make sure that you set up a solid foundation to work from. This means that you need to have the latest version of WordPress installed on your web server and know how to upgrade it when WordPress releases a new version of its software, which it does approximately once every 120 days.

This chapter takes you through installing WordPress correctly, step by step, so you have a solid foundation to work from. That foundation allows you to concentrate more on your design work and coding and less on the back-end, server-related issues that may pop up if you don't pay attention to those initial installation steps.

If you plan on designing and developing WordPress themes for yourself, for public release, or for paid clients, you need to understand the release schedule of WordPress development, versions, and nightly builds, or *bleeding edge* versions, which are released prior to official releases. This chapter gives you the resources you need to stay up to date with WordPress development.

Installing WordPress

Before you're ready to install WordPress, you need to do the following:

- Purchase the domain name registration for your account.
- Obtain a hosting service on a web server for your site.

✔ Establish your hosting account username, password, and File Transfer Protocol (FTP) address.

✔ Acquire an FTP client for transferring files to your hosting account.

If you've missed any of the first three items listed, see Chapter 2 for details. For more on acquiring and using an FTP client, see Chapter 5.

Some web hosts offer a one-click installation process for WordPress through scripts like *Fantastico,* which is the most popular script installer available. If this is the case for you, you can simply follow the instructions provided by your web host (and skip ahead to the "Discovering WordPress Release Cycles" section, later in this chapter). The instructions in this section are for manually installing WordPress on your web server.

If you have to install WordPress manually, here's where the rubber meets the road — that is, you're putting WordPress's famous five-minute installation to the test. Set your watch and see whether you can meet that five-minute mark.

The famous five-minute installation includes the time it takes to install only the software. It doesn't include the time to register a domain name; obtain and set up your web-hosting service; and download, install, configure, and figure out how to use the FTP software.

Without further ado, here are the general steps to install WordPress:

1. **Get the latest version of the WordPress software at** `http://wordpress.org/download`**.**

   WordPress gives you two compression formats for the software: `.zip` and `tar.gz`. I recommend getting the Zip file because it's the most common format for compressed files.

2. **Download the WordPress software to your computer and *decompress* (or unpack or unzip) it to a folder on your computer's hard drive.**

   You can use a free web application such as WinZip (`www.winzip.com`) to decompress the file.

3. **Set up a MySQL database so that it's ready to accept the installation.**

4. ***Upload* (transfer) the WordPress files from your hard drive to your web-server account (the one you obtain in Chapter 2).**

5. **Connect the WordPress software you uploaded to the MySQL database.**

I discuss Steps 3 through 5 in more detail in the following sections.

Setting up the MySQL database

WordPress software is a personal publishing system that uses a PHP/MySQL platform, which provides everything you need to create your own website and publish your own content dynamically without knowing how to code those pages. In short, all your content (such as options, posts, comments, and so on) is stored in a MySQL database in your hosting account.

Every time visitors go to your website to read your content, they make a request that's sent to your server. The PHP programming language receives that request, obtains the requested information from the MySQL database, and then presents the requested information to your visitors through their web browsers.

Every web host is different in how it gives you access to set up and manage your MySQL database(s) for your account. In this section, I use *cPanel*, a popular hosting interface. If your host provides a different interface, the same basic steps apply; just the interface setup that your web host provides may be different.

To set up the MySQL database for your WordPress site with cPanel, follow these steps:

1. **Log in to your hosting account administration interface with the username and password assigned to you by your web host.**

   I use the cPanel administration interface, but your host may provide NetAdmin or Plesk, for example.

2. **Locate the MySQL Database Administration icon in your cPanel.**

   In cPanel, click the MySQL Databases icon.

   The MySQL Databases page appears, as shown in Figure 3-1.

3. **Enter a name for your database in the New Database text box.**

   Be sure to make note of the database name because you need it when installing WordPress.

   Usually, I give my database a name that I'll easily recognize later. This practice is especially helpful if you run more than one MySQL database in your account. If I name this database something like *WordPress* or *wpblog,* I can be reasonably certain — a year from now when I want to access my database to make some configuration changes — that I know exactly which one I need to deal with.

4. **Click the Create Database button.**

   A message appears, confirming that the database has been created.

Figure 3-1: The MySQL Databases page in cPanel.

5. **Click the Go Back link or the Back button on your browser toolbar.**

   This returns you to the MySQL Databases page where your newly created database is listed under Current Databases.

6. **Scroll down the page to the Add New User area, enter a username and password for your database, and then click the Create User button.**

   A confirmation message appears, stating that the username was created with the password you specified.

   For security reasons, make sure that your password isn't something that sneaky hackers can guess easily. During the database-creation process, cPanel gives you a handy tool to create a password using a very secure combination of numbers, letters, and symbols that makes it virtually uncrackable.

Make absolutely sure that you note the database name (from step 3), username, and password that you set up during this process. You need them in the next section before officially installing WordPress on your web server. Jot them down on a piece of paper or copy and paste them into a text editor; either way, just make sure you have them handy.

7. **Click the Go Back link or the Back button on your browser toolbar.**

   This returns you to the MySQL Databases page.

8. **In the Add Users to Database section, choose the user you just set up from the User drop-down list and then choose the database from the Database drop-down list.**

   The MySQL Account Maintenance, Manage User Privileges page appears.

9. **Select the All Privileges check box to assign user privileges.**

   Because you're the administrator (owner) of this database, make sure you assign all privileges to the new user you just created.

10. **Click the Make Changes button.**

    A page opens with a confirmation message that you've added the selected user to the selected database.

11. **Click the Go Back link to return to the MySQL Databases page to see your new MySQL database and user listed on the MySQL Databases page.**

Uploading the WordPress files

To upload the WordPress files to your host, return to the folder on your computer where you unpacked the WordPress software that you downloaded earlier. Figure 3-2 displays the WordPress files on my local computer on the left side of the figure, with the same files displayed on my web server on the right side.

Using your FTP client, connect to your web server and upload all these files into the root directory of your hosting account. (I discuss this process in more detail in Chapter 5.)

If you don't know what your root directory is, contact your hosting provider and ask. Every hosting provider's setup is different. On my web server, my root directory is the `public_html` folder; some of my clients have a root directory in the `httpdocs` folder. The answer really depends on what type of setup your hosting provider has. When in doubt, ask!

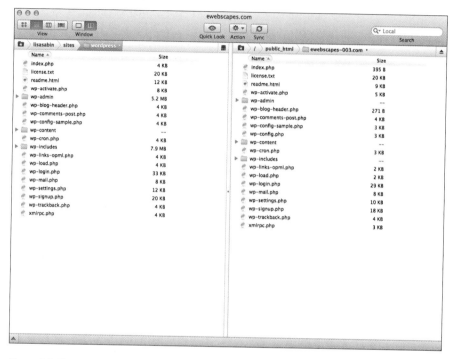

Figure 3-2: Using an FTP client makes file transfers easy.

Here are a few things to keep in mind when you upload your files:

- **Upload the *contents* of the `/wordpress` folder to your web server — not the folder itself.** Most FTP client software lets you select all the files and drag and drop them to your web server. Other programs have you highlight the files and click a Transfer button.

- **Choose the correct transfer mode.** File transfers via FTP have two forms: ASCII and binary. Most FTP clients are configured to autodetect the transfer mode. Understanding the difference as it pertains to this WordPress installation is important so that you can troubleshoot any problems you may have later:

    - *Binary transfer mode* is how images (such as JPG, GIF, BMP, and PNG files) are transferred via FTP.

    - *ASCII transfer mode* is for everything else (text files, PHP files, JavaScript, and so on).

For the most part, having the transfer mode of your FTP client set to auto-detect is a safe bet. But if you experience issues with how those files load on your site, retransfer the files using the appropriate transfer mode.

✔ **You can choose a different folder from the root.** You aren't required to transfer the files to the root directory of your web server. You can choose to run WordPress on a subdomain or in a different folder on your account. If you want your blog address to be `http://your domain.com/blog`, for example, you'd transfer the WordPress files into a `/blog` folder.

✔ **Choose the correct file permissions.** *File permissions* tell the web server how these files can be handled on your server — whether they're files that can be written to. As a general rule, PHP files need to have a permission (`chmod`) of 666, whereas file folders need a permission of 755. Almost all FTP clients let you check and change the permissions on the files, if you need to. Typically, you can find the option to change file permissions within the menu options of your FTP client. (I discuss file permissions in more detail in Chapter 5.)

Some hosting providers run their PHP software in a more secure format — *safe mode.* If this is the case with your host, you need to set the PHP files to 644. If you're unsure, ask your hosting provider what permissions you need to set for PHP files.

Running the install script

The final step in the installation procedure for WordPress is connecting the WordPress software you uploaded to the MySQL database. Follow these steps:

1. **Type the following URL in the address box of your browser, replacing** *yourdomain.com* **with your own domain name:**

   `http://yourdomain.com/wp-admin/install.php`

   If you installed WordPress in a different folder from the root directory of your account, make sure you indicate this in the URL for the install script. If you transferred the WordPress software files to a `/blog` folder, for example, you'd point your browser to the following URL to run the installation: `http://yourdomain.com/blog/wp-admin/install.php`.

   Assuming that you did everything correctly (see Table 3-1 later in this chapter for help with common installation problems), you see the message shown in Figure 3-3.

2. **Click the Create a Configuration File button.**

   The Welcome to WordPress page, which gives you the information you need to proceed with the installation, opens.

3. **Click the Let's Go button at the bottom of the page.**

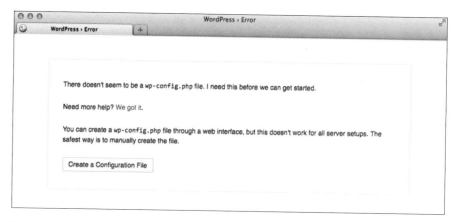

Figure 3-3: WordPress prompts you to create a configuration file.

4. **Dig out the database name, username, and password that you saved earlier (see the "Setting up the MySQL database" section, earlier in this chapter), and then use that information to fill in the following fields, as shown in Figure 3-4:**

   • *Database Name:* Type the database name you used when you created the MySQL database before this installation. Because hosts differ in configurations, you need to enter either the database name or the database name with your hosting account username appended.

   If you named your database wordpress, for example, you'd enter that in this text box. Or if your host requires you to append the database name with your hosting account username, you'd enter ***username*_wordpress**, substituting your hosting username for *username.* My username is lisasabin, so I entered lisasabin_wordpress.

   • *User Name:* Type the username you used when you created the MySQL database before this installation. Depending on what your host requires, you may need to append this username to your hosting account username.

   • *Password:* Type the password you used when you set up the MySQL database. You don't need to append the password to your hosting account username here.

   • *Database Host:* Ninety-nine percent of the time, leave this field set to localhost. Some hosts, depending on their configurations, have different hosts set for the MySQL database server. If localhost doesn't work, contact your hosting provider to find out the MySQL database host.

- *Table Prefix:* Leave this field set to wp_.

It's acceptable practice to leave the database table prefix to the default: wp_. However, if you want a bit more security on your WordPress install, set the database table prefix to something unique because people are out there on the Internet making attempts to hack WordPress databases, and one of the first things they check for is the default database table prefix. If you set this to a unique prefix, it becomes impossible for anyone to access your database unless they know your prefix. For example, I would set mine to something like: lswwp_. This practice isn't necessary, but it's recommended for a more secure WordPress installation.

5. **After you have all that information filled in, click the Submit button.**

   You see a message that says, "*All right, sparky! You've made it through this part of the installation. WordPress can now communicate with your database. If you're ready, time now to run the install!*"

6. **Click the Run the Install button.**

   You see another welcome page with a message welcoming you to the famous five-minute WordPress installation process, as shown in Figure 3-5.

WordPress › Setup Configuration File

WordPress › Setup Configuratio...   +

WORDPRESS

Below you should enter your database connection details. If you're not sure about these, contact your host.

Database Name	wordpress	The name of the database you want to run WP in.
User Name	username	Your MySQL username
Password	password	...and your MySQL password.
Database Host	localhost	You should be able to get this info from your web host, if localhost does not work.
Table Prefix	wp_	If you want to run multiple WordPress installations in a single database, change this.

Submit

Figure 3-4: Enter the database name, username, and password.

Figure 3-5: Information is needed to finish the WordPress installation.

7. Enter or change the following information:

- *Site Title:* Enter the title you want to give your site. The title you enter isn't written in stone; you can change it at a later date, if you like.

- *Username:* This is the name you use to log in to WordPress. By default, the username is `admin`, and you can leave it that way. However, for security reasons, I recommend you change your username to something unique to you.

- *Password, Twice:* Type your desired password in the first text box and then type it again in the second text box to confirm that you've typed it correctly. If the two versions of your password don't match, WordPress alerts you with an error message. If you don't enter a password, one is generated automatically for you.

For security reasons (and so other people can't make a lucky guess), passwords need to be at least seven characters long with as many different characters in as many combinations as possible. Use a mixture of uppercase and lowercase letters, numbers, and symbols, such as ! " ? $ % ^ &.

- *Your E-mail:* Enter the e-mail address you want to use to be notified of administrative information about your website. You can change this address at a later date, too.

- *Allow search engines to index this site:* By default this check box is selected, which lets the search engines index the contents of your website and include your website in search results. To keep your website out of the search engines, deselect this check box.

8. Click the Install WordPress button.

The WordPress installation machine works its magic and creates all the tables within the database that contain the default data for your website. WordPress displays the login information you need to access the WordPress Dashboard. Make note of this username and password before you leave this page; scribble it on a piece of paper or copy it into a text editor such as Notepad.

After you click the Install WordPress button, WordPress sends you an e-mail with the login information and login URL. This information is handy if you're called away during this part of the installation process. So go ahead and let the dog out, answer the phone, brew a cup of coffee, or take a 15-minute power nap. If you somehow get distracted from the page displaying your username and password, the e-mail sent to you contains the information you need to successfully log in to your WordPress website.

9. Click the Log In button to log in to WordPress.

If you happen to lose the login page before clicking the Log In button, you can always find your way to the login page by entering your domain followed by the call to the login file (for example, http://yourdomain. com/wp-login.php).

You know that you're finished with the installation process when you see the login page, as shown in Figure 3-6. Check out Table 3-1 if you experience any problems during this installation process; it covers some of the common problems users run into.

So do tell — how much time does your watch show for the installation? Was it five minutes? Stop by my blog (http://lisasabin-wilson.com) sometime and let me know whether WordPress stood up to its famous five minute-installation reputation. I'm a curious sort.

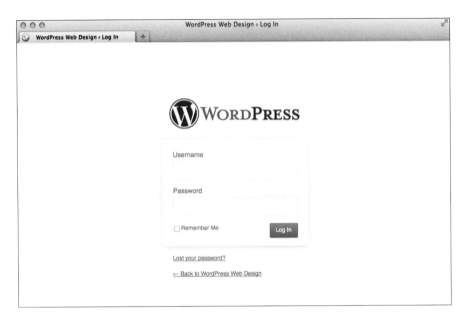

Figure 3-6: You know you've run a successful WordPress installation when you see the login page.

The good news is — you're done! Were you expecting a marching band? WordPress isn't that fancy . . . yet. Give it time, though; if anyone can produce it, the folks at WordPress can.

Table 3-1	Common WordPress Installation Problems	
Error Message	**Common Cause**	**Solution**
Error Connecting to the Database	The database name, username, password, or host was entered incorrectly.	Revisit your MySQL database to obtain the database name, username, password, and host and then reenter that information.
Headers Already Sent Error Messages	A syntax error occurred in the wp-config.php file.	Open the wp-config.php file in a text editor. The first line should contain only this text: <?php. The last line should contain only this text: ?>. Make sure that those lines contain nothing else — not even white space. Save the file changes.

Error Message	Common Cause	Solution
`500: Internal Server Error`	Permissions on PHP files are set incorrectly.	Try setting the permissions (`chmod`) on the PHP files to 666 (see Chapter 5). If that change doesn't work, set them to 644. Each web server has different settings for how it lets PHP execute on its servers.
`404: Page Not Found`	The URL for the login page is incorrect.	Double-check that the URL you're using to get to the login page is the same as the location of your WordPress installation (such as `http://yourdomain.com/wp-login.php`).
`403: Forbidden Access`	An `index.html` or `index.htm` file exists in the WordPress installation directory.	WordPress is a PHP application, so the default home page is `index.php`. Look in the WordPress installation folder on your web server. If an `index.html` or `index.htm` file is there, delete it.

Now, with WordPress fully and correctly installed, you have a solid foundation to start working with and designing themes.

Discovering WordPress Release Cycles

In Chapter 1, I introduce the concept of open-source software (OSS) and discuss how the WordPress development community is made up of, primarily, volunteer developers who donate their time and talents to the WordPress platform. The development of WordPress is a collaborative effort, and with each new release, you can count sometimes more than 300 developers who have contributed in one way or another.

The publicly stated schedule for new WordPress releases is, roughly, once every 120 days, so you can expect a new release of the WordPress software about three times per year. I've used WordPress since 2003, and in those ten years, the WordPress development team has stuck to that schedule pretty closely, with only some exceptions here and there. When WordPress makes exceptions to its 120-day rule, it usually makes a public announcement so that users know what to expect and the estimated time frame for the new release.

Interruptions in that 120-day schedule can — and do — happen, mainly because the development of WordPress is primarily on a volunteer basis. Only a few developers actually get paid to develop for WordPress — and those are employees of *Automattic,* the company behind the hosted WordPress.com service. Because of the volunteer nature of the development crew, the progress of WordPress development depends on volunteer developers making time in their schedules to work on the software in a timely manner. Generally, they do, and you can count on new updates to WordPress on a regular basis.

From a practical standpoint, you can expect to update your WordPress installation at least three, if not four, times per year.

Understanding why you need to upgrade regularly

Don't get discouraged by how many times you need to upgrade your WordPress installation in a year. The WordPress development team constantly strives to improve the user experience and bring exciting and fun new features to the WordPress platform. With each new upgrade, you find improved security and new features that you can use to improve the experience on your website.

The following list provides some reasons why upgrading your WordPress installation is important and something every WordPress website owner needs to do every time a new version is released:

- **Security:** As WordPress versions come and go, outdated versions are no longer supported and are the most vulnerable to malicious attacks and hacker attempts. If you've heard anything negative about WordPress security, 99.99 percent of the time it's because the users were using an outdated version on their websites. To make sure you have the most up-to-date and secure version running, make sure you upgrade to the latest version as soon as you can.

- **New features:** With major WordPress releases, you always find great new features and tools that improve your experience, boost your efficiency and productivity in maintaining your website, improve your visitors' experiences, and are fun to use. (See the sidebar "Major versus point releases," later in the chapter.) Upgrading your WordPress installation ensures you always have access to the latest and greatest tools and features that WordPress has to offer.

- **Plugins and themes:** Most plugin and theme developers work hard to make sure their products are up- to- date and compatible with the latest WordPress version. Therefore, plugin and theme developers generally don't worry about *backward compatibility,* or working with out-of-date WordPress versions, because keeping their products relevant to the current WordPress version is challenging enough. To be sure that the plugins and themes you use are current and don't break any of the features on your site (for example, they stop working or cause errors), make sure you use the latest WordPress version and the latest version of your chosen plugins and themes.

Examining release cycles

By the time you upgrade to the latest WordPress installation, that installation has gone through several *iterations,* or versions, before it lands in your hands. This section helps you understand what it takes to get the latest version to your website, and the terminology used, so when you see it bantered about in blogs and Twitter posts, you at least know the basics of what people are talking about.

The steps and terminology involved in the release of a new version of WordPress include the following:

- **Alpha:** This is the first phase of the new version, typically the *idea* phase in which developers gather ideas from one another, from users, and from community members. During the alpha phase, developers determine which features to include in the new release and develop an outline and project plan. After features are decided, developers develop and testers test until they reach the *feature freeze* — the point in the development cycle when all new features are considered complete and the development moves on to the *beta* cycle in which developers perfect new features through user testing and bug fixes.

- **Beta:** This cycle is in place to fix bugs and any problems reported by testers. Beta cycles can last 4–6 weeks, if not more, and many times, WordPress releases several beta versions that look something like WordPress version 3.0 Beta, WordPress version 3.0 Beta 1, and so on. This continues until the development team decides that the software is ready to move into the next phase of the development cycle.

- **Release candidate (RC):** A version is issued as a *release candidate* when it's been determined that the bugs from the beta versions have been fixed and the version is almost ready for the final release. You can sometimes see several iterations referred to as RC-1, RC-2, and so on.

- **Final release:** When a version has gone through full testing in several (hopefully all) types of environments (browser systems, different web server configurations, and so on) and user experiences; when no major bugs are reported; and when all bugs from the alpha, beta, and RC phases have been squashed; the development team releases the final version of the WordPress software.

Major versus point releases

Notice that when you install your first WordPress version and when you make subsequent upgrades with each new release, WordPress versions are numbered. These numbers show the progress of the software development, but the numbers are also *software versioning,* which is a method of assigning unique numbers to each version release. Regardless of the version number, whenever WordPress puts out a new release, you should always upgrade to keep your WordPress software as up to date as possible.

✓ **Point release:** Point releases usually only increase numerically by a point or two, indicating that it's a relatively minor release and includes things like minor bug fixes. For example, when the version number jumps from 3.0 to 3.0.1, you can be pretty certain that the new version (3.0.1) was released to fix existing minor bugs or cleanups in the source code, rather than to add new features.

✓ **Major release:** A major release most often contains new features, and you generally see a large jump in version numbers. For example, when WordPress went from 2.9 to 3.0, it was considered a major release because it jumped a whole number, rather than incrementally increasing by decimal points (although version 2.9 did get versioned into 2.9.1 and 2.9.2 before it jumped to 3.0). This large jump is a sign that this version includes a few new features, rather than just bug fixes or code cleanup. The larger the jump in version number, the more major the release. For example, if a version number suddenly jumped from 3.0 to 3.5, that would be an indication of some pretty major new features in that release.

After a version is issued as a final release, the WordPress development team starts all over again in the alpha phase, gearing up to go through the development cycle again, ready for the next major version.

Typically, one development cycle lasts approximately 120 days, but any number of things can happen during a development cycle, from developer delays to particularly difficult bugs that take longer to fix than expected. Legend has it that during the 3.0 development cycle, the final release was delayed by several weeks because of a kitten that required lots of time and TLC (http://cheezburger.com/View/3444964352).

Keeping Track of WordPress Development

If you know where to look, keeping track of the development cycle of a WordPress project is pretty easy because the development team tries to make the development process transparent. Not only can you keep track by reading about the cycle in various spots on the Internet, but you can also eavesdrop on the conversations between developers and, if you feel so inclined, jump in and lend a hand where you can.

You can stay up to date on what's going on in the WordPress-development world through blog posts, live chats, development meetings, tracking tickets, and bug reports, just to name a few. This list gives you a solid starting point on where you can go to stay informed:

- **Make WordPress Core:** The official blog of the WordPress development team (`http://make.wordpress.org/core/` where you can follow and keep track of the progress of the WordPress software project as it happens, as shown in Figure 3-7. Here you find agendas, schedules, meeting minutes, and discussions surrounding the development cycles.

- **WordPress Developer Chat:** Using an Internet Chat Relay (IRC) program, WordPress developers gather weekly to discuss a predetermined agenda of items that need to be discussed during the development cycle (`http://freenode.net/irc_servers.shtml` in the `#wordpress-dev` chat channel). You're invited to join the IRC chat room to listen in or participate. You can download the free mIRC program (PC) from `www.mirc.com` or the Ircle program (Mac) from `www.ircle.com`. Follow the program's user manual for instructions on how to use IRC to chat over the Internet.

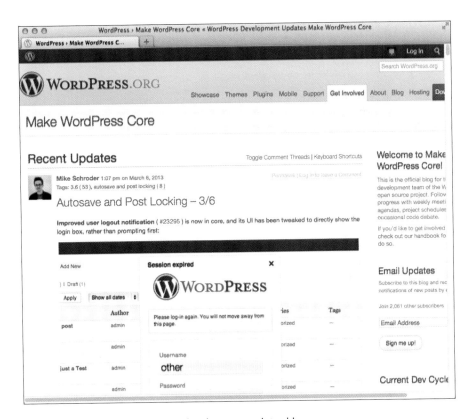

Figure 3-7: The official WordPress development updates blog.

✔ **WordPress Trac:** You can follow along here (`http://trac.wordpress.org`) with the changes in WordPress development by

- *Following the Timeline:* `http://core.trac.wordpress.org/timeline`

- *Viewing the Roadmap:* `http://core.trac.wordpress.org/roadmap`

- *Reading available reports:* `http://core.trac.wordpress.org/report`

- *Performing a search:* `http://core.trac.wordpress.org/search`

✔ **WordPress Mailing Lists:** Join mailing lists focused on different aspects of WordPress development, such as bug testing, documentation, and hacking WordPress (`http://codex.wordpress.org/Mailing_Lists`).

4

Managing Content with WordPress

In This Chapter

▶ Archiving your content

▶ Working with permalinks

▶ Feeding your readers with RSS

*W*ordPress provides you with many ways to organize, categorize, and archive content on your website or blog (or both!). Packaged within the WordPress software is the capability for you to maintain chronological and categorized archives of your publishing history, enabling your website visitors to easily find and read the content they're interested in. WordPress uses PHP and MySQL technology to sort and organize everything you publish in an order that you, and your readers, can access by date and category. This archiving process is done automatically with every post you publish to your blog.

In this chapter, you find out all about WordPress archiving, from categories to tags and more. You also discover how to take advantage of the built-in permalink system that creates Search Engine Optimization–friendly permalinks for your site. Finally, this chapter takes you through all the types of content you can build within WordPress. When people refer to *content,* they assume you mean posts and pages that you publish, which is true; but there are other types of content and ways to organize it that help you build a more dynamic and informative website.

Archiving Content with WordPress

When you create a post on your WordPress site, you can file that post under a category that you specify. This feature makes for a very nifty archiving system in which you and your readers can find articles/posts that you've placed within a specific category. Articles that you post are also sorted and organized by date (day/month/year) to make it easy to locate articles that you've posted at a certain time. The archives page on my business website (see it at `http://webdevstudios.com/sitemap`) contains a list of pages, a list of months content was published in, and a list of topics. Clicking a month on that page, for example, takes you to a page listing articles from that month, which are linked to the individual articles, as shown in Figure 4-1.

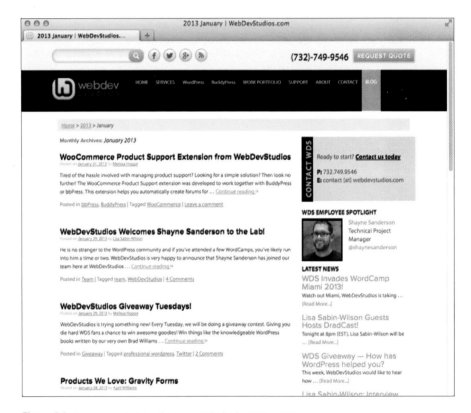

Figure 4-1: An archive listing of posts made in January 2013.

Dates and categories aren't the only ways WordPress archives and organizes your content. There are several others as well, and in this chapter, I give you an overview of them. In later chapters in this book, I show you how you can leverage those archive types to create a dynamic website that's easy for your visitors to navigate. The different types of archives and content include

✓ **Categories:** Create categories of topics to file your articles in to create easy archiving of relevant topics. A popular way that websites display content is by category — typically referred to as a *Magazine Theme* — where all content is displayed by topic, rather than a simple chronological listing. An example of a Magazine Theme (the Modern Blogger by StartBox at `http://demo.wpstartbox.com/?theme=modern-blogger`) is shown in Figure 4-2.

You can find out how to create a theme of your own by using the information in Part III of this book, which deals with WordPress themes; also be sure to check out Chapter 12 to discover how to use template tags to display category-specific content — exciting stuff!

✓ **Tags:** Tagging your posts with micro-keywords, or *tags,* helps drill down related content, which is good for *search engine optimization* (SEO) purposes, and also provides additional navigation pieces for your readers to find relevant content on your site. See the sidebar "What are tags, and how/why do you use them?" later in this chapter, to find out how tags differ from categories.

Figure 4-2: An example of a Magazine Theme created with WordPress.

✔ **Date based:** Your content is automatically archived by date based on the day, month, year, and time you published it.

✔ **Author:** Content is automatically archived by author based on the author of the post and/or page. Creating an author archive is possible for those sites that have multiple content contributors.

✔ **Keyword (or search):** WordPress has a built-in search function that allows you, and your readers, to search for keywords to see an archive listing of content that's relevant to your chosen keyword.

✔ **Custom post types:** You can build custom post types based on the kind of content your site offers — you can find more information on this topic in Chapter 12.

✔ **Attachments:** WordPress has a built-in media library where you upload different media files such as photos, images, documents, videos, and audio files (to name a few). You can build an archive of those files to create things like photo galleries, e-book archives (PDFs), or video galleries.

Building categories

In WordPress, a *category* is what you determine to be the main topic of a blog post. Through categories, you can file your blog posts into topics by subject. To improve your readers' experiences in navigating through your blog, WordPress organizes posts by the categories you assign to them. Visitors can click the categories they're interested in to see the blog posts you've written on those particular topics. You should know ahead of time that the list of categories you set up can be displayed on your blog in a few places, including the

✔ **Body of the post:** In most WordPress themes, you see the title followed by a statement, such as "Filed In: *Category 1, Category 2.*" The reader can click the category name to go to a page that lists all the posts you've made in that particular category. You can assign a single post to more than one category.

✔ **Sidebar of your blog theme:** You can place a full list of category titles in the sidebar by using the Categories widget included in your WordPress installation. (Widgets are covered in Chapter 12.) A reader can click any category and go to a page on your site that lists the posts you've made within that particular category.

Subcategories (or *category children)* can further refine the main category topic by listing specific topics related to the main *(parent)* category. In your WordPress Dashboard on the Manage Categories page (choose Posts➪Categories), subcategories are listed directly below the main category. Here's an example:

Books I Enjoy (main category)

Fiction (subcategory)

Nonfiction (subcategory)

Trashy Romance (subcategory)

Biographies (subcategory)

For Dummies (subcategory)

Changing the name of a category

Upon installation, WordPress gives you one default category — *Uncategorized* — as shown on the Categories page in Figure 4-3. That category name is pretty generic, so you definitely want to change it to one that's more specific to you. (On my blog, I changed it to *Life in General.* Although that name's still a bit on the generic side, it doesn't sound quite so . . . well, uncategorized.)

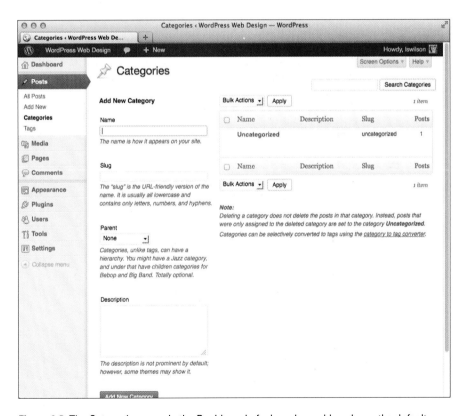

Figure 4-3: The Categories page in the Dashboard of a brand-new blog shows the default Uncategorized category.

What are tags, and how/why do you use them?

Tags are not to be confused with categories, but a lot of people do confuse them. *Tags* are clickable, comma-separated keywords that help you microcategorize a post by defining the topics in it. Unlike WordPress categories, tags do not have a hierarchy; there are no parent tags and child tags. If you write a post about your dog, for example, you can put that post in the Pets category — but you can also add some specific tags that let you get a whole lot more specific, such as `poodle`, or `small dogs`. If visitors click your `poodle` tag, they find all the posts you've ever made that contain the `poodle` tag.

Another reason to use tags: When they crawl your site, search-engine spiders harvest tags, so tags help other people find your site when they search for specific keywords.

You can manage your tags in the WordPress Dashboard by choosing Posts➪Tags. The Tags page opens where you can view, edit, delete, and add new tags.

The default category also serves as kind of a fail-safe. If you publish a post to your blog and don't assign that post to a category, WordPress automatically assigns that post to the default category, no matter what you name the category.

So how do you change the name of that default category? When you're logged in to your WordPress Dashboard, just follow these steps:

1. **Choose Posts➪Categories.**

   The Categories page opens, containing all the tools you need to set up and edit category titles for your blog.

2. **Click the title of the category you want to edit.**

   For example, if you want to change the Uncategorized category, click the Uncategorized link. The Edit Category page appears, as shown in Figure 4-4.

3. **Type the new name for the category in the Name text box and then type the new slug in the Slug text box.**

   Slug refers to the word(s) used in the web address for the specific category. For example, the Books category has a web address of

   ```
   http://yourdomain.com/category/books
   ```

   If you change the slug to Books I Like, the web address is

   ```
   http://yourdomain.com/category/books-i-like
   ```

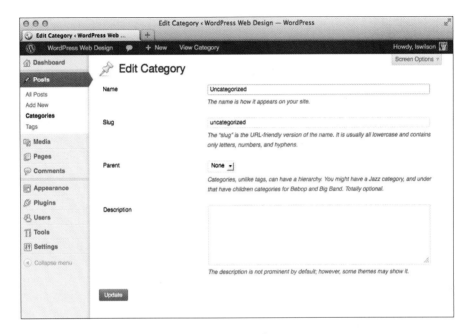

Figure 4-4: Edit a category in WordPress on the Edit Category page.

WordPress automatically inserts a dash between the slug words in the web address.

4. Choose a parent category from the Parent drop-down list.

If you want this category to be a main category, not a subcategory, choose None.

5. (Optional) Type a description of the category in the Description text box.

Use this description to remind yourself what your category is about. Some WordPress themes display the category description on your site, which can be helpful for your visitors. You'll know whether your theme is coded in this way if your site displays the category description on the category page(s). (See Part III of this book for more about themes.)

6. Click the Update button.

The information you just edited is saved, and the Categories page reloads, showing your new category name.

Creating new categories

Today, tomorrow, next month, next year — as your blog grows in size and age, you'll continue adding new categories to further define and archive the history of your blog posts. You aren't limited in the number of categories and subcategories you can create in your blog.

Creating a new category is as easy as following these steps:

1. **Choose Posts⇨Categories.**

   The Categories page opens. The left side of the Categories page displays the Add New Category section, shown in Figure 4-5.

2. **Type the name of your new category in the Name text box.**

   Suppose that you want to create a category in which you file all your posts about the books you read. In the Name text box, type something like **Books I Enjoy**.

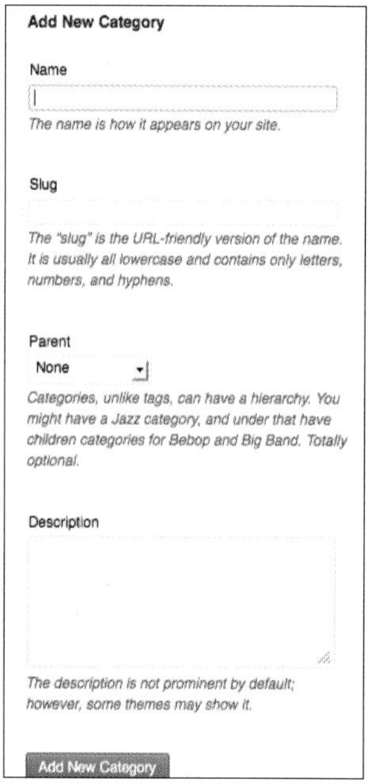

Add New Category

Name

The name is how it appears on your site.

Slug

The "slug" is the URL-friendly version of the name. It is usually all lowercase and contains only letters, numbers, and hyphens.

Parent

None

Categories, unlike tags, can have a hierarchy. You might have a Jazz category, and under that have children categories for Bebop and Big Band. Totally optional.

Description

The description is not prominent by default; however, some themes may show it.

Add New Category

Figure 4-5: Create a new category on your blog.

3. Type a name in the Slug text box.

The slug creates the link to the category page that lists all the posts you've made in this category. If you leave this field blank, WordPress automatically creates a slug based on the category name. If the category is Books I Enjoy, WordPress automatically creates a category slug like this:

```
http://yourdomain.com/category/books-i-enjoy
```

4. Choose the category's parent from the Parent drop-down list.

Choose None if you want this new category to be a parent (or top-level) category. If you want this category to be a subcategory of another category, choose the category you want to be the parent of this one.

5. (Optional) Type a description of the category in the Description text box.

6. Click the Add New Category button.

That's it — you've added a new category to your blog. Armed with this information, you can add an unlimited number of categories to your blog.

You can delete a category on your blog by hovering your mouse pointer over the title of the category you want to delete, and then clicking the Delete link that appears underneath the category title.

Deleting a category doesn't delete the posts and links in that category. Instead, posts in the deleted category are assigned to the Uncategorized category (or whatever you've named the default category).

If you have an established WordPress blog with categories already created, you can convert some or all of your categories to tags. To do so, look for the Category to Tag Converter link on the right side of the Categories page (refer to Figure 4-3) — click it to convert your categories to tags. (See the earlier sidebar "What are tags, and how/why do you use them?" for more information on tags.)

The `WP_Query();` class (described in Chapter 12) enables you to take advantage of categories in WordPress to build a dynamic theme that displays your content in a way that highlights the different topics available on your site. In Chapter 12, you also find out how to use WordPress template tags to manipulate category archives for display and distribution on your website.

Using static page parents and children

People use the Pages feature on their sites to create *static* content (content that does not often change), such as an About Me or Contact Me page. Click the Pages menu in the WordPress Dashboard to reveal the submenu links:

- **Edit:** This link opens the Edit Pages screen where you can search, view, edit, and delete pages in your WordPress site.
- **Add New:** This link opens the Add New Page screen where you can compose, save, and publish a new page on your blog.

Pages are different from posts on a WordPress website because users typically create a smaller amount of pages with static content, whereas when users have a blog on their site, they are, generally, adding blog posts regularly. WordPress separates posts from pages to distinguish the two types of content. Table 4-1 illustrates the differences between a post and a page in WordPress.

Table 4-1	The Differences between a Post and a Page	
WordPress Options	*Page*	*Post*
Appears in blog post listings	No	Yes
Appears as a static page	Yes	No
Appears in category archives	No	Yes
Appears in monthly archives	No	Yes
Appears in Recent Posts listings	No	Yes
Appears in site RSS feed	No	Yes
Appears in search results	Yes	Yes

WordPress allows pages to have a hierarchal structure, which can be helpful in your navigation plans for your site, as well as grouping together pages that relate to one another topically.

For example, I can create an About Me page that contains a brief biography of me as an author, designer, and public speaker. This About Me page is considered a parent page because it's a top-level page created at, for example, http://yourdomain.com/about. Then, I can create child pages underneath the parent page that relate to it, in terms of content. For example, I can create three pages: Design, Books, and Speaking. Each of those pages contains expanded content about each topic, individually. The navigation structure would look something like this:

About Me (`http://yourdomain.com/about`)

Design (`http://yourdomain.com/about/design`)

Books (`http://yourdomain.com/about/books`)

Speaking (`http://yourdomain.com/about/speaking`)

You can see where the grouping of those pages together as parent/child pages makes sense from a navigation perspective and a content delivery perspective. In Chapter 10, you find out how to build custom navigation menus using the built-in menu feature in WordPress. In Chapter 12, you discover how to use WordPress template tags to call different menus into your themes, and in Chapter 14, you find some CSS tips and tricks that help you style those menus to your satisfaction.

Customizing Permalinks

Each WordPress blog post is assigned its own web page, and the address (or URL) of that page is a *permalink*. Posts that you see in WordPress blogs usually have the post permalink in four typical areas:

- The title of the blog post
- The Comments link below the post
- A Permalink link that appears (in most themes) below the post
- The titles of posts in a Recent Posts sidebar

Permalinks are meant to be permanent links to your blog posts (which is where *perma* comes from, in case you're wondering). Other bloggers can use a post permalink to refer to that particular blog post. So ideally, the permalink of a post never changes. WordPress creates the permalink automatically when you publish a new post.

By default, a blog post permalink in WordPress looks like this:

```
http://yourdomain.com/?p=100/
```

The p stands for *post,* and `100` is the ID assigned to the individual post. You can leave the permalinks in this format, if you don't mind letting WordPress associate each post with an ID number.

WordPress, however, lets you take your permalinks to the beauty salon for a bit of a makeover so you can create pretty permalinks. I bet you didn't know that permalinks could be pretty, did you? They certainly can. Allow me to explain.

Making your post links pretty

Pretty permalinks are links that are more pleasing to the eye than standard links and, ultimately, more pleasing to search engine spiders. (See Chapter 15 for an explanation of why search engines like pretty permalinks.) Pretty permalinks look something like this:

```
http://yourdomain.com/2008/01/01/pretty-permalinks/
```

Break down that URL, and you see the date when the post was made, in year/month/day format. You also see the topic of the post.

To choose how your permalinks look, choose Settings⟹Permalinks. The Permalink Settings page opens, as shown in Figure 4-6.

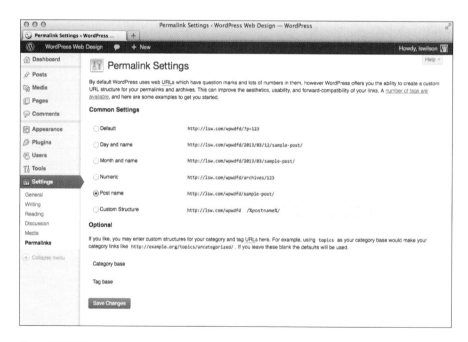

Figure 4-6: Make your permalinks pretty.

On this page, you find several options for creating permalinks:

- **Default (ugly permalinks):** WordPress assigns an ID number to each blog post and creates the URL in this format: `http://yourdomain.com/?p=100`.

- **Day and Name (pretty permalinks):** For each post, WordPress generates a permalink URL that includes the year, month, day, and post slug/title: `http://yourdomain.com/2008/01/01/sample-post/`.

✐ **Month and Name (pretty permalinks):** For each post, WordPress generates a permalink URL that includes the year, month, and post slug/title: `http://yourdomain.com/2008/01/sample-post/`.

✐ **Numeric (not so pretty):** WordPress assigns a numerical value to the permalink. The URL is created in this format: `http://yourdomain.com/archives/123`.

✐ **Post Name (recommended):** WordPress takes the title of the post or the page and turns it into a permalink slug like this: `http://yourdomain.com/post-name`

✐ **Custom Structure:** WordPress creates permalinks in the format you choose. You can create a custom permalink structure by using tags or variables, as I discuss in the next section.

To create the pretty-permalink structure, select the Day and Name (or Month and Name) radio button; then click the Save Changes button at the bottom of the page.

For optimization reasons, my preferred permalink structure is Post Name, which uses the tag `%postname%` in the Custom Structure field found on the Permalink Settings page (refer to Figure 4-6). I prefer this structure because it strips all the date information and leaves only the post name, or slug, itself. For example, using the Day and Name structure for my permalinks, my posts' permalinks look like this: `http://lisasabin-wilson.com/2013/06/02/post-title/`; however, if I use my preferred method of `%postname%`, my permalinks look like this: `http://lisasabin-wilson.com/post-name`. See how it shortens the permalink URL considerably? This is a better method for search engine optimization, and it just looks better.

Customizing your permalinks

A *custom permalink structure* lets you define which variables you want to see in your permalinks by using the tags listed in Table 4-2.

Table 4-2	Custom Permalinks
Permalink Tag	**Results**
`%year%`	4-digit year (such as `2007`)
`%monthnum%`	2-digit month (such as `02` for February)
`%day%`	2-digit day (such as `30`)
`%hour%`	2-digit hour of the day (such as `15` for 3 p.m.)

(continued)

Table 4-2 *(continued)*

Permalink Tag	Results
`%minute%`	2-digit minute (such as `45`)
`%second%`	2-digit second (such as `10`)
`%postname%`	Text — usually the post name — separated by hyphens (such as `making-pretty-permalinks`)
`%post_id%`	The unique numerical ID of the post (such as `344`)
`%category%`	The text of the category name that you filed the post in (such as `books-i-read`)
`%author%`	The text of the post author's name (such as `lisa-sabin-wilson`)

If you want your permalink to show the year, month, day, category, and post name, select the Custom Structure radio button in the Permalink Settings page and type the following tags in the Custom Structure text box:

```
/%year%/%monthnum%/%day%/%category%/%postname%/
```

Under this permalink format, the link for the *WordPress For Dummies* post made on February 1, 2008, filed in the Books I Read category, would look like this:

```
http://yourdomain.com/2008/02/01/books-i-read/wordpress-for-dummies/
```

Be sure to include the slashes before tags, between tags, and at the very end of the string of tags. This format ensures that WordPress creates correct, working permalinks by using the correct `re_write` rules located in the `.htaccess` file for your site. (See the following section for more information on `re_write` rules and `.htaccess` files.)

Changing the structure of your permalinks in the future affects the permalinks for all the posts on your blog . . . new and old. Keep this fact in mind if you ever decide to change the permalink structure. An especially important reason: Search engines (such as Google and Yahoo!) index the posts on your site by their permalinks, so changing the permalink structure makes all those indexed links obsolete.

Don't forget to click the Save Changes button at the bottom of the Permalink Settings page; otherwise, your permalink changes won't be saved!

Making sure that your permalinks work with your server

After you set the format for the permalinks for your site by using any options other than the default, WordPress writes specific rules, or directives, to the `.htaccess` file on your web server. The `.htaccess` file communicates to your web server how it should serve up the permalinks, according to the permalink structure you've chosen to use.

To use an `.htaccess` file, you need to know the answers to two questions:

- ✓ Does your web server configuration use and give you access to the `.htaccess` file?
- ✓ Does your web server run Apache with the `mod_rewrite` module?

If you don't know the answers, contact your hosting provider to find out.

If the answer to both questions is yes, proceed to the next section. If the answer is no, skip to the "Working with servers that don't use Apache mod_rewrite" section.

Creating .htaccess files

You and WordPress work together in glorious harmony to create the `.htaccess` file that lets you use a pretty permalink structure in your blog. To create an `.htaccess` file on your web server and set the correct permissions for it, follow these steps:

1. **Using a plain-text editor, such as Notepad (Windows) or TextMate (`http://macromates.com`) (Mac), create a blank file, name it htaccess.txt, and upload it to your web server via FTP.**

   You may not have to create the file (as instructed in Step 1); if the `.htaccess` file already exists, you can find it in the root of your directory on your web server — that is, the same directory where you find your `wp-config.php` file. If you don't see the file in the root directory, try changing the options of your FTP client to show hidden files. (Because the `.htaccess` file starts with a period, it may not be visible until you configure your FTP client to show hidden files. See Chapter 5 for details.)

2. **After the file is uploaded to your web server, rename the file `.htaccess` (notice the period at the beginning) and make sure that it's writable by the server by changing permissions to either 755 or 777.**

   See Chapter 5 for information about FTP and details on changing permissions on server files.

3. **Create the permalink structure in the Permalink Settings page on your WordPress Dashboard.**

   See the section "Making your post links pretty," earlier in this chapter.

4. **Click the Save Changes button at the bottom of the Permalink Settings page.**

   WordPress inserts into the `.htaccess` file the specific rules necessary for making the permalink structure functional in your blog.

Now you have an `.htaccess` file on your web server that has the correct permissions set so that WordPress can write the correct rules to it. Your pretty permalink structure works flawlessly. Kudos!

If you open the `.htaccess` file and look at it now, it's no longer blank. The file should have a set of *rewrite rules* code, which looks something like this:

```
# BEGIN WordPress
<IfModule mod_rewrite.c>
RewriteEngine On
RewriteBase /
RewriteCond %{REQUEST_FILENAME} !-f
RewriteCond %{REQUEST_FILENAME} !-d
RewriteRule . /index.php [L]
</IfModule>
# END WordPress
```

I could delve deeply into `.htaccess` and all the things you can do with this file, but I'm restricting this section to how it applies to WordPress permalink structures. If you want to unlock more mysteries about `.htaccess`, check out `http://javascriptkit.com/howto/htaccess.shtml`.

Working with servers that don't use Apache mod_rewrite

Using permalink structures requires that your web hosting provider has a specific Apache module option — `mod_rewrite` — activated on its servers. If your web hosting provider doesn't have this option activated on its servers or if you're hosting your site on a Windows server, the custom permalinks work only if you type **/index.php** in front of any custom permalink tags.

For example, create the custom permalink tags like this:

```
/index.php/%year%/%month%/%date%/%postname%/
```

This format creates a permalink like this:

```
http://yourdomain.com/index.php/2008/02/01/wordpress-for-dummies
```

You don't need an `.htaccess` file to use this permalink structure.

Through my experiences over the years, Yahoo! hosting doesn't allow users access to the .htaccess file on their servers, and it doesn't use mod_ rewrite. So if you're hosting on Yahoo!, you need to use the custom permalink technique that I describe in this section.

Syndicating Your Content with RSS Feeds

RSS stands for *really simple syndication.* An *RSS feed* is a standard feature that blog readers have come to expect. So what is it, really?

The Introduction to RSS page on WebReference.com (www.webreference. com/authoring/languages/xml/rss/intro) defines RSS as "a lightweight XML format designed for sharing headlines and other Web content. Think of it as a distributable 'What's New' for your site."

Introducing feed readers

Users can use *feed readers* to download your RSS feed. The feed readers are set up to automatically discover new content (such as posts and comments) from your blog and download that content for users' consumption. Users can download several RSS feed readers, for either a PC or a Mac — and there are also popular and accessible online RSS feed readers available on the Internet. *Feedly* (http://feedly.com) a free RSS reader with applications for the Chrome browser, iPhones, and so on, is a popular online RSS reader on the web. With Feedly, readers can keep up with their favorite blogs and websites that have syndicated (RSS) content.

Most browser systems alert visitors to the RSS feed on your site by displaying the universally recognized orange RSS feed icon, shown here in the margin.

Keep in mind that almost all browser systems have built-in RSS readers. Just look for the small RSS icon in the address bar of your favorite browser (such as Internet Explorer or Mozilla Firefox) and click it. The RSS feeds you've saved appear directly in your browser window.

For the readers of your blog to stay updated with the latest and greatest content you post to your site, they need to subscribe to your RSS feed. Most blogging platforms allow the RSS feeds to be *autodiscovered* by the various feed readers — meaning that the user needs only to enter your site's URL, and the program automatically finds your RSS feed.

WordPress has built-in RSS feeds in several formats. Because the feeds are built in to the software platform, you don't need to do anything to provide your readers with an RSS feed of your content.

Discovering the many WordPress RSS options

RSS feeds come in different flavors, including RSS 0.92, RDF/RSS 1.0, RSS 2.0, and Atom. The differences among them lie within the base code that makes up the functionality of the syndication feed. What's important is that WordPress supports all versions of RSS — which means that anyone can subscribe to your RSS feed with any type of feed reader available.

WordPress is very intuitive, and this section on RSS feeds is a shining example of a feature that WordPress automates. WordPress has a built-in feed generator that works behind the scenes to create feeds. This feed generator creates feeds from your posts, comments, and even categories.

The RSS feed for your blog posts is *autodiscoverable* — almost all RSS feed readers and even some browsers (Firefox, Internet Explorer 8, and Safari, for example) automatically detect the RSS feed URL for a WordPress blog. Table 4-3 gives you some guidelines on how to find the RSS feed URLs for the different sections of your blog.

Table 4-3	URLs for Built-In WordPress Feeds
Feed Type	*Example Feed URL*
RSS 0.92	`http://yourdomain.com/wp-rss.php` or `http://yourdomain.com/?feed=rss`
RDF/RSS 1.0	`http://yourdomain.com/wp-rss2.php` or `http://yourdomain.com/?feed=rdf`
RSS 2.0	`http://yourdomain.com/wp-rss2.php` or `http://yourdomain.com/?feed=rss2`
Atom	`http://yourdomain.com/wp-atom.php` or `http://yourdomain.com/?feed=atom`
Comments RSS	`http://yourdomain.com/?feed=rss&p=50` `p` stands for *post,* and `50` is the post ID. You can find the post ID in the Dashboard by clicking the Posts link.
Category RSS	`http://yourdomain.com/wp-rss2.php?cat=50` `cat` stands for *category,* and `50` is the category ID. You can find the category ID in the Dashboard by clicking the Categories link in the Posts menu.

If you're using custom permalinks (see "Making your post links pretty," earlier in this chapter), you can simply add `/feed` to the end of any URL on your blog to find the RSS feed. Some of your links look similar to these:

✔ http://*yourdomain.com*/feed: Your main RSS feed

✔ http://*yourdomain.com*/comments/feed: Your comments RSS feed

✔ http://*yourdomain.com*/tag/tag-name/feed: RSS feed for a tag

✔ http://*yourdomain.com*/category/cat-name/feed: RSS feed for a category

Try adding /feed with any URL on your site. You get the RSS feed for that page.

RSS feeds are important parts of delivering content from your blog to your readers. RSS feeds are expected these days, so the fact that WordPress has taken care of the feeds for you, is compliant with all RSS formats, and offers so many internal feeds, gives the software a huge advantage over any of the other blog-software platforms.

If you intend to use the Atom publishing protocol, you need to enable it manually because it's disabled by default. On the Dashboard, choose Settings⟳Writing, and then select the two check boxes in the Remote Publishing section to enable Atom publishing in WordPress.

Using your RSS feeds with your social media accounts

RSS feed technology is an important part of publishing content on a blog or website. RSS doesn't only give your readers an option to subscribe to syndicated content from your website. Website publishers are also involved in other social networks that use the RSS feeds from their sites to publish, market, and help other Internet browsers discover their content, including

✔ **Twitter:** This very popular social media network is full of would-be visitors to websites. Tools, which I outline in Chapter 16, allow you to publish new blog posts and content to your Twitter stream, as well. This is a powerful marketing tool that many site owners use. (http://twitter.com)

✔ **Facebook:** This is another extremely popular social media community that allows you to automatically publish your blog and website content into your Facebook profile, which puts your content in front of hundreds of eyes within the network. Figure 4-7 shows my personal Facebook profile where the content from my business site (http://webdevstudios.com) is automatically displayed on my profile page. This happens through the magic of sharing my RSS feed from my website with my Facebook account. (www.facebook.com)

Figure 4-7: My website RSS feed shared on my Facebook profile.

Additionally, WordPress has a handy widget that allows you to display content from an RSS feed of your choice on your website. You can find more information on working with WordPress widgets in Chapter 12.

Part II
Choosing the Right Tools

Discover three helpful add-ons for the Mozilla Firefox browser that will assist you with your day-to-day web designing needs at www.dummies.com/extras/ wordpresswebdesign.

In this part . . .

- ✔ Assemble the right tools for the job of web designing with WordPress.

- ✔ Explore several text editors that you can use to efficiently write code, including HTML and CSS.

- ✔ Discover a few different FTP (File Transfer Protocol) tools to use to make transferring files to and from your web server quick and easy.

- ✔ Start formulating a plan for your web design projects, including the right questions to ask, information to gather, and content to collect.

5

Exploring Editors, Browsers, and FTP

I started in web design in 1998 and have learned a great many things during my journey through designing my little corner of the web. One thing that's certain is that technology moves at a pretty rapid pace, and if you're really serious about making a career — or even a serious hobby — out of web design, you need to keep up. Being a full-time web designer and developer is like being back in school because you're constantly discovering and teaching yourself new and emerging technologies.

I've also learned that when you sit down at the computer to begin any web design project, large or small, it's vital that you have the right tools at your fingertips. Having the right tools makes a world of difference in the quality, efficiency, and overall experience in designing a website.

In this chapter, you discover different tools for things like editing HTML, CSS, and PHP. You also explore different web browser platforms, such as Internet Explorer and Mozilla Firefox, including tools and add-ons that you can add to a browser to make it work better for your web designing needs. Finally, you uncover the mysteries of File Transfer Protocol (FTP), including what it means, how to use it, and different types of programs that you can use.

In some cases, the tools I mention in this chapter aren't necessarily required; however, you'll be very thankful when you find tools that make your web designing life a lot easier.

Choosing the Right Text Editor for You

In Part III of this book, you dig in to WordPress themes, work with CSS and HTML, and type template tags and a bit of PHP. This chapter arms you with the tools you need to prepare for a smooth and efficient experience.

Next to reliable ol' pen and paper, nothing beats a good, solid text editor. I admit, I'm a little old school, so for things like grocery lists and jotting down ideas, I stick with a pad of paper and a pen. Unfortunately, writing code is difficult with a pen and paper, and it doesn't translate very well when I need to publish it to the Internet. That's when a basic text-editor program comes in handy. I always have one open on my computer (usually several instances of my favored text editor, actually) and use it for writing Cascading Style Sheets (CSS) and HTML as well as coding WordPress templates and themes.

Make sure that you use a *text editor* and not a *word processor,* such as Microsoft Word, to write any code because a word processing program automatically inserts formatting, characters, and hidden spaces. When you're writing code, the last thing you want is anything but your own code inserted into the document — so stick with a basic text editor.

The text editors I describe in this section are programs that you install on your computer. Some of them are available only for Windows, and some only for Macs — I specify as such in their descriptions.

Notepad (Windows)

Notepad is a basic text editor that you can use to write code without the fuss and worry of text formatting. Notepad doesn't support any special document formatting or characters, which makes it great for writing code and web documents.

Notepad is the go-to text editor for most Windows users because it's a Microsoft product that's packaged in every Windows operating system. Often, people use Notepad to view and edit text files with the .txt extension, but many people, including myself, use it to create basic CSS and HTML files, as well.

Notepad, by default, saves files with a .txt extension. With WordPress templates and theme files, you typically save files with a .php or .css extension, so make sure you save them correctly. To save a file with a .php or .css extension with Notepad, follow these quick steps in Windows 7:

1. **Choose Start➪All Programs➪Accessories➪Notepad.**

   Notepad opens, and you can start typing your code.

2. **Create your CSS or PHP document.**

   Check out Chapter 14 for details on how to create CSS.

3. **Choose File⇨Save As, and then choose the location on your computer where you want to save the file.**

4. **Type the filename, including the extension, in the File Name field.**

   In Figure 5-1, the name of my PHP file is `header.php`. However, if you're saving a CSS document, the extension is `.css`, such as `style.css`.

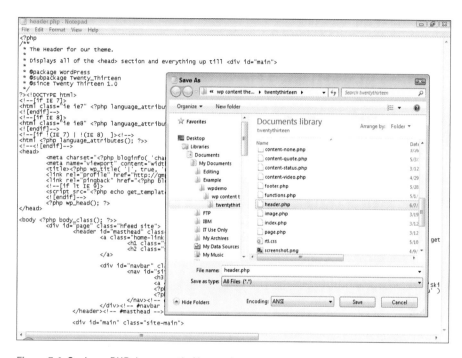

Figure 5-1: Saving a PHP document in Notepad.

5. **Choose All Files in the Save as Type drop-down list (see Figure 5-1).**

   By default, Notepad wants to save the file with the file type Text Documents (*.txt).

6. **Leave ANSI chosen in the Encoding field.**

   This is default character encoding and is okay to leave as is.

7. **Click Save.**

Notepad++ (Windows)

Notepad++ is a text editor for Windows and is often referred to as "Notepad on steroids" because the interface looks a lot like regular Notepad — but that's where the similarities end. Notepad++ has advanced features such as color-coded syntax (see the nearby sidebar "Code syntax highlighting"), code indentation, and line numbering, which make it an extremely useful and help-ful application for writing and editing code. Figure 5-2 demonstrates the code syntax formatting of this editor.

Notepad++ supports many programming languages, including the main ones you use for this book: CSS, HTML, and PHP. Notepad++ is free open-source software (see Chapter 1)! You can download it to your computer from `http://notepad-plus-plus.org/download`.

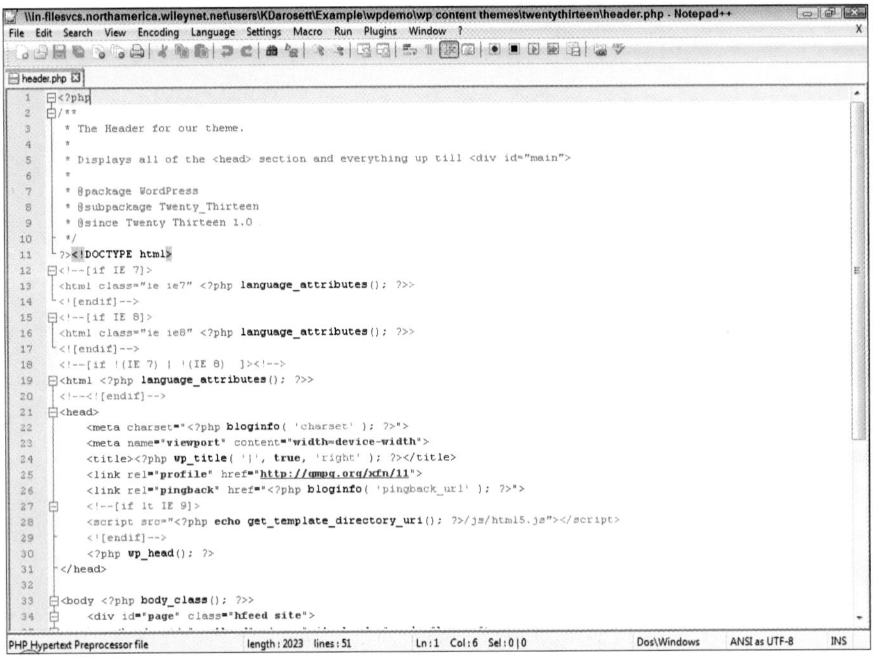

Figure 5-2: Notepad++ with color-coded syntax.

Code syntax highlighting

Excluding Notepad, all the text editors I mention in this chapter are considered *syntax editors* — they follow code syntax highlighting formats for different types of code like PHP, JavaScript, HTML, and CSS. Notice that lines of code are highlighted by different colors, making it easy for you to read and separate the type of code and markup you're looking at. The way the code executes isn't affected; the highlighting is purely a readability feature that makes reading through lines and lines of code easier on the eyes and on the brain.

TextMate (Mac)

TextMate is an Apple product and, as such, can be used only on a Mac. TextMate is the most popular text editor for Mac and is referred to as "the missing editor." Like Notepad++, TextMate is a *syntax editor* — it color-codes the markup and code that you write and has several features expected of most syntax editors, including

- Easy searching and replacing
- Auto-indenting and color-coding markup and code
- Opening several documents, each in their own tab, when applicable
- Working as an external editor for FTP programs

TextMate isn't free, however. You can download a free 30-day trial from `http://macromates.com`. After the free trial ends, you can buy a single-user license for $56.

Understanding and Choosing a Web Browser

Knowing which web browser to use as your primary browser can be confusing because so many are available. Everyone has their favorite browser, and if you don't already, one will emerge as your favorite for one reason or another. Each browser system has a different look and feel as well as different features and tools. You'll find that a certain browser's features and tools will make it your preferred browser for your personal browsing experience.

One thing you need to keep in mind, however, is that you must have access to all major browsers so that you can test and view your web designs in different browsers to make sure they render and look the same.

If you can, download and install all the browsers I discuss in this section so you have them at your fingertips to test your designs across the systems. Some browsers are system-specific (either only for Windows or only for Macs), so use the ones that are for your system.

Discovering browsers and tools

A multitude of browser systems are available on the web. This section takes you through five major browsers that are the most popular among Internet users. Additionally, you find some helpful tools, add-ons, and extensions that assist you with your web design efforts in the different browser systems. These include some of my favorite and must-have tools I use on a regular basis.

As far as the design and development communities are concerned, the choice over which web browser to use typically falls on how compliant the browser is with open web standards developed by the *World Wide Web Consortium (W3C),* an international community that develops web standards to ensure long-term web growth (www.w3.org). As a designer, you should at least have a working knowledge of what the W3C is and the standards it supports and promotes. You can read about the W3C vision and mission statement at www.w3.org/consortium/mission.html.

Google Chrome

Google *Chrome* (www.google.com/chrome) is the most popular web browser today, according to W3Schools report on browser statistics and trends: www.w3schools.com/browsers/browsers_stats.asp. Chrome was developed and released by Internet search giant, Google. Chrome has an active development community and has add-ons, or extensions, that you can install it easily on your computer on a Mac, Windows, or Linux.

You can find web development–related extensions for Google Chrome at https://chrome.google.com/extensions/featured/Web_dev.

Internet Explorer

Internet Explorer (IE) is by far one of the most popular browsers because it's part and parcel of all Microsoft Windows operating systems. Over the years, IE has struggled with its reputation of not keeping up or being compliant with web standards and CSS rendering that the development and design communities have come to love and expect from other browser systems. This is largely because of the layout engine in use at the foundation of IE. (For more on layout engines, see "Understanding cross-browser compatibility," later in this chapter.)

One of the challenges that designers come across is the different versions of Internet Explorer that are widely used across the web. With each new version, Microsoft's flagship browser comes closer and closer to compliance with open web standards, however. But because IE is the browser present with millions of operating systems across the world, not every individual user or company is quick to adopt the new versions as they are released. This results in several versions of IE in use across the world, and designers generally make an effort to ensure their designs render correctly on, at least, the last two to three recent versions of IE.

Currently, the versions of Internet Explorer that are supported by the majority of designers are versions 8, 9 and 10, with most designers gradually dropping support for versions 6 and 7 (commonly referred to as IE6 and IE7, respectively).

Trying to test designs on different versions of Internet Explorer is difficult because attempting to install different versions on your computer can cause some big headaches if you don't know exactly what you're doing. I use a few tools for overall browser testing (see the later section "Understanding cross-browser compatibility" in this chapter), but a tool called IETester comes in handy for specifically testing different IE versions. You can download IETester from `www.my-debugbar.com/wiki/IETester`. In Figure 5-3, buttons across the top are labeled for specific IE versions: IE5.5, IE6, IE7, IE8, IE9, and IE10. The figure displays the WordPress website in IE7.

Figure 5-3: Test different IE versions with IETester.

Mozilla Firefox

Firefox is the second most popular web browser and has emerged over the years as a solid IE competitor. Designers and developers tend to prefer Firefox over IE because *Mozilla* (the makers of Firefox) uses a solid layout engine that adheres closely to open web standards and supports and renders CSS better.

Firefox is available for download and use on Windows, Mac, and Linux operating systems and in more than 70 languages. You can download it from the Mozilla website at `http://mozilla.com`.

One of the main reasons Firefox is my personal browser of choice goes beyond the fact that it adheres to open web standards and renders CSS as it was meant to be rendered. Firefox is also an open-source software project with a vibrant development community that releases very helpful add-ons and tools, which extend its capabilities beyond just a web browser, turning it into a web development tool, in many cases.

You can find Firefox add-ons at `https://addons.mozilla.org/firefox` for just about everything from the appearance of your Firefox browser to browser-based games.

And the rest

A couple other web browsers are used regularly but aren't quite as popular as Chrome, IE, or Firefox. However, they're worth checking out:

- **Opera:** Opera (`www.opera.com`) is available for Windows, Mac, and Linux and markets itself as fast, secure, and completely in line with open web standards, including cutting-edge development languages like HTML5 and CSS3. Opera has add-ons available as well, which you can find at `http://addons.opera.com`.

- **Safari:** Safari (`www.apple.com/safari`) is installed on every Mac, from large iMacs to MacBook laptops to iPads and iPhones. In short, Safari is an Apple product; however, it can also be installed on Windows. Instead of a bunch of add-ons that you can download and install for web development, Safari has built-in web developer tools, such as

  - A developer toolbar with tools for website manipulation, testing, and debugging

  - A Web Inspector with a wealth of web development tools, including an Element pane where you can inspect CSS markup

  - A Resources pane that displays a website's resources by date, size, and speed

  - A JavaScript Debugger that displays any problems your site is experiencing due to JavaScript that is in use

  - A Timeline pane that analyzes a website's behavior over time

  - A JavaScript Profiler that lists the performance characteristics of scripts that run on a website

  - A Console pane for debugging

  - A Snippet Editor to test HTML markup

Understanding cross-browser compatibility

Cross-browser compatibility is the practice of testing designs across all major browser systems and is important in web design because you don't just design websites for yourself, but for an entire audience on the web. Because you have no idea what browser your audience uses, you must test your designs in all the systems to ensure that all your website visitors have the same experience.

The problem that web designers run into with web browsers is that each browser system uses a different *layout engine* (the browser's underlying code that powers the way the browser interprets design language such as CSS and HTML) that renders CSS differently. The difference in CSS rendering can sometimes make it a real challenge to adjust your CSS styling so that it takes into account the different layout engines available. Additionally, not every layout engine supports all CSS versions. Table 5-1 illustrates the different layout engines, browsers, and CSS versions the layout engine supports to give you an idea of what you're dealing with in different browser systems. You can find more information on CSS versions, support, and validation in Chapter 14.

Table 5-1	Layout Engines, Browser Types, and CSS Version Support	
Layout Engine	*Browser System*	*Supports CSS Version*
Gecko	Mozilla Firefox	CSS v1, v2, v3 (partially)
Presto	Opera	CSS v1, v2, v3 (partially)
Trident	Internet Explorer	CSS v1, v2, v3 (slightly)
WebKit	Google Chrome, Safari	CSS v1, v2, v3 (partially)

In Table 5-1, partially means that the browser system supports most of the features of the CSS version; slightly means that the browser system supports very few features.

The absolute best way to test your website across the major browser systems is to download the browsers to your computer and then load your website in each browser, checking for correct rendering as you go. However, if you have only a Windows computer, you can't really test your website on a Mac, and vice versa. Don't fret, though, because here are two alternatives that I use when I need to test my sites on a browser I don't have access to:

- ✔ **Browsershots:** This is an online, browser-based tool. Visit the Browsershots website (http://browsershots.org), enter your desired web address in the Enter URL Here field at the top of the page, and then choose your desired browsers and operating systems. Browsershots takes a screenshot of your website in each of the browsers that you indicate so you can see what your website looks like. From there, you can fix any problems and retest again, if needed.

- ✔ **BrowserStack:** BrowserStack is another online cross-browser compatibility testing tool that gives you real-time views of your website using a Flash interface. This service is free; however, option premium upgrades are available for a cost at http://browserstack.com.

Introducing File Transfer Protocol (FTP)

Throughout this book, you run into the term *File Transfer Protocol (FTP)*. You use FTP to perform various tasks, such as uploading and downloading WordPress files, editing files, and changing file permissions.

This section introduces you to the basic FTP elements. The ability to use FTP with your hosting account is a given for almost every web host on the market. FTP is a way of moving files from one place to another, such as

- **Uploading:** Transferring files from your local computer to your web server

- **Downloading:** Transferring files from your web server to your local computer

You can do several other things with FTP:

- **View files:** After you log in via FTP, you can see all the files that are located on your web server.

- **See dates when files were modified:** You can see the date the file(s) was last modified, which can sometimes be helpful when troubleshooting problems.

- **See file sizes:** You can see the size of each file on your web server, which is helpful especially if you need to manage the disk space on your account.

- **Edit files:** Almost all FTP clients allow you to open and edit files through the client interface, which is a convenient way to get the job done.

- **Change permissions:** Commonly referred to as CHMOD (change mode), it controls what type of read/write/execute permissions the files on your web server have.

Using FTP to transfer files requires an FTP *client,* or program. Many FTP clients are available for download. Following are some good (and free) ones:

- **WS_FTP LE (Windows):** www.wsftple.com

- **SmartFTP (Windows):** www.smartftp.com/download

- **FileZilla (Windows or Mac):** http://sourceforge.net/projects/filezilla

- **Cyberduck (Windows or Mac):** http://cyberduck.ch

- **FTP Explorer (Windows):** www.ftpx.com

Your web host gives you a username and password for your account, including an FTP IP address. (Usually, the FTP address is the same as your domain name, but check with your web host because addresses may vary.) It is this information — the username, password, and FTP IP address — that you insert into the FTP program to connect it to your hosting account. (See the next section for details on connecting to your web hosting account via FTP.)

Figure 5-4 shows my FTP client connected to my hosting account. The directory on the left is the listing of files on my computer; the directory on the right shows the listing of files on my hosting account.

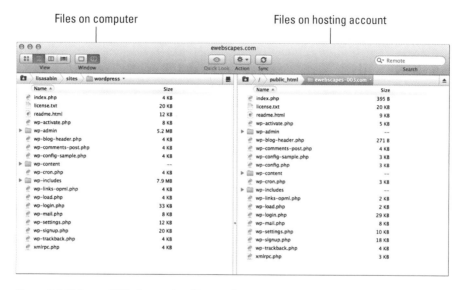

Figure 5-4: Using an FTP client makes file transfers easy.

FTP clients make it easy to transfer files from your computer to your hosting account by using a drag-and-drop method. Simply click the file on your computer that you want to transfer, drag it over to the side that lists the directory on your hosting account, and drop it. Depending on the FTP client you've chosen to work with, you can refer to its user manuals or support documentation for detailed information on how to use the program.

Setting Up FTP on Your Hosting Account

Many web hosts offer FTP as part of their hosting packages, so just confirm that your hosting provider makes FTP available to you for your account. In Chapter 2, I discuss in detail the specifics of a web-hosting environment, and most web hosts provide *cPanel* — a hosting account management interface. cPanel is by far the most popular hosting account management software used by many hosts on the web. Others, such as Plesk and Netadmin, are widely used as well but aren't as popular.

In this chapter, I use cPanel; if your hosting provider gives you a different interface to work with, the concepts are the same, but refer to your hosting provider for the specifics to adapt my directions to your specific environment.

By and large, the FTP for your hosting account is set up automatically. Follow these few steps to get to the FTP Accounts page, shown in Figure 5-5, to view and set up your FTP account:

1. **Log in to the cPanel for your hosting account:**

   a. *Browse to* `http://yourdomain.com/cpanel` *to bring up the login screen for your cPanel (where* `yourdomain` *is your actual domain name).*

   b. *Enter your specific hosting account username and password in the login fields and then click OK.*

2. **Click the FTP Accounts link and/or icon in your cPanel to open the FTP Accounts page, shown in Figure 5-5.**

3. **Check to see if you have an existing FTP Account.**

   If you already have an existing FTP Account, you can skip the rest of the steps in this section.

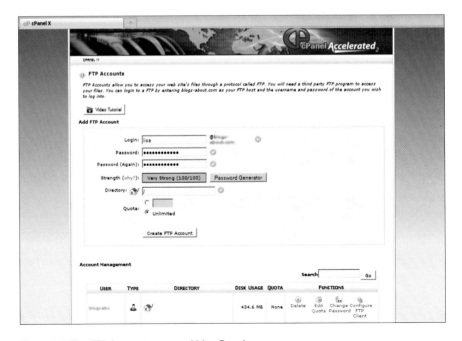

Figure 5-5: The FTP Accounts page within cPanel.

If your hosting provider automatically sets you up with an FTP account, you see it in the Account Management section. Ninety-nine percent of the time, the default FTP account uses the same username and password combination as your hosting account, or the login information you used to log in to your cPanel in Step 1.

4. **(Optional) Create a new FTP Account.**

   If the FTP Accounts page doesn't show a default FTP user in the Account Management section, create one in the Add FTP Account section with these steps:

   a. *Type your desired username in the Login text field.*

      This creates the username of `username@yourdomain.com` (in which *username* is the desired username you typed and *your domain.com* is your specific domain name).

   b. *Type your desired password in the Password text field and then retype it in the Password (Again) text box to validate it.*

      You can either type your own chosen password or click the Password Generator button to have the server generate a secure password for you.

   c. *Check the Strength indicator.*

      The server tells you whether your password is Very Weak, Weak, Good, Strong, or Very Strong, as shown in Figure 5-5. You want a Very Strong password for your FTP account so it's very hard for hackers and malicious Internet users to guess and crack.

   d. *Leave the Directory text box blank.*

      Leaving this field blank gives you access to the root level of your hosting account, which as the site owner, you want. Therefore, leave this field blank. (In the future, if you set up FTP accounts for other users, you can lock their access to your hosting directory by indicating which directory the FTP user has access to.)

   e. *Leave the default Unlimited radio button selected to indicate the space limitations in the Quota text field.*

      In the future, if you add a new FTP user, you can limit the amount of space, in megabytes (MB), by selecting the other radio button and typing the numerical amount, such as **50MB**, in the text box.

   f. *Click the Create FTP Account button.*

      A new screen loads with a message that the account was created successfully; it also displays the settings for this new FTP account.

   g. *Copy and paste these settings into a text editor, such as Notepad or TextMate.*

      These settings contain the connection details you need to connect via FTP and looks like this (the FTP username, password, and server are specific to your domain and the information you entered in the preceding steps):

FTP Username: lisa@yourdomain.com

Password: {W?$s((7Tqi

FTP Server: ftp.yourdomain.com

FTP Server Port: 21 (your web server automatically assigns the FTP Port)

Quota: Unlimited MB

At any time, you can revisit the FTP Accounts page to delete the FTP accounts you've created, change the quota, change the password, or find the connection details specific to that account.

Transferring Files with an FTP Client

After you create an FTP account on your web server, as described in the preceding section, you're ready to connect your FTP client to your web server so you can begin transferring files.

Connecting to the web server via FTP

For the purposes of this chapter, I use the Mozilla FileZilla FTP client (http://sourceforge.net/projects/filezilla). FileZilla is my favorite FTP client software because it's easy to use and the cost is free ninety-nine (that's open-source geek speak for *free!*).

My FileZilla client is shown in Figure 5-6; it's not yet connected to any server. On the left of the window is a directory listing of files and folders on my local computer. The right side of the window doesn't display anything . . . yet; it will, however, when I connect to my web server.

If you use different FTP client software than FileZilla, the steps and look of the software differ from what I share with you in this chapter. Adapt your steps and practice for the specific FTP client software you use.

Connecting to a web server is a pretty easy process. Before you begin, however, you need the FTP settings from Step 4 in the preceding section. Then to connect to your web server via the FileZilla FTP client, follow these few steps:

1. **Launch the FTP client software on your local computer.**

2. **Choose File⇨Site Manager to open the Site Manager, as shown in Figure 5-7.**

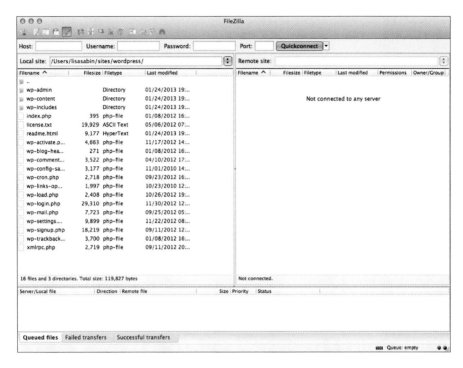

Figure 5-6: FileZilla FTP client software.

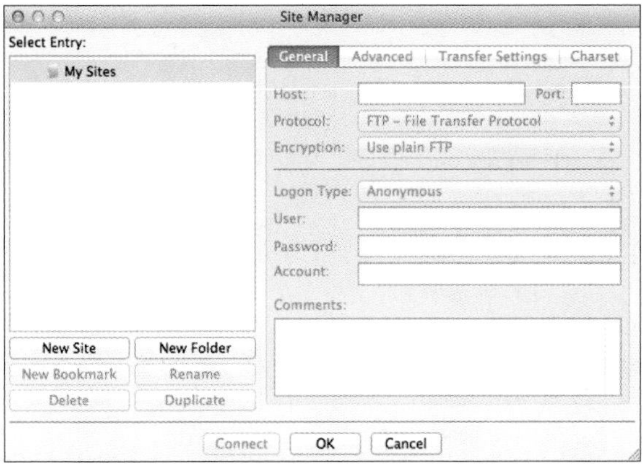

Figure 5-7: The Site Manager in FileZilla.

3. **Click the New Site button and name your site.**

You can give the new site a name to help you identify it. This site name can be anything you want because it's not part of the connection data that you add in the next steps. (In Figure 5-8, I named mine *My Site* — pretty original, I know.)

4. **Enter the FTP server in the Host text field.**

   The *host name* is the same as the FTP server information provided to you when you set up the FTP account on your web server. My FTP server is `mydomain.com` (where `mydomain.com` is your actual domain name), so I typed that in the Host text field, as shown in Figure 5-8.

5. **Enter the FTP port in the Port text field.**

   My port is 21. Typically, in most hosting environments, FTP uses port 21 and SFTP (secure FTP) uses port 22, and this never changes — just be sure to double-check your port number and enter it in the Port text field, as shown in Figure 5-8 (check with your web host about which protocol you should be using).

6. **Choose FTP – File Transfer Protocol from the Protocol drop-down list and then choose Normal in the Logon Type drop-down list (see Figure 5-8).**

7. **Type your username in the User text field and then type your password in the Password text field.**

   This is the username and password given to you in the FTP settings. For example, my username is `lisa@yourdomain.com`, and my password is `{W?$s((7Tqi`.

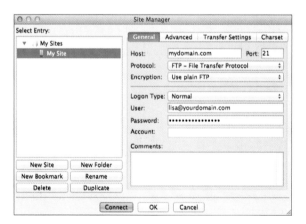

Figure 5-8: The FileZilla Site Manager with FTP account information.

8. **Click the Connect button.**

   Your computer connects to your web server. The directory of folders and files from your local computer appears on the left of the FileZilla FTP client window, and the directory of folders and files on your web server is displayed on the right.

Now you can take advantage of all the tools and features FTP offers.

Transferring files from point A to point B

After your local computer is connected to your web server, transferring files between the two couldn't be easier. Within the FTP client software, you can browse the directories and folders on your local computer on the left and browse the directories and folders on your web server on the right.

FTP clients make it easy to transfer files from your computer to your hosting account by using a drag-and-drop method. There are two ways of transferring files. Here's what they are and how you use them:

- **Upload:** This generally means that you transfer files from your local computer to your web server, or *upload* files. Click the file you want to transfer from your local computer and drag and drop it over to the right side (the web server side) to upload a file from your computer to your web server.

- **Download:** This means that you transfer files from you web server to your local computer, or *download* files. Click the file you want to transfer from your web server and drag and drop it over to the left side (the local computer side) to download a file from your web server to your local computer.

Downloading files from your web server is an efficient, easy, and smart way of backing up files to your local computer. Keeping your files, especially theme files and plugins, safe is always a good idea.

Editing files by using FTP

You will run into situations where you need to edit files that live on your web server. You can use the methods I describe earlier: Download a file from your web server, open it, edit it, save it, and then upload it back to your web server. Or, you can use the built-in edit feature that exists in most FTP client software by following these steps:

1. **Connect your FTP client to your web server and then locate the file you want to edit.**

2. **To use the internal FTP editor, right-click the file and choose View/Edit.**

   Remember, for the example, I'm using FileZilla — your FTP client may name this command something like Open or Edit. Usually, the FTP client uses a program that already exists on your computer, such as Notepad (Windows) or TextMate (Mac), to edit the files. Occasionally, depending on the FTP client software, it may have its own internal text editor. FileZilla uses a text-editing program that's already on your computer.

3. **Edit the file to your liking, click the Save icon or choose File⇨Save to save the changes you made to the file, and re-upload the file to your web server.**

After you save the file, a window opens in FileZilla that alerts you that the file's been changed and asks whether you wish to upload the file back to the server.

4. **Click the Yes button.**

The newly edited file replaces the old one.

That is really all there is to it. Use the FTP edit feature to edit, save, and re-upload files as you need to.

When you edit files using the FTP edit feature, you edit files in a *live* environment, meaning that when you save the changes and re-upload a file, the changes take effect immediately and affect your live website. For this reason, I always strongly recommend downloading a copy of the original file to your local computer before making changes. That way, if you happen to make a typo on the saved file and your website goes haywire, you have a copy of the original to re-upload quickly to restore it to its original state.

Changing file permissions

Every file and folder that exists on your web server has a set of attributions, or *permissions,* assigned that tells the web server three things about the folder or file. On a very simplistic level, these permissions include

- ✔ **Read:** Determines whether the file/folder is readable by the web server
- ✔ **Write:** Determines whether the file/folder is writeable by the web server
- ✔ **Execute:** Determines whether the file/folder is executable by the web server

Each set of permissions has a numerical code assigned it, identifying what type of permissions are assigned to that file or folder. There are a lot of them, but here are the most common ones that you run into and deal with when running a WordPress website:

- ✔ **644:** Files with permissions set to 644 are readable by everyone and writeable only by the file/folder owner.
- ✔ **755:** Files with permissions set to 755 are readable and executable by everyone, but only writeable by the file/folder owner.
- ✔ **777:** Files with permissions set to 777 are readable, writeable, and executable by everyone. Don't use this set of permissions, for security reasons, on your web server unless absolutely necessary.

Typically, folders and files within your web server have already been assigned permissions of either 644 or 755. You usually see PHP files with permissions set to 644 if the web server is configured to use PHP Safe Mode.

I'm giving you a very basic look at file permissions here because you usually don't need to mess with file permissions on your web server. In case you need to dig further into this topic, here's a great reference on file permissions from Elated: www.elated.com/articles/understanding-permissions/.

You may run across a situation in which you're asked to edit and change the file permissions on a particular file on your web server. With WordPress sites, this usually happens when dealing with plugins or theme files. This practice is also referred to as *CHMOD*, or *Change Mode*. When someone says, "You need to CHMOD that file to 755," you'll know what she's talking about.

Here are some quick and easy steps for using your FTP program to CHMOD a file, or edit its permissions on your web server:

1. **Connect your FTP client to your web server and then locate the file you want to CHMOD.**

2. **In FileZilla, right-click the file on your web server and choose File Permissions to open the file attributes.**

   Your FTP client may use different terminology.

   The Change File Attributes dialog box opens, as shown in Figure 5-9.

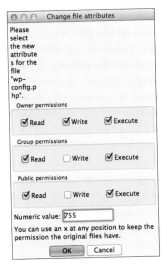

Figure 5-9: The Change File Attributes dialog box in FileZilla.

3. **Type the correct number in the Numeric Value text field.**

   This is the number assigned to the permissions you want to give the file. Most often, you're given directions by the plugin or theme developer on which permissions number to assign to the file or folder, and typically, it's either 644 or 755. In Figure 5-9, you see the permissions are assigned with 755.

4. **Click OK.**

   The file saves with the new permissions assigned.

6

Choosing Graphics and Software Resources

*T*hese days, the term *designer* encompasses many things relating to the world of web design. A *graphic designer* has the ability and creativity to create graphics from scratch, or to modify existing photos or graphics to suit a particular need using image-editing software. Other *web designers* don't necessarily create any graphic designs, but they master the art of manipulating images and photos to display on a website for a nice visual presentation.

This chapter takes a look at some of the popular graphic-editing software available (such as Adobe Photoshop and Illustrator and Corel PaintShop Pro), as well as some great and inexpensive image and graphic resources to add to your toolbox. You also find out the differences among various image formats and how to optimize images for a website so pages load faster while the images look sharp and clean.

Exploring Image Types and Formats

Graphics software packages don't come cheap, so before you make a decision on which one to use, you need to determine what type of graphic work you'll do for your web design projects. Web designers fall into three standard categories, and your design style may fall into one, two, or all three:

✓ **Graphic designer:** You may consider yourself an illustrator because you create all the graphics that you use from scratch. You start with a blank slate, and through different tools and techniques used in your favorite image-editing software, you create your own unique graphics.

✔ **Graphic manipulator:** You're a master at taking graphics, or photos, that someone else created and manipulating them for use in your web design projects. Through the use of different tools and techniques, you can do things like adjust colors and sizes, and even change the shapes and positions of the different elements of a graphic (particularly if you're working with vector graphics, covered in the next section).

✔ **Graphic consumer:** You download images from resources on the web (check out my list of resources later in this chapter), and you use those images to add color and visual design elements to your website projects.

As I state earlier, you may fit one, two, or all three of these categories, and that's perfectly acceptable when designing themes for websites as long as you abide by copyright and licensing restrictions on graphics you use (if you're a graphics manipulator and/or consumer). Additionally, it is important to understand the types of graphics that you can use to accomplish your goals for your web design projects. The following sections cover different types of graphics and file formats to help you understand which types of graphics you need to use for different purposes.

Comparing raster and vector images

As a graphic designer, you'll most likely work with two types of graphics — raster and vector. As a web designer, you'll definitely work with raster images, and you may work with vector images. The software program that you use to edit and create graphics depends on the type of image file you're working with. Here is a brief rundown of the differences between the raster and vector images:

✔ **Raster:** These images are made up of hundreds of little dots, or *pixels*. Each pixel can be a different color, allowing for rich, full-color images and photographs. Creating and editing a raster image calls for a raster-based editing program, such as Corel's PaintShop Pro or Photoshop.

✔ **Vector:** These images are made up of *curves* rather than pixels. Vector images have four vector points, one in each corner of the image, and you connect the dots with curves. Then, the curves can be filled with colors and effects.

The following sections go into more detail about raster and vector images and how you may use them in your web designs.

Raster images

Raster images, such as photographs and graphics used in the website theme design, are most often used for web design and display on websites. Raster images don't scale well; if you try to resize the image larger or smaller, you see a noticeable loss in the image quality because the pixels get resized and the image becomes grainy. Raster images are *flat* — there's only one layer to the image elements — making it difficult (and sometimes impossible) to edit some of the different image elements within the graphic file. For use on the web, however, raster images load quickly because they usually have a small file size and don't require a lot of bandwidth to transfer.

Figure 6-1 shows a raster image file open in Photoshop. On the right side, on the Layers tab, there is only one layer — Background — to this raster image. Common file formats for raster images include JPG, GIF, and PNG. (I discuss file formats for images in the section "Looking at image file formats," later in this chapter.)

Figure 6-1: A raster image in Photoshop.

Vector images

Vector images are used for print design, such as business cards, brochures, magazine ads, and billboards. Because vector images are made up of curves rather than static pixels, vector images can be resized without any quality loss. Therefore, you can reduce a vector image to the size of a postage stamp or increase its size to fit the side of a large truck, and the image quality remains the same. That's why vector images are ideal for logos and print work. Typically, vector images are *layered* — each element of the image has its own layer — allowing you to use your favorite vector image editor, such as Illustrator, to manipulate and change the different elements within the vector image file.

The file sizes of vector images can get quite large, so they're not ideal for displaying on a website; you'll want to use raster images instead. However, you can start out working with a vector file for your web design work and then save the final file in a raster format that's optimized for the web.

Figure 6-2 displays a vector image file open in Illustrator. On the bottom right, on the Layers tab, you see several layers available for editing on this particular image. Common file formats for vector images include AI, EPS, and CDR. (I discuss these file formats in the next section, "Looking at image file formats.")

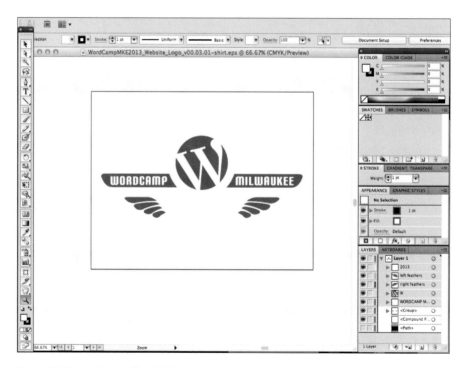

Figure 6-2: Vector image file with layers open in Illustrator.

Looking at image file formats

Before I discuss recommended graphic-editing software, you need to understand the types of image file formats you will work with for designing on the web. As I mention earlier, the images — whether photos or logos — you save and use on your website should be raster file types because of the smaller file size and rich color display. In the following sections, you find out how compression affects the size of raster images and discover what types of file formats you may use in your own projects.

Understanding compression

When you use raster images in your web design, they need to have a certain amount of *compression,* or a decrease in the overall size of the file. Image compression occurs when you save a raster image file as a JPG, GIF, or PNG. Compressing a file decreases the size of the image file so that the image loads quicker on a web page.

The larger the image file size, the longer it takes for that image to load on your web page.

Compressing image files can use two different algorithms, depending on the file format you've chosen for your image file. For digital image files, compression happens in one of two ways:

- **Lossless compression:** All data from the image file is retained during and after compression, usually resulting in zero loss of quality from the original image file.

- **Lossy compression:** This reduces the size of an image file by removing certain bits of data from the original file or by combining parts of the image that are similar to one another. This usually results in image-quality loss from the original file.

Determining which file types to use for your projects

Table 6-1 lists six common file formats you'll work with for web design and the type of file and compression. Although the final image files that you save and use in your web design work should be raster, you may begin with vector images to edit and manipulate graphics to suit the needs of your web design projects.

Table 6-1	Image File Format, Compression, and Type	
Image File Format	*Image File Type*	*Compression Type*
JPG	Raster	Lossy
GIF	Raster	Lossless
PNG	Raster	Lossless
AI	Vector	N/A*
EPS	Vector	N/A*
CDR	Vector	N/A*

*Vector images do not experience compression.

Here are the three main vector image formats that you'll probably come across in your work with graphic design:

- ✔ **AI:** Adobe Illustrator, a proprietary file developed by Adobe for representing vector images

- ✔ **EPS:** Encapsulated PostScript vector image format

- ✔ **CDR:** CorelDRAW proprietary graphic file developed by Corel for representing vector images

When deciding what raster image file format to use in your project, take into account the characteristics of each format. In addition to different types of compression, the file formats also contain varying amounts of color. The characteristics of the three most common raster image file formats include

- ✔ **JPG:** This format is suited for photographs and smaller images used in your web design projects. Although the JPG format compresses with lossy compression, you can adjust the amount of compression that occurs when you save the file. You can choose a compression level from 1 to 100, and you usually don't see a great deal of image quality loss with compression levels 1–20.

- ✔ **PNG:** This format is suited for larger graphics used in web design, such as the logo or main header graphic that identifies the brand and the overall, visual look of the website. PNG uses lossless image compression and, therefore, suffers no data loss during compression, creating a cleaner, sharper image. PNG files can also be created and saved on a transparent canvas, whereas JPG files can't. JPG files must have at least a white *canvas* (background), or some other color that you've designated.

- ✔ **GIF:** Compression of a GIF file is *lossless*, rendering the image exactly as you designed it without quality loss. However, GIF files are limited to 256 colors. For higher-color images, GIF isn't the greatest format to use; use the PNG format instead.

Exploring Graphic Design Software

In the following sections, I introduce you to four software programs that designers use to create graphics and edit images, as well as provide you with some valuable resources that you can use to figure out the intricacies of the software programs presented here.

Graphic design software can get expensive; however, the software packages that I mention in this section offer trial versions that allow you to test drive the software before you fork out the cash — I recommend the practice of try-before-you-buy to make sure the software fits your needs.

The type of image file or format you're working with determines which type of software you use for that particular image. Raster images require a raster-based program, and likewise, vector images require a vector-based program. (See the earlier section "Comparing raster and vector images.")

Using raster-based software

The two most common raster-based graphic software programs used by designers are Photoshop and PaintShop Pro. Although these programs have vector capabilities as well, they aren't known as vector-editing programs, and their vector capabilities are somewhat limited. When you work with raster images, you need at least one of these two programs in your arsenal to create your designs.

Adobe Creative Cloud

Available from Adobe Systems, which has several graphics programs and design software suites, Photoshop is the most popular software for raster images, and Illustrator is the most popular software for editing and working with vector images. Everything you need is available online via the Creative Cloud from Adobe at `www.adobe.com/products/creativecloud.html`. The cost for a new Creative Cloud member is $49.99 per month, but there are a variety of other less costly plans that may also suit your needs.

With graphic and web designers using Photoshop, the most popular format is a PSD file. A *PSD file* is a single image file with multiple layers that contain complex image effects and text layers that compose a full image. PSD files are often used and developed to create full website designs. You can lay out an entire design look for a web page in one file, and then using different layers and elements, you can create one, flat raster image for use in the overall design.

Figure 6-3 displays a PSD file in Photoshop. On the bottom-right side on the Layers tab are several layers that compose the file. The PSD file shown in Figure 6-3 is a website project I developed for one of my clients. I can open a PSD file anytime to change or edit any of the graphics, and then save the graphic as a single file in JPG, PNG, or GIF formats to use on the web.

Figure 6-3: A PSD file in Photoshop.

You can add several tools (developed by either Adobe or third-party developers) to the Photoshop software to help you create effects and elements for your graphic design, including

✔ **Plugins:** These small add-on programs created by Adobe, or third-party developers, add new features and effects to Photoshop, such as the array of Photoshop plugins available from Alien Skin (www. alienskin.com).

✔ **Brushes:** These small graphics created by Adobe, or third-party designers, give you some great effects to use with the Paintbrush tool in Photoshop.

✔ **Patterns and textures:** These small graphic files created by Adobe, or third-party designers, give you interesting textures and pattern effects to use in your graphic design.

Photoshop is also well-known for its built-in tools for editing and enhancing photographs. Many photographers use Photoshop for this purpose, and as a web designer, you can also take advantage of the photo-editing tools in Photoshop to enhance and optimize photographs for your website designs.

If you're interested in finding out more about how to use Photoshop, check out *Photoshop CS6 All-in-One For Dummies* (Wiley) by Barbara Obermeier or any of the online resources listed in Table 6-2.

Table 6-2	Online Photoshop Resources
Resource Name	**Description**
Photoshop.com	The official Photoshop marketplace where you can find and download Photoshop tools like brushes and textures, as well as find tips and tutorials: `http://photoshop.com`
Psdtuts+	A popular blog that covers Photoshop tutorials from beginner to advanced levels of experience and knowledge: `http://psd.tutsplus.com`
Planet Photoshop	A website where you find several Photoshop tutorials, resources, and reviews: `http://planetphotoshop.com`

Corel PaintShop Pro

Available from Corel, well-known for its suite of graphic-editing and photo-manipulation software, is the PaintShop Pro X5 image and photo-editing software available for purchase and download at `http://corel.com`. PaintShop Pro is available for download as a single product ($49.99), or as part of the larger Paint Shop Pro X5 Ultimate software suite that bundles several digital image, photo-editing, and design products ($59.99). Currently, Corel PaintShop Pro is available only for Windows.

Figure 6-4 shows how you can control the amount of compression that's applied to JPG files when saving them in PaintShop Pro. (See the earlier section "Understanding compression.") In the figure, I apply a compression level of 10 to the photo that I'm saving. This amount of compression is a good trade-off between reducing the file size and retaining much of the original image quality. PaintShop Pro allows you to preview the compressed image before you save it, so you can decide whether or not you like how much compression you've added, and can adjust if needed.

PaintShop Pro makes several add-on tools and utilities available to extend the capabilities of the program, enabling you to increase its feature set for methods and techniques you can use to create and edit images, including

✔ **Plugins:** These add-on programs developed by Corel or third-party developers extend the features of the program. Photoshop has plugins as well, and you can use those plugins with PaintShop Pro because they're compatible.

 ✔ **Masks and tubes:** These small image files created by Corel or third-party designers give you some different image effects and graphics you can use in your designs.

 ✔ **Brushes and textures:** These small image files created by Corel or third-party designers allow you to add different effects and elements to your design work.

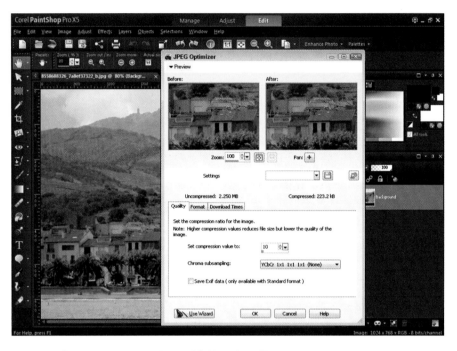

Figure 6-4: Compressing and saving a JPG file in PaintShop Pro.

Table 6-3 gives you a few PaintShop Pro resources, including downloadable add-ons, tutorials, and discussion forums to extend your knowledge base and improve your techniques.

Table 6-3	PaintShop Pro Online Resources
Resource Name	*Description*
Corel Resources page	Contains tutorials, tips, and tricks: `www.corel.com/servlet/Satellite/us/en/Content/1152796555465`
PaintShop Pro Forum	PaintShop Pro forum: `http://forum.corel.com/EN/viewforum.php?f=56`

I am asked a lot whether Photoshop or PaintShop Pro is the best for raster-based image files. I use both for different cases; however, I can say that Photoshop is the most popular mainly because it's available for Windows and Mac, whereas PaintShop Pro is available only for Windows. Also, with Photoshop, you can create layered PSD files for full website designs, whereas with PaintShop Pro, you can't (but you can edit them, with some limitations). Of course, Photoshop is much more expensive, so if price is a big consideration for you, you may want to opt for the more affordable PaintShop Pro.

Using vector-based software

Vector-based editing software lets you create quality vector graphics and illustrations that can then be saved in raster format for web use. Many illustrators, cartoonists, and logo designers start with vector editing programs to create vector images. (See the earlier section "Comparing raster and vector images.")

Two of the most popular vector-based editing programs are Illustrator and CorelDRAW. Whether you create vector files from scratch or edit/manipulate existing vector files, you need to have a vector-based editing program to take full advantage of all the editing tools and features.

Vector image files often have several layers containing complex and extensive design elements that add to the overall image. Programs like Photoshop or PaintShop Pro (which I describe in the preceding section) don't allow you to expand the layers available in a vector image.

Adobe Illustrator

Illustrator is a vector-image creation and editing program available as part of Adobe's Creative Cloud at `http://creative.adobe.com`.

With Illustrator, you can open an existing vector file and manipulate it easily by discovering the layers embedded in it. Refer to Figure 6-2 to see a simple illustration of a logo with multiple layers available for editing in Illustrator's Layers tab (shown in the bottom right). Figure 6-5 shows the same file opened in Photoshop; with the Layers tab, the different layers aren't available because Photoshop flattens the image. Illustrator leaves the different layers intact for editing and manipulation.

The file types that you most commonly work with and come across for Illustrator are AI and EPS. These are vector image files that you can easily open and edit in Illustrator.

If you're interested in finding out more about how to use Illustrator for your design needs, check out *Adobe Creative Suite 6 Design & Web Premium All-in-One For Dummies* by Jennifer Smith, Christopher Smith, and Fred Gerantabee (Wiley), or either of the handy online resources in Table 6-4.

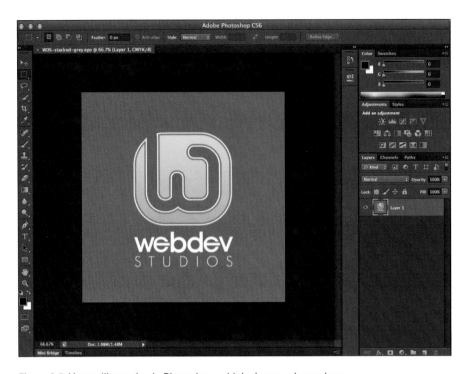

Figure 6-5: Vector illustration in Photoshop, which shows only one layer.

Table 6-4	Illustrator Online Resources
Resource Name	*Description*
N.Design Studio	Illustrator tutorials from the talented designers at N.Design Studio: www.ndesign-studio.com/tutorials
Vectortuts+	A site filled with tutorials, tips, and tricks: http://vector.tutsplus.com

CorelDRAW

CorelDRAW is a vector-based editing software available as part of the CorelDRAW Graphics Suite X6 ($479; http://corel.com). CorelDRAW is currently available only for Windows.

Like Illustrator, CorelDRAW lets you create and edit vector-based images by manipulating the available layers embedded within the vector image file.

Within the program, click the layer or curve to select what you need to edit and make it active on your editing screen, allowing you to apply different effects and edit it to your liking.

You can easily open regular vector image file formats, such as AI and EPS, as well as the Corel-specific vector format, CDR. Table 6-5 gives you a few helpful online resources to find out more about using CorelDRAW for creating and editing vector images.

Table 6-5	CorelDRAW Online Resources
Resource Name	*Description*
Association of CorelDRAW Professionals	Includes newsletters, an online magazine, tutorials, tips, and advice from other users: `www.coreldrawpro.com`
Graphics Unleashed	CorelDRAW books and online training classes: `www.unleash.com`

Using Online Image-Optimization Tools

Earlier in this chapter, I recommend four image-editing software programs that you, the designer, can use to edit and manipulate images for use in your web designs. You can use these image programs to compress your image files as much as possible without losing image quality. However, what do you do when clients ask how they can compress their images, but don't have access to the same type of software as you? Your clients will use their WordPress website to upload photographs and images within their blog posts and pages, and you can advise them on a few easy online tools to help them compress the images to keep their website load time down as much as possible.

Here are a few nifty, free, online, image optimization tools that you and your clients can use:

✔ **Dynamic Drive:** This tool lets you input the web address of the image you want to compress, or upload an image from your computer. The image optimizer lets you choose what type of image you want to output — PNG, GIF, or JPG — or you can choose all three. After this tool gives you the optimized, compressed images, you can save them to your local computer (usually by right-clicking the images and choosing Save Image As) to use on your website later. (`http://tools.dynamicdrive.com/imageoptimizer`)

✔ **Yahoo! Smush.it:** This tool lets you upload an image from your computer or enter the URL of the image, and it optimizes and compresses the image to make it available for you to download. Smush.it also reports on the results of the image compression by telling you, in percentages, how much it was able to *smush,* or compress, your image. (`http://smushit.com`)

✔ **Image Optimizer:** Image Optimizer is another free online service that compresses and resizes your images in a downloadable format for you to use on your website. It's also available as an application that you can download to your computer so you can use it locally, rather than using the Image Optimizer website to compress your images. (`www.image optimizer.net`)

✔ **Web Resizer:** The Web Resizer tool does the same as the previous tools, allowing you to upload an image that it compresses and then makes available for download to your computer. This tool also provides other image-editing tools like resizing, cropping, adding borders, and changing the tint and contrast of the image. (`http://webresizer.com/ resizer`)

Finding Online Image Libraries

After you assemble your graphic- and image-editing software tools and understand the types of image files you're working with, locate some great image and photo libraries to add to your web design toolbox.

Frequently, when prospective clients approach you to design their websites, they provide some basic requirements, or specifications, they hope you can provide for their website designs. These requirements include things like color schemes, layout and format, content and features, and images for logos, header files, and design elements. If you're lucky, your clients come to you with their image files in hand, ready for you to use. If not, they look to you to either create those images or find suitable images from stock photo or stock illustration websites. Lucky for you, many are out there — and here are the top three that I look to in these situations:

✔ **iStockphoto:** An extensive library of stock photography, vector illustrations, video and audio clips, and Flash media. You can sign up for an account and search through its libraries of image files to find the one that suits you, or your client, best. The files that you use from iStockphoto aren't free — and be absolutely sure that you read the license for each image you use. iStockphoto has several licenses, and the cheapest one is its Standard license, which has some limitations. For example, you can use an illustration from iStockphoto in one website design, but you can't use that same illustration in a theme design that you intend to sell multiple times over (for example, in a premium theme marketplace). Be sure to read the fine print. (http://istockphoto.com)

✔ **Dreamstime:** Dreamstime is a major supplier of stock photography and digital images. Sign up for an account and search through its huge library of digital image offerings. Dreamstime offers free images occasionally — so keep your eyes out for those. Also, Dreamstime has different licenses for its image files that you need to pay close attention to. One really nice feature is its Royalty Free licensing option, which allows you to pay only once for the image and then use it as many times as you want; however, you can't redistribute the image in the same website theme over and over again, such as in one template, sold to the public multiple times. (http://dreamstime.com)

✔ **VectorStock:** VectorStock offers royalty-free vector-only illustrations and graphics for sale. You won't find stock photography here because VectorStock is limited to only vector illustrations. (You need a vector-based editing program like Illustrator or CorelDRAW to open and use these images.) As with other digital-image resources and libraries, licenses apply to the images that you purchase and use — be sure to read about the license of the image you purchase before using it in your web design projects. (www.vectorstock.com)

7

Choosing Colors and Fonts

In This Chapter

▶ Considering color schemes and palettes

▶ Finding color tools and resources

▶ Understanding font basics

▶ Finding fonts for your project

Two of the many decisions you'll make about a website design, whether for your site or your client's, are the color scheme and the fonts that'll be used in and around the site. Sometimes these choices will be easy because you, or your client, already have an established color scheme and chosen fonts. However, some design projects will require that you make new decisions on color choices and fonts.

Sometimes, making the decision on a color scheme that's just right can be very time-consuming because as a designer, you know that first impressions count, and color scheme is an important part of the start of any design process. Selecting the right fonts that you want to use is also an important part of branding an online identity, so knowing where to find the right fonts and tools to help you make the right choices gives you a good head start.

This chapter introduces you to the concepts of color schemes and palettes. I share tools and resources you can use to put together a fantastic color scheme. I also introduce you to the basic concepts of typography and web-safe fonts, and help you understand font licensing and where to find fonts that you can use in your web designs.

Understanding Color

If I've learned something in more than ten years in the web design industry, it's that people interpret colors differently, and what looks good to me doesn't necessarily look good to you, and vice versa. Many clients have asked me to create designs based on a color combination that I'll always remember simply because I thought it was so awful; but my client liked it, so

I completed the project with the full understanding that I could walk away when the project was over and never look at it ever again.

Color and preferences in color combinations are completely subjective and based on what looks good to each individual's eye. Because of this adage, I don't spend time telling you what colors look good and which color combinations work the best because those ideas are mainly based on preference and experience. The following sections introduce you to basic color theory and terminology to give you a good grasp of the concepts to help guide you toward choosing color and schemes with confidence and certainty.

Checking out the color wheel

Almost every graphic design program or web-based color scheme includes a red, green, blue (RGB) color wheel (shown in Figure 7-1) that basically separates colors into three groups:

- ✔ **Primary colors:** Includes the three main colors — red, green, and blue

- ✔ **Secondary colors:** Includes colors that you get when you mix equal amounts of primary colors together, such as mixing red and blue to create purple

- ✔ **Tertiary colors:** Includes colors that you get when you mix primary colors with secondary colors, such as cyan (blue-green), magenta (red-purple), or vermillion (red-orange)

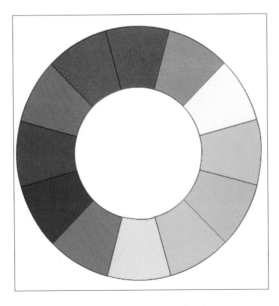

Figure 7-1: The standard RGB color wheel.

Additionally, you can use the color wheel to discover two main color groups, or *schemes:*

- ✔ **Complementary colors:** A pair, or group, of colors that exist directly opposite one another on the color wheel. Using the color wheel in Figure 7-1 as the guide, an example would be yellow and blue.

- ✔ **Analogous colors:** A pair, or group, of colors that are grouped closely together on the color wheel. Have a look at the color wheel in Figure 7-1, and you find analogous colors like orange and yellow, or red and orange.

You can find an easy-to-use online color wheel at `www.colorspire.com/rgb-color-wheel`. To use this wheel, simply click in the color square on the left to find complementary or analogous color schemes on the color wheel to the right.

Examining the RGB and hex color models

In web design, the two main color models that you'll deal with on a regular basis are the RGB and the hexadecimal (hex) systems, with the hex system being the most popular method to define colors in a Cascading Style Sheet (CSS). (See Chapter 14 for more on CSS.)

RGB

RGB is a model used to represent the display of colors through electronic devices, such as mobile devices and computer monitors. The RGB color model is based on the idea that any color can be created by combining different levels of red, green, and blue. Because you're designing for websites that are viewed through computer monitors and mobile devices, the RGB color model is the standard basis of color in web design.

RGB colors are represented by three numbers, each of which is indicative of how much red, green, and blue exist within the specific color. Each color has a numerical range of 256 levels of brightness represented by 0–255. You can mix and match colors by increasing or decreasing the numbers of each individual color until you find the color you like. Based on the 256 values available for each color, using the 0–255 numbers, here's what each color equals:

- ✔ **Red:** R: 255 G: 0 B: 0 (255, 0, 0)
- ✔ **Green:** R: 0 G: 255 B: 0 (0, 255, 0)
- ✔ **Blue:** R: 0 G: 0 B: 255 (0, 0, 255)

Luckily, interactive color wheels, such as the one shown in Figure 7-1 and the ones you find in your preferred graphics program, make it easy to point and click to mix and match colors to find their individual RGB values.

Hex

The most popular way that color is represented in web design is through the use of *hex* codes, or *hexadecimals,* that represent the colors in the RGB model. Two hexadecimal numbers together are a *byte* and represent up to 256 different colors. (Remember the RGB model also is based on 256 possible color values.) Each of the colors (red, blue, and green) is represented by two hexadecimals; those hexadecimals use combinations of 0–9 and A–F.

Table 7-1 lists hex codes for commonly used colors. Actually, when I was a kid, I learned a good mnemonic device to help me remember the colors of the rainbow — Roy G. Biv (red, orange, yellow, green, blue, indigo, and violet). Table 7-1 gives you the hex codes for all the colors of the rainbow as well as the standard white and black.

Table 7-1	Common Colors and Hex Codes
Color	*Hex Code*
White	#FFFFFF
Black	#000000
Red	#FF0000
Orange	#FFA500
Yellow	#FFFF00
Green	#008000
Blue	#0000FF
Indigo	#4B0082
Violet	#EE82EE

Creating Color Schemes with Helpful Tools

You can spend a lot of time creating different color schemes by using the online color wheel described earlier; however, you can find other tools to help you create just the right color scheme, as described in the following sections.

Exploring different color combinations

Here are several online tools and places on the web where I find color inspiration and ideas:

✔ **COLOURlovers:** The COLOURlovers website lets you browse through millions of different color combinations and palettes that you can use in your designs. Figure 7-2 shows the results of the palettes I found by searching for an orange color using the hex code #F8981F in the search feature. Members of the website submit and share their favorite colors and schemes with other members — so it's a social network based around colors. (www.colourlovers.com)

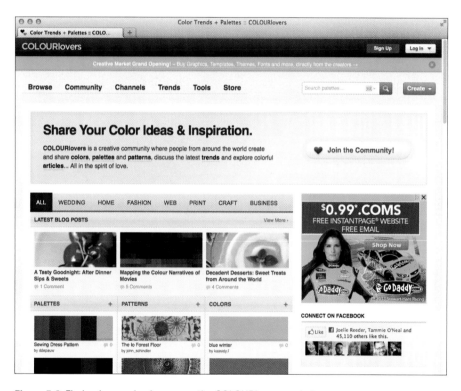

Figure 7-2: Find colors and schemes on the COLOURlovers website.

✔ **Kuler from Adobe:** Adobe's Kuler is a web-based application where you can share and experiment with different color combinations. Kuler is a community where members share their color schemes and experiments with other members to help inspire one another in the area of color. (https://kuler.adobe.com/create/color-wheel/)

 ✔ **ColorSchemer Studio 2:** ColorSchemer Studio 2 ($49.99) is an application for mixing and matching colors to develop a color scheme to use on your website design project. Download the app from the ColorSchemer website and install it on your computer. From there, use its visual color wheel to create your preferred color schemes. This application is available for Windows and Mac. (`www.colorschemer.com`)

Finding RGB and hex codes

Sometimes you already have a color scheme defined for you before the design project begins; for example, if a client comes to you with her logo and wants the color scheme to match it. I've also had clients come to me with a preferred color scheme based on a favorite photo or just by saying, "I like blue and green together" or "I really like the colors used on that website." In these circumstances, pull out the following tools to determine quickly and easily the RGB or hex codes of the colors presented:

 ✔ **Color Cop:** Color Cop is a very handy small application that you download from the Color Cop website (`http://colorcop.net`) and install on your computer (currently available only for Windows). After it's installed, you can find the Color Cop icon on your Windows Quick Launch toolbar. Follow these steps to quickly pick a color from a website you're viewing in your browser:

 1. *Click the Color Cop icon on your Windows Quick Launch toolbar.*

 A small Color Cop window opens.

 2. *Click and drag the eyedropper to your desired color location.*

 The eyedropper symbol is located on the middle of the left side of the window. You can drag the eyedropper to any location on your monitor to select your preferred color.

 3. *Note the RGB and hex codes of your preferred color.*

 The RGB code appears in the upper-left section of the Color Cop window, and the hex code appears in the middle, underneath the main color box. Figure 7-3 shows the color red in the Color Cop window, which I discovered by dragging the eyedropper over the red in the Google logo at `www.google.com`.

 4. *When you're done, close the application by clicking the X button in the top-right corner of the window.*

Figure 7-3: Use the Color Cop eyedropper to find specific colors from a web page.

- **Color Palette Generator:** This is an online tool; you can upload an image, such as a logo provided by a client or a photograph with a preferred color scheme, and the website analyzes the image and returns a color scheme based on the colors found in the image you uploaded. Figure 7-4 shows the Color Palette Generator results after I uploaded a photograph of my parrot. You can see that the tool returns the main colors found in that image, and from there, I can hover over each color with my mouse pointer to discover the specific hex code to use in my design project. (http://jrm.cc/color-palette-generator)

- **I Like Your Colors:** I Like Your Colors lets you discover a specific color scheme of another website by simply entering its *URL* (web address) and clicking the Submit button. I Like Your Colors then returns a listing of colors found on the website you entered. This is a handy tool when a client comes to you and says, "I love the color scheme on Google — I want to use that scheme!" You can then enter Google's URL and find out the exact hex codes for the colors it uses. (http://redalt.com/ilyc)

If all else fails, most graphic design and image-editing programs have color pickers, or eyedroppers, that you can use to drag over an image to select a particular color. Between your graphics program and the tools and information presented in this chapter, you're all set to create your own color schemes.

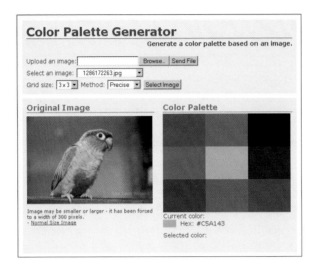

Figure 7-4: Discover colors from a photograph at the Color Palette Generator website.

Understanding Typography Essentials

Typography refers to the art, design, and visual look of the typeface used in print and website design, most likely known as *fonts*. You see creative uses of typography in everything from newspapers and magazines to greeting cards and billboards, but you also see it used on websites — both in the content body and in graphics and logos.

As a web designer, you use typography styling on your website design projects in two ways:

- ✔ **Body content:** These are the fonts, including the size, style, and colors you use for the content, such as published articles, pages, posts, and so on. The typography styling used in this area is controlled by Cascading Style Sheets (CSS) through the use of style definitions. You can find more information about CSS, including the font styling and spacing used to ensure easy readability and nicer displays, in Chapter 14.

- ✔ **Graphics and logos:** This refers to the fonts you use to create graphics for logos, icons, buttons, and other graphics designed for the website project, typically using your preferred design and image-editing software, such as Photoshop.

In the following sections, you find out more about different font styles and discover what fonts are considered web-safe.

Exploring font styles

Fonts come in different shapes and sizes and, for the most part, can be grouped into common categories in terms of their style and type:

- **Serif:** These fonts have decorative elements, such as tails or curlicues, at the edges of letters.

- **Sans-serif:** These fonts have straight edges and don't have decorative elements. Generally, sans-serif fonts are considered easier to read on computer monitors and mobile devices.

- **Script or decorative:** These fonts resemble cursive or handwritten type. These are generally not used to display content because they can be difficult to read at small sizes.

- **Monospace:** These fonts have letters that are all the same size and width, with no variation. Monospace fonts are typically used to display programming code.

Figure 7-5 illustrates these four font styles in a quick graphic I created in Photoshop. These categories of font styles are generic styles that reference fonts commonly used in web content (see the next section "Discovering web-safe fonts for content"); however, hundreds of font styles are available to use in designing graphics, logos, and other design elements created in your preferred software. See the section "Finding and Using Fonts for Graphic Design" toward the end of this chapter for information on resources you can use to find and discover such fonts.

Discovering web-safe fonts for content

The web is actually kind of picky about how it displays fonts and what kind of fonts you can use because not all fonts are viewed correctly on the web. The concept of web-safe fonts is easy to understand if you keep in mind that for a font to appear correctly on a website for any of your readers, the actual font used must be a system font on that reader's computer.

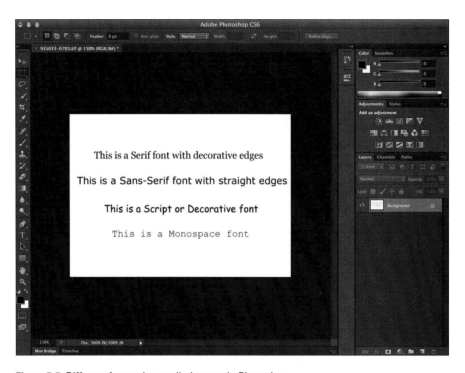

Figure 7-5: Different font styles applied to text in Photoshop.

If a font doesn't exist on a reader's computer, the web browser he's using automatically displays the default font set in his web browser options. Because of this, you need to know the common fonts that exist within all operating systems to ensure each reader views your website the way you intended him to. The following minitable illustrates some common fonts that are safe to use in your stylesheets and website content areas:

Font Name	Font Style
Arial, Arial Helvetica, **Arial Black**	Sans-serif
Georgia, New Times Roman	Serif
Tahoma, Geneva	Sans-serif
Trebuchet MS, **Verdana**	Sans-serif
Comic Sans MS	Cursive
Courier New, Lucida Console, Monaco	Monospace
Palatino, Palatino Linotype, Book Antiqua	Serif

You can find additional information on different font families, styles, and types in Chapter 14, which covers how to use CSS to define the typography styling for your web content.

You're not restricted regarding the type of fonts and font styles you can use on web graphics, including logos, header images, buttons, and so on. Because those are graphics rather than dynamic content generated by the user's web browser, the fonts you use in graphic design always appear as you intend. Web-safe fonts refer only to font families that you include in the style definitions in the CSS for the website format. See the "Font replacement technology" sidebar to find some resources on how you can replace web-safe fonts with your favorite font in your content.

Font replacement technology

With basic CSS practices, you are restricted on the types of font families that you can use and display in your web design projects. However, some really nifty tools that use plugins for WordPress allow you to replace standard, web-safe fonts with fonts of your choosing. Typically, the only fonts you'd be able to use are fonts that are included in most of the major operating systems (such as the fonts listed in the section "Discovering web-safe fonts for content"), but here are some WordPress plugins you can use to replace those fonts with any font you would like and make sure it appears correctly in your users' browsers:

✔ **WP-Cufon** (http://wordpress.org/extend/plugins/wp-cufon): This plugin for WordPress makes it easy to use the Cufon JavaScript tool to convert your favorite font files to regular text on your WordPress website.

✔ **Typekit Fonts for WordPress** (http://wordpress.org/extend/plugins/typekit-fonts-for-wordpress): This plugin allows you to easily embed fonts from Typekit (http://typekit.com) on your WordPress website. You can replace some, or all, of the fonts that handle text within your content.

✔ **Facelift Image Replacement (FLIR)** (http://wordpress.org/extend/plugins/facelift-image-replacement): This plugin replaces text on your WordPress website with an image created by your chosen font files, essentially turning your text into images generated using JavaScript, allowing your text to appear using the font of your choice.

The best way to discover the type of font you want to use for the content of your website is to try different fonts in your stylesheet to see which one you like best. A real handy tool is the Typetester (www.typetester.org). On its website, you can insert a paragraph of text and then easily change the font styles in the web browser with its tools. As a matter of fact, I added a sentence to the Typetester website and applied different font styling to it, as you can see in Figure 7-6.

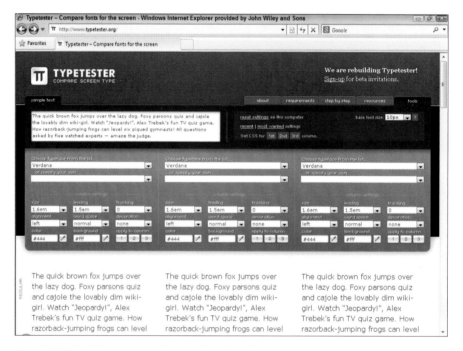

Figure 7-6: Using Typetester to choose a font for web content.

The Typetester website is an especially handy tool if your clients have no idea what type of font they want to use. Send them to that website, and then tell them to test the various fonts available and report back to you with their preferred findings.

Finding and Using Fonts for Graphic Design

As I mention in the preceding section, you're not limited to the types of fonts you can use in graphic design — the sky's the limit. Literally hundreds of thousands, if not millions, of fonts are available on the web. If you're a fontaholic like me, you can get lost in the vast number of font libraries that you find on the web while searching for just the right font to suit your tastes. I can't tell you how many hours have ticked by while I've browsed through and admired different font galleries looking for, and usually finding, inspiration.

As beautiful and gorgeous as some of the fonts are, they're not all free for you to use. Some of them cost money (in some cases, a great deal of money), and many have specific licenses attached to them that designate circumstances under which you can use them. Be sure to read the license attached to the font, if there is one (usually a file called `license.txt` bundled in the download file), to be sure you're fully licensed to use the font in your web project.

Finding the right fonts for your project

Here's a quick list of free font resources that have some really great fonts available for download and use:

- ✔ **UrbanFonts.com:** `www.urbanfonts.com`
- ✔ **Google Fonts:** `www.google.com/fonts/`
- ✔ **daFont.com:** `www.dafont.com`
- ✔ **FontFreak.com:** `www.fontfreak.com`
- ✔ **Font Squirrel:** `www.fontsquirrel.com`

For your web design projects, you may have to bite the bullet and purchase a font or two; or maybe your clients find a font they absolutely *must* use in their design but will have to purchase. Some premium font resources include

- ✔ **Fonts.com:** `http://fonts.com`
- ✔ **MyFonts:** `http://myfonts.com`

One last, but extremely helpful, resource for finding the font you need is the WhatTheFont web page (`www.myfonts.com/WhatTheFont/`) on the MyFonts site. Use this resource when you have a font but don't know its name or how to locate it. This tool is particularly helpful if a client comes to you and says, "I love the font on that site — I want to use the same one." You can either upload an image file that displays the font in question or indicate the URL where the font is located. After you do so, WhatTheFont generates a listing of possible fonts that match the one you indicated. From there, you can purchase the font (if it's not free) and then download it to your computer for use in your web design project.

Installing fonts on your computer

After you find the font that you want to use, install it on your computer so it appears in the font list within your preferred graphic design program. On the Windows 8 operating system, Microsoft makes it easy to install a font by simply double-clicking the font file and then clicking install. Additionally, you can select multiple font files and right-click to install in bulk.

Alternatively, you can follow these steps to install a font on the Windows 8 operating system:

1. **Download the font to your computer and save it in a location you're sure to remember.**

2. **Unzip the download file.**

   Typically, font downloads are packaged within a Zip file, requiring that you use a popular archiving program, such as WinZip (www.winzip.com), to unzip (uncompress) the file.

3. **Save the unzipped file to a location on your computer and right-click the font filename.**

   Font files have a .ttf (TrueType Font) or .otf (OpenType Font) extension.

4. **Select Copy.**

5. **Browse to C:\Windows\Fonts.**

6. **Right-click inside the C:\Windows\Fonts directory and select Paste.**

   This moves the font file from its original location to the Fonts directory (C:\Windows\Fonts) on your computer, and a dialog box opens, indicating that the font is being installed. The dialog box closes when the font installation is complete.

The new font is now installed on your computer.

8

Planning Your Design Strategy

In This Chapter

- Selecting a fluid or fixed width
- Deciding on the number of columns in the layout
- Determining your menu navigation
- Choosing how to display your content
- Understanding responsive design concepts
- Creating a sandbox environment for testing

*W*ith every new web design project you begin, you need to answer several preliminary questions before you can proceed with starting the design and development processes of the website. If you're working on a design project for a client, communicate with her to make sure you understand the requirements before you proceed — same thing if you're working on a project of your own. You have to evaluate the overall project in terms of content, type, and purpose to determine what your design strategy will be. Without a plan in place from day one, you're likely to struggle through the entire design process, so developing a solid plan first is a good practice for every project you approach, no matter how big or small.

In this chapter, I discuss some of those preliminary decisions to make for your project, such as which type of layout to use, how many columns to include, and what the navigation structure will look like for menus. I also explore several ways to present content on a website, such as using full content versus excerpts, using photographs versus thumbnails to provide a visual component, and presenting content (for example, chronologically, by topic, by most popular, and so on). Also in this chapter are concepts and factors to consider for *responsive design,* or making sure your site looks good on mobile devices such as smartphones and tablets.

Finally, I take you through the steps of creating your own WordPress *sandbox* (development environment) *locally* (on your own computer) so you can develop and test your website design before you officially launch it on the Internet.

Choosing the Width of Your Website

Every website starts with a layout that takes width into consideration. Here are the primary types of widths to consider when you start to design your website:

- ✔ **Fixed:** This is a static width that's determined by a set number of pixels. This type of layout stays the same size no matter how big or small the user's computer monitor and resolution are.

- ✔ **Fluid:** This is a flexible width determined by percentages that create an experience in which your website fills the entire width of your readers' browsers, no matter how big or small their monitor size and/or screen resolution is.

- ✔ **Responsive:** This type of layout is considered *device agnostic.* In other words, the size of the device the visitor is using to browse the website doesn't matter — the site will display perfectly on very large monitors down to the smallest mobile phone device. This layout is called *responsive* because it responds to the size of the viewing device.

When choosing between fixed, fluid, and responsive layouts, keep in mind that computer monitors and resolutions come in several sizes, and people who surf the web use their browsers in many ways. Some users fully maximize their browser windows so that they take up the full height and width of the screen. Other users do the same, but use different toolbars and sidebars in their browsers that decrease the screen size that displays your website. Also in practice are users who use a *portrait* (vertical) and a *landscape* (horizontal) layout on tablets and mobile devices. Your challenge as a web designer is to design your website so that it fits correctly in your visitors' browsers, no matter what their setups are.

Screen resolution, another factor to strongly consider, is a setting on each computer system that can vary greatly among your website visitors. *Screen resolution* is the number of pixels wide followed by the number of pixels high that a computer monitor uses to display content; the greater the numbers, the higher the resolution. So, for example, a resolution of 1600 x 900 (or 1600 pixels wide by 900 pixels high) is a greater resolution than 800 x 600.

W3Schools is a website that leads the way in providing tools and resources for web designers; it keeps track of the statistics on what screen resolutions are most, and least, used on the web from year to year, and the results are then published to help designers understand how people use the Internet. The site's most recent report for 2013 indicates that the majority of people who browse the web use a screen resolution greater than 1024 x 768 (www. w3schools.com/browsers/browsers_display.asp).

The type of layout — fixed or fluid or responsive — that you decide to use greatly depends on your own preferences or the preferences of your client.

Some designers are completely married to one type of layout over the other; however, as computer monitor sizes get bigger and bigger for desktop and laptops and then smaller and smaller for mobile devices and tablets, designers are finding that they may have to alter their regular design techniques to account for the various screen sizes out there.

In the following sections, I go into more detail about fixed and fluid width and responsive layout designs and the pros and cons to each choice.

Designing with a fixed width

A *fixed width* website has a container that's a set width, in pixels, and everything within it remains contained within the width defined in the Cascading Style Sheet (CSS). (I discuss CSS in detail in Chapter 14.) If a fixed width container is set to 960 pixels, for example, it doesn't move wider than 960 pixels, no matter what the visitor's screen size or resolution is. So if a visitor browses at a 1600-pixel-width resolution, the website still displays a 960-pixel-width container.

Figure 8-1 displays a popular 960-pixel-wide layout. In the figure, the header and footer of the site are 960 pixels wide; the content area is 520 pixels wide; the two sidebars are 200 pixels wide; and the content area and first sidebar are separated by 20-pixel right margins.

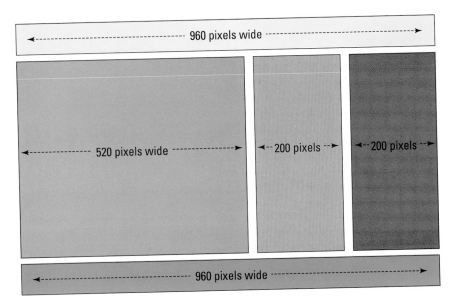

Figure 8-1: A sample fixed-width layout at 960 pixels in width.

The CSS for the layout shown in Figure 8-1 looks something like this:

```
body {
background: #ffffff;
margin:0;
font-family: arial, verdana, helvetica, sans-serif;
}

#container {
width: 960px;
margin:0 auto;
}

#header {
width: 960px;
height: 100px;
margin-bottom: 20px;
background: #eee;
}

.content {
width: 520px;
margin-right: 20px;
float:left;
background: #eee;
}

.sidebar1 {
width: 200px;
margin-right: 20px;
float:left;
background: #eee;
}

.sidebar2 {
width: 200px;
float:left;
background: #eee;
}

#footer {
float:left;
width: 960px;
height: 100px;
margin-top: 20px;
margin-bottom: 20px;
background: #eee;
clear:both;
}
```

And the HTML markup for the layout in Figure 8-1 looks like this (and corresponds to the preceding CSS example):

```
<!doctype html>
<html lang="en" class="no-js">
<head>
<meta charset="utf-8">
<title>Your Site Title</title>
</head>
<body>
<div id="container">
<header>This is the Site Header</header>
<div class="content">
<p>This is the content area</p>
</div>
<div class="sidebar1">This is the first sidebar</div>
<div class="sidebar2">This is the second sidebar</div>
<div id="footer">This is the footer area</div>
</div>
</body>
</html>
```

A 960-pixel-wide layout is the most popular, and most standard, fixed width layout because designers create sites with the assumption that 1024 x 768, or greater, is the most popular screen resolution in use. So a 960-pixel-wide layout appears perfectly on a 1024-pixel-wide resolution when you take into account the browser's toolbar and scroll bars. Anything larger than 960 pixels creates a horizontal scroll bar along the bottom of the browser window, and you don't want your readers to scroll horizontally while reading your website. A resource you may find helpful is the 960 Grid System website at http://960.gs, which offers basic Photoshop templates created with a 960-pixel-wide layout.

Using a fixed width layout has its advantages and disadvantages. One of the biggest advantages is that you can more easily control design elements such as graphics, icons, and banners. Because a fixed width layout is set to a static pixel width, you can be pretty confident that what you see on your computer screen is what your website visitors see, too. Because you know the exact width of the website, it's easy to plan for the insertion of videos, photos, and other media elements, and you can be certain that the files will display correctly within the container of the overall site design.

One disadvantage to a fixed width layout is how it looks on larger computer monitors. A layout that's 960 pixels in width shows a lot of empty space on a monitor that displays content in a 1600 x 950 resolution. In this case, you'd have 640 pixels of empty space. Although this may bother some people, it's not enough to dissuade some designers from using this model.

Figure 8-2 shows my website, which is a fixed layout at 960 pixels in width for a 1024-pixel-wide screen resolution. I chose a fixed width layout for my site because I find it an easier layout to work with. Figure 8-3 demonstrates how the 960-pixel-wide, fixed layout appears in a 1600-pixel-wide screen resolution. You can see how differently the site appears, in terms of the empty space to the left and right of the design container on the 1600-pixel-wide resolution display.

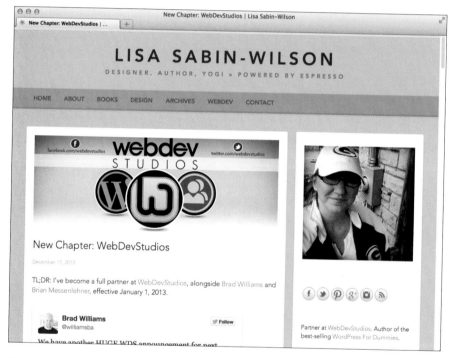

Figure 8-2: A fixed layout at 960 pixels displayed on a 1024-pixel-wide screen resolution.

Figure 8-3: A fixed layout at 960 pixels displayed on a 1600-pixel-wide screen resolution.

Designing with a fluid width

A website designed with a fluid width layout has a flexible width. The container of the website content is determined by percentages rather than static pixels. Unlike the fixed width layout, which I discuss in the preceding section, the fluid width layout can expand or contract in width based on the screen resolution used by the visitor's browser. In the earlier example for the fixed width layout, I used a 960-pixel-wide example; the container of the website is exactly 960 pixels in width, and that never changes. With a fluid width layout, you change the 960 pixels in width to 90 percent in width. The container takes up 90 percent of the browser, no matter how big or small.

Figure 8-4 displays a popular 90-percent-width layout. The header and footer of the site are 90-percent wide; the content area is 50-percent wide; the two sidebars are 20-percent wide; and the content area and first sidebar are separated by 5-percent margins.

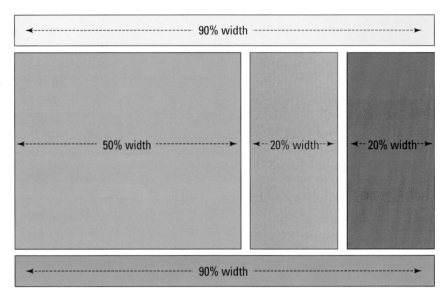

Figure 8-4: A sample fluid width layout at a 90-percent width.

The CSS for the layout shown in Figure 8-4 looks something like this:

```
body {
background: #ffffff;
margin:0;
font-family: arial, verdana, helvetica, sans-serif;
}

#container {
width: 90%;
margin:0 auto;
}

#header {
width: 90%;
height: 100px;
margin-bottom: 20px;
background: #eee;
}

.content {
width:50%;
margin-right: 5%;
float:left;
background: #eee;
}

.sidebar1 {
width: 20%;
```

```
margin-right: 5%;
float:left;
background: #eee;
}

.sidebar2 {
width: 20%;
float:left;
background: #eee;
}

#footer {
float:left;
width: 90%;
height: 100px;
margin-top: 20px;
margin-bottom: 20px;
background: #eee;
}
```

Combine this fluid width CSS example with the HTML markup I provide in the preceding section, and you see the difference in layout. The fluid width layout, with the width calculated in percentages, creates an elastic layout that changes its width based on the screen size your site visitor uses.

Fluid width has a few advantages — the most important is that it uses all the space — or *real estate* — of a browser. No real estate goes to waste. Fluid width adjusts to the visitor's screen resolution and creates what some feel is a better user environment. Also, in screen resolutions smaller than 1024 pixels in width, it eliminates the horizontal scroll bar across the bottom of the browser that often appears with a fixed- width design created for resolutions greater than 1024.

However, fluid width has several disadvantages that you need to be aware of. Many of these disadvantages are what cause designers to shy away from a fluid-width design. Here are some of these disadvantages:

- ✔ **Multimedia display:** One major problem accounts for multimedia files such as photographs, videos, and images within the content of a website. If, for example, you embed a video that is 500 pixels in width and place it within the 50-percent width container (refer to Figure 8-4), you can never be sure that every site visitor's browser creates a content area greater than 500 pixels. If the visitor uses a smaller resolution, the embedded video, at 500 pixels in width, may overlap other areas of the site design, which isn't your intended result.

  You do have workarounds for this problem, however, by using CSS properties like `min-width` and `max-width`, which I cover in Chapter 14; however, these properties aren't supported by Internet Explorer (like they are in Firefox and Chrome browsers), which means you have to work harder to create Internet Explorer–specific expressions that resolve the problem, using the `height` and `overflow` CSS properties.

✔ **Readability:** Visitors that have very large monitors or screen resolution settings may cause a fluid width website to span the entire width of the screen, making it sometimes difficult to read — unless you use CSS solutions to create a minimum or maximum width, which I discuss in Chapter 14.

Speaking of CSS, it's sometimes difficult to get a fluid width website to appear correctly in all major browser systems without a lot of work — and undesired browser-specific CSS hacks to force it into working and appearing the way it should. Getting the site to appear correctly isn't impossible, but the extra time and work (and brain power) involved in making it happen make some designers stick with a fixed- width layout method of designing websites, which is a perfectly acceptable practice.

At the end of the day, whichever method of laying out websites you're most comfortable with is what you should stick with. But, by all means, experiment with different layouts and solutions to find the ones that you like best.

Designing a responsive layout

A website that has a responsive layout takes the size of any viewing device into consideration. It doesn't matter if it's the largest television monitor or the smallest mobile phone or tablet device; the website layout is prepared to handle any size on any device. It is called *responsive* because the layout responds to its environment — or in the case of the website, the layout responds to the size of the viewing device (monitors, smartphones, tablets, and so on).

The number of devices, platforms, and browser systems available for users to view websites grows every day, it seems. Most website owners want to make sure they're paying attention to their mobile and tablet readers, as well as their traditional visitors on regular computers. Having a responsive layout in place accomplishes this goal and is an important design aspect for your website, particularly if a majority of website visitors are using handheld devices such as smartphones or tablets.

Refer to Figure 8-2 to see what my personal website looks like on a regular computer monitor at a resolution of 1024 x 768, and to Figure 8-3 to see what it looks like on an even larger computer monitor with a resolution of 1600 x 1200. In Figure 8-5, you see an example of responsive design in practice as it shows how my personal website looks on an iPhone 5, and in Figure 8-6, you see you it looks on an iPad tablet. Responsive layouts are accomplished with a mix of grids and layouts that are flexible enough to respond to any size viewing environment. As website visitors switch their viewing devices, or even flip their view from portrait to landscape, the layout automatically switches to accommodate the size — and this includes navigation menus, images, media, and content areas.

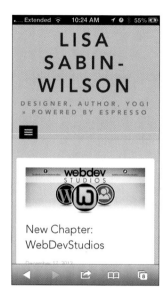

Figure 8-5: Responsive design on an iPhone 5.

Figure 8-6: Responsive design on an iPad tablet.

You can design a responsive layout a number of different ways, but most importantly, you want to make sure that you're using efficient techniques and tools and doing the job the right way. The following list describes some great resources to start with for designing responsively — definitely check these out and consider them as potential starting points and tools to add to your web designer toolkit:

- **Smashing Magazine:** "Responsive Web Design: What Is It and How to Use It," an article on responsive design that covers concepts and techniques (`http://coding.smashingmagazine.com/2011/01/12/guidelines-for-responsive-web-design/`)

- **Bootstrap from Twitter:** A front-end framework including HTML, CSS, and JavaScript that makes responsive web design faster and easier (`http://twitter.github.io/bootstrap/`)

- **Responsinator:** A handy web-based tool that allows you to test how your website looks on several different mobile devices, including smartphones and tablets (`www.responsinator.com/`)

- **Media Queries:** A fantastic site that showcases responsive design techniques in practice today — a great place for inspiration (`http://mediaqueri.es/`)

If digging into responsive design practices is a little intimidating or something you'd like to put off for now, WordPress has a handful of plugins that will provide mobile layout for any website, regardless of whether it has a responsive layout in place. Keep in mind that these plugins will provide you with a mobile/tablet view; however, it is not always as customized or visually appealing as you may want it to be. The only way you have full control over how your website looks on any device is by getting into the practice of responsive design. Here are a few plugins from WordPress that will provide a mobile view for your website:

- **JetPack:** A plugin with several different modules, including a Mobile module that will give your website viewers the opportunity to browse your website on any mobile device or tablet (`http://wordpress.org/plugins/jetpack/`)

- **WPTouch:** A popular plugin that transforms your WordPress website for mobile devices (`http://wordpress.org/plugins/wptouch/`)

- **WordPress Mobile Pack:** A toolkit that provides a mobile view for your website and includes different themes, widgets, and a mobile admin panel (`http://wordpress.org/plugins/wordpress-mobile-pack/`)

Choosing the Number of Columns

Most websites are laid out in columns that span the width of the visitor's computer screen and rows that span the length. When you develop a plan for your website design layout, you need to decide how many columns you'll use to display content. The options are literally endless, but keep in mind that the more columns you use in a website design, the smaller they need to be for them to appear across the width of the screen. (Rows, on the other hand, because they are vertical, can be used endlessly because you are not limited in the amount of vertical space you have available in your browser window.)

A website that uses a one-column layout has one column that spans the full width of the computer monitor, whereas a website that uses a four-column layout has four smaller columns that span the width of the screen. Most layouts are anywhere from one to three columns, with each column holding different types of content, such as blog posts, navigation menus, advertisement banners, and so on. A two-column layout is the most popular, followed by a three-column layout, and in some cases, you do see a one-column layout.

Take into account the following factors when deciding how many columns to use in a site design:

- ✏ The type of content being presented
- ✏ How much content there is
- ✏ Whether you, or your client, intend to advertise, sell products, or host videos or audio files

The answers to those questions help determine how many columns the website needs to cleanly accommodate and present all the different content to website visitors. You want the website to have a clean and organized feel, as well as to make sure it's not too cluttered and confusing to visitors. If you have a lot of content to display, consider using a larger number of columns to present the content in an orderly way.

Figures 8-7, 8-8, and 8-9 show examples of one-, two-, and three-column layouts, respectively. (They are all WordPress-powered websites, by the way!)

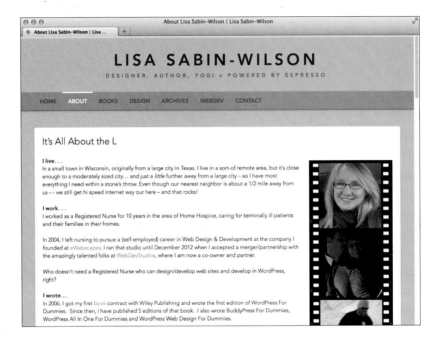

Figure 8-7: An example of a one-column layout at `http://lisasabin-wilson.com`.

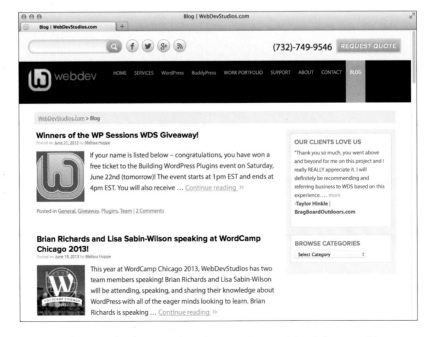

Figure 8-8: An example of a two-column layout at `http://webdevstudios.com`.

Figure 8-9: An example of a three-column layout at `http://safemama.com`.

Determining Website Navigation

All good websites provide visitors with an easy way to navigate the different areas of the sites. To provide your visitors with a way to read internal pages and archives and to navigate to a page where they can get in touch with you, you have to provide a menu of links, or a *navigation menu*. A navigation menu displays prominently on a website so that your readers don't have to hunt around to find the information they want.

In Chapter 10, I discuss how you can use the built-in Custom Menus feature in WordPress to build menus, which makes it easy to include navigation menus on your site. Your job as a web designer is to determine what type of navigational structure makes sense for your client, or your site visitors, and what kind of information and links you want to include in those menus. Here are the various ways to accomplish your navigational structure:

- A horizontal navigation menu across the top of your site
- A vertical navigation menu down one side of your site
- A series of different menus with groupings of related links
- A horizontal navigation menu in the footer of your site

The possibilities for providing navigation menus to your visitors are really endless, especially with how easy the WordPress platform makes it for you. As a designer developing a site, you need to answer these questions:

- **Should you even have a navigation menu?** Some sites don't require a full navigation menu, particularly if they're smaller sites with little content or information to offer. However, most websites have more than one page, and you want to provide a method for your site visitors to easily navigate to those pages and back to the home page.

- **Where should you place the navigation menu?** A popular location for the navigation menu is near the top of the website, below the website name and/or header graphic. My website at WebDevStudios (`http://webdevstudios.com`) has a theme, as shown in Figure 8-10, that has a horizontal navigation menu (with drop-down menus) prominently displayed below the site header to make it easy for visitors to navigate to the various areas within the site.

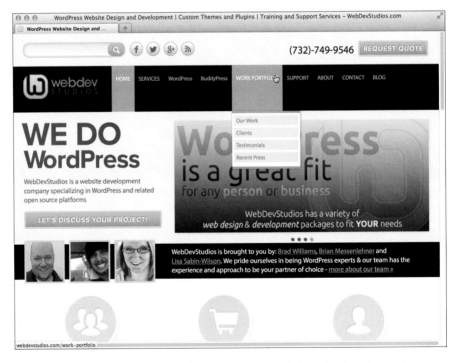

Figure 8-10: An example of a horizontal navigation menu with links that drop down, at WebDevStudios.com.

✔ **What links should you include in the navigation menu?** You (or your client) should have a good idea of what links and information should be presented in the navigation menu. Generally, you include links to important internal pages (such as an About Me or Contact page), categories or archives, and links to external websites, such as the site's Twitter or Facebook page.

Before writing a single line of code for the website development, knowing what the navigation structure should include will help you put a plan in place to build and display the navigation menu on the website. For example, websites with a great number of links for the menu benefit from a horizontal structure with *drop-down lists* — links that drop down when you hover over the menu titles (shown in Figure 8-10). Likewise, websites with a small number of links may benefit from a smaller, more compact vertical menu in the sidebar.

Understanding Content Display Options

With a WordPress-powered website, several options are available to display content, such as

✔ Full articles

✔ Excerpts

✔ Photo galleries

✔ Chronological order

✔ Grouped by topic

✔ Most popular

Deciding how to display different types of content on your website is greatly determined by what type of content your website offers. Here are a few examples:

✔ **An online store:** A website that sells products to its visitors wants a prominent display of the product information, including photos, descriptions, pricing, and purchasing options. This type of e-commerce setup is designed to sell products and make money, so making sure those products and the purpose of the website are prominently displayed when a visitor first sees the site is important. See Chapter 16 for a detailed explanation of e-commerce options for WordPress.

✔ **A news or magazine site:** This type of site focuses on the delivery of *content,* or articles and stories that have been written for reader consumption. This type of site should display the content in a fashion that's easily accessible by readers. You may consider grouping the content into topical archives with *excerpts* (short snippets or teasers that require the reader to click a Read More link to access the full article) to compact the content in areas on the website that are easy to navigate. I cover the different WordPress template tags and code for accomplishing excerpts and topical archives in Chapter 12.

✔ **A photography site:** A site may focus completely on photography or imagery, in which case the emphasis is on the visual offerings of the website. Explore options for how to display photos or video galleries in Chapter 16.

✔ **A site with a blog:** A simple, typical blog layout, for example, displays full blog posts in chronological order (from the most recent posts to the oldest). This type of content presentation is typically reserved for a website that has a blog on its front page or a website that contains a blog as part of its content offerings. In Chapter 15, I cover using WordPress as a content management system (CMS) so that you can use different types of layouts for different pages on the website. For example, the front page of the website can be all about e-commerce and products, and an internal page (any page other than your front page) can have a completely different layout of blog posts and articles.

You have many options for content delivery with a WordPress website, and before you design or code the site, knowing what type of content will be presented and how it should look is important information to include in your overall plan.

Testing Your Design in a Sandbox Environment

As a website designer and developer, it's very helpful to have a sandbox to play in. A *sandbox,* in this case, is a website or local development area where you can work on a website design and test different layouts and methods of content delivery before launching the site live on a client's (or your) hosted domain. As a professional designer who creates several websites per year for my clients, a sandbox environment is extremely vital to what I do. The sandbox allows me a private space to create the site design and present my work to my client where we can work, back and forth, to get the site design and features in line with what my client expects. After the client gives me final approval on the overall website design and layout, I can transfer the site from my sandbox domain to the client's live domain within a matter of minutes. (I explain how to accomplish that transfer at the end of this chapter.)

Additionally, creating a sandbox environment helps me a great deal when I work with platforms that change as quickly as WordPress and related plugins because I can install and run beta versions of the software (as I discuss in Chapter 3). In a test environment, working with new features before they release to the public in an official version upgrade can be highly beneficial. The advantages of doing this include

- ✔ Becoming adept at using new features so that when you upgrade your site, you're informed enough to advise your users.

- ✔ The opportunity to install and test new plugins or themes before you commit to making those changes on your site.

- ✔ Testing early, beta versions of WordPress to help discover bugs and then using WordPress Trac to report any problems. You don't have to be a programmer to contribute to the WordPress project. You can be a tester and help the developers and programmers fix issues for WordPress users worldwide.

In the following sections, you find out how to create your own sandbox environment as well as how to transfer a site from your sandbox domain to the live domain.

Creating a sandbox environment

You can create a test environment in several ways, and everyone's mileage will vary on how they prefer to create one. Here are the steps you can take to create a sandbox environment:

1. **Find out whether your hosting provider lets you create subdomains.**

   Generally, most hosting providers give you this option. I use the cPanel hosting account manager to create my subdomain, but your hosting account may offer you a different management tool, such as NetAdmin or Plesk.

   A *subdomain* is the second level of your current domain that can handle unique content separately from content in your main domain. Subdomains operate underneath your main domain and can function as a wholly different section of your site, independent from your existing domain name.

   In Steps 3 and 4, I use my domain, ewebscapes.com, to create the subdomain http://testing.ewebscapes.com. The prefix testing in that web address (or URL) is a subdomain that branches off eweb scapes.com that, when set up, handles completely different content from what's currently installed on my main domain.

2. **Log in to cPanel (or the hosting account manager tool provided to you).**

   If you're using a management tool other than cPanel, the steps will likely be different from what I've described in this section. Please refer to your web-hosting provider's documentation for assistance with the tool you're using.

3. **Locate and then click the Subdomains icon in the cPanel interface.**

   The arrangement of icons on the cPanel interface varies from hosting provider to hosting provider.

   The Subdomains page within cPanel appears, as shown in Figure 8-11.

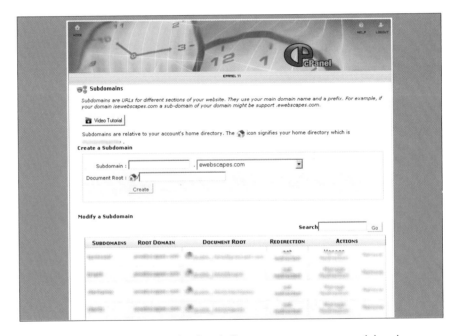

Figure 8-11: The Subdomains page in cPanel allows you to create a new subdomain.

4. **Type the name of your subdomain in the Subdomain text box.**

   For the purposes of making this straightforward and easy, type **testing** in the text box.

5. **From the drop-down list, choose the name of the domain on which you want to add the subdomain.**

   In Figure 8-11, the drop-down list shows the domain ewebscapes.com. In this example, you're creating the subdomain on this domain, so the new subdomain is http://testing.ewebscapes.com.

A unique folder name for your new subdomain appears in the Document Root text box. Don't alter this text because this tells your web server where to install the necessary WordPress files.

6. **Click the Create button.**

   After a few seconds, the page refreshes and displays a message that the new subdomain has been created, as shown in Figure 8-12.

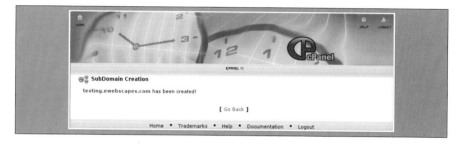

Figure 8-12: A successful subdomain-creation message in cPanel.

Now that you have a subdomain set up on your hosting account, you can install WordPress into the folder that was created when you added the subdomain. For example, if you created a `testing` subdomain, you'll install WordPress into the `/testing` folder. Flip to Chapter 3 for the steps to install WordPress.

With your new subdomain created, you can work on your new WordPress website design and development without disrupting anything on the live site (or the intended domain where the website will eventually be after it's completed).

To go one step further, you can use the Members Only WordPress plugin to lock down your sandbox environment and keep it away from prying eyes and search engines. The Members Only plugin lets you show the website to only those people whom you give access to by providing them with a username and password to log in to the sandbox test site. You can find the Members Only plugin on the Plugin Directory page at `http://wordpress.org/extend/plugins/members-only`. (See Chapter 16 for the lowdown on installing plugins.)

Using a plugin to back up and transfer from your sandbox

I use the BackupBuddy plugin on a regular basis to move a WordPress website from one hosting environment to another. BackupBuddy is not a free plugin available on the WordPress Plugin Directory page. You have to pay for this plugin, but it's worth every penny because it takes the entire backup and migration (or transfer) process and makes mincemeat out of it. Translation: BackupBuddy makes the backup and migration of your website very easy, and can be done in minutes.

You can use the BackupBuddy plugin to back up and transfer from your sandbox environment to your client's destination server and vice versa. Follow these steps to use this plugin to move the website from your sandbox environment to your or your client's server:

1. **Purchase and download the BackupBuddy plugin from** `http://ithemes.com/purchase/backupbuddy.`

   At this time, the cost for the plugin starts at $80.

2. **Install the plugin on your current WordPress website.**

   By *current,* I mean your sandbox environment, not the destination server yet.

3. **In WordPress Dashboard, choose Plugins⟳BackupBuddy⟳Activate under the BackupBuddy plugin name.**

   WordPress activates the plugin.

4. **Choose BackupBuddy⟳Backups.**

   The Backups page appears.

5. **Click the Full Backup button.**

   This initiates a full backup of your database, files, and content and then packages it neatly into one Zip file for you to store on your local computer, in a location of your choosing.

6. **Download the `importbuddy.php` file by clicking the `importbuddy.php` link on the Backups page and downloading it to your local computer.**

   Preferably, place this file in the same directory as the backup file you downloaded in Step 5.

7. **Connect to the destination web server via FTP.**

   See Chapter 5 for the lowdown on connecting to your web server and transferring files with FTP.

8. **Upload the `backup.zip` file and the `importbuddy.php` file.**

   These files are uploaded in the root, or top-level, directory on your web server. On some web servers, this is the `/public_html` folder, but on others, it may be the `/httpdocs` folder. If you aren't sure what your root directory is, your hosting provider can tell you.

9. **Create a new database on your new hosting account.**

   You can find the steps for creating a database in Chapter 3.

10. **Navigate to the `importbuddy.php` file in your web browser.**

    This URL looks like `http://yourdomain.com/importbuddy.php` (where *yourdomain.com* is your actual domain name).

    The BackupBuddy page loads in your web browser.

11. **Follow the steps provided on the BackupBuddy page to import the backup file and install WordPress.**

    These steps include adding the database information needed, such as the database username, database name, password, and host (see Chapter 3).

    This entire process takes about 5–10 minutes, maybe more depending on the size of your website.

12. **Type the URL of your website in your web browser address bar and press Enter.**

    This loads your website in your browser window, and after BackupBuddy does its thing, the new website is completely loaded onto the new server and is an absolute duplicate of what you have in your sandbox environment.

Using this method to back up and transfer a full WordPress website from one server to another takes about 5–10 minutes, which is a huge time-saver. If you had to transfer and back up the site manually (by taking manual backups of separate elements, such as images, content, themes, plugins, settings, and so on), it'd take a couple hours to complete. The BackupBuddy plugin is an essential tool in my WordPress toolkit that I use several times per week, at least.

Part III
Working with WordPress Themes

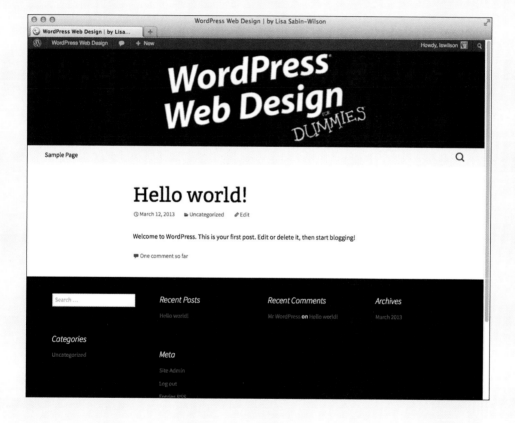

WordPress commercial themes cost money, and they aren't found in the WordPress Themes Directory; however, commercial themes offer you theme options with features that have professional-level quality in design and development. Learn more at www. dummies.com/extras/wordpresswebdesign.

In this part . . .

- ✔ Step into the code and development of WordPress themes, starting with a basic run-through that explores the anatomy of a theme.

- ✔ Get an in-depth look into the default WordPress theme, Twenty Thirteen, which is provided in every WordPress software installation.

- ✔ Dissect themes and template files, and learn important information about template tags, parameters, and built-in features that you can use to liven up any WordPress website.

- ✔ "Get your geek on" while turning the pages in this part as I take you through a comprehensive look at page templates, custom post types, post formats, navigation menus, post thumbnails, and post queries.

9

Finding and Installing a WordPress Theme

In This Chapter

▶ Finding, previewing, downloading, and installing themes

▶ Deciding whether to use premium themes

*W*ordPress *themes* are simply a group of files, called templates, bundled together that, when activated in WordPress, determine the look and basic function of your site. WordPress comes packaged with one very useful default theme — *Twenty Thirteen* (named after the year it was released in version 3.5 of WordPress). Most bloggers who use WordPress usually don't waste any time finding a theme that they like better than Twenty Thirteen. Although you're not limited to the default theme, it's very functional for a basic site. (See Chapter 10 for more on the Twenty Thirteen theme.)

This chapter discusses other WordPress themes that you can download and use as a foundation for your overall design work. Not all WordPress themes are created equal, and it's important for you to know the differences between free and premium themes:

▶ **Free:** These themes are free, period. You can download and use them on your website at absolutely no cost. As a courtesy, you can include a link to the designer in your footer — but you can even remove that link if you want to.

▶ **Premium:** These themes cost money. You usually find premium themes available for download only after you pay anywhere from $10 to $500. The designer feels that these themes are a cut above the rest and, therefore, are worth the money you spend for them. Most premium themes come with a full support package and access to future upgrades of the theme as they're released.

In this chapter, you discover how to find, install, and activate free themes on your site. Additionally, I introduce premium themes.

You can also create your own theme from scratch, as I cover in Chapters 11 and 12, but sometimes using an existing theme keeps you from completely reinventing the wheel because the framework is already done.

Finding and Installing a Theme from the Themes Directory

Free WordPress themes are popular because of their appealing designs, easy installation and use, and mostly their price tag — free. They're great tools to use when you launch your new site, and if you dabble a bit in graphic design and Cascading Style Sheets (CSS), you can customize one to fit your needs. (See Chapter 14 for HTML resources and CSS information.)

By using free themes, you can have your site up and running with a new design — without the help of a professional — pretty fast. You can change your theme as often as you want. Trying several free themes is like trying on different outfits for your site; you can change outfits until you find just the right theme. Finding the theme that fits you best may take some time, but with thousands available, you'll eventually find one that suits you.

The WordPress platform gives an easy way to browse the Themes Directory page to find, preview, and install themes on your site without ever leaving the comfort of the WordPress Dashboard. The following steps show you how:

1. **Choose Appearance⇨Themes on the WordPress Dashboard and then click the Install Themes tab at the top of the Manage Themes page.**

   The Install Themes page opens, as shown in Figure 9-1.

2. **Search for a new theme by entering a keyword, author, or tag in the Search box. You can filter the results by using the Feature Filter check boxes to filter theme results by colors, columns, width, features, and subjects.**

3. **After you've entered your search criteria, click the Search button to the right of the Search box.**

   The search results page displays a list of themes for you to choose from.

4. **(Optional) Click the Preview link underneath the theme of your choice to view a sample of how the theme looks. To return to the search results page, click the Close link in the upper-left corner of the preview window.**

   Figure 9-2 shows a preview of the Path theme, which I found by searching for the keyword *Responsive* on the Install Themes page.

5. **After you find a theme you like, click the Install link underneath the theme name to install the theme on your site.**

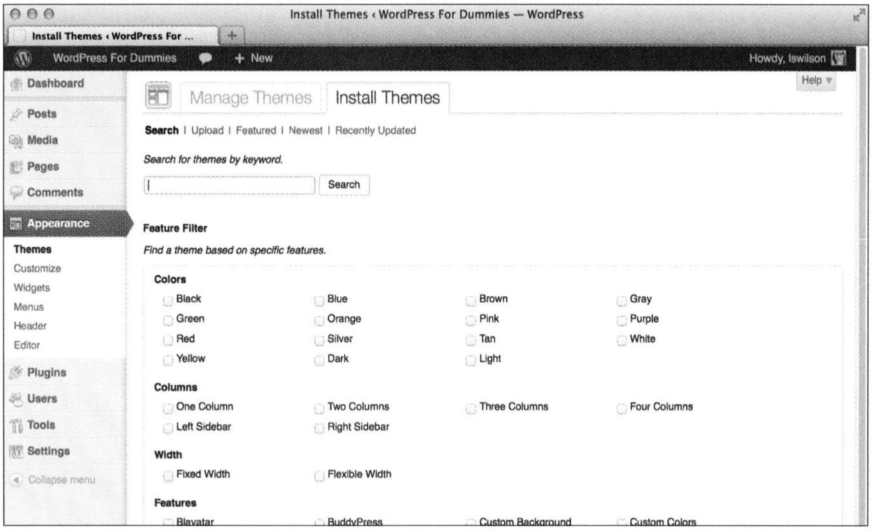

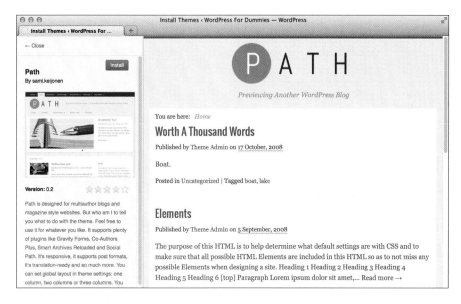

Figure 9-1: Find new themes on the Install Themes page on the Dashboard.

Figure 9-2: A preview of the Path theme on the Install Themes page.

6. **Click the Install New button to complete the installation.**

   The window closes, and the Installing Theme page appears.

7. **Click Activate to activate and display the new theme on your site.**

   The Manage Themes page refreshes and displays the activated theme under the Current Theme header, indicating that it's the theme currently in use on your website.

Themes found in the official WordPress Themes Directory have been vetted by the WordPress folks. Your Dashboard hooks into the Themes Directory page on the WordPress.org website (http://wordpress.org/extend/themes), so you find only those themes that are free and safe. *Safe* themes are free of spam and malicious code and contain basic WordPress functions to ensure that your WordPress site functions with the minimum requirements.

Deciding to Use a Premium Theme

Premium WordPress themes have become a very popular way for talented designers to provide a service they're passionate about — designing themes — while making a little money for their efforts. There are many schools of thought as to what makes a theme *premium*. Actually, the topic of what is and isn't considered premium is guaranteed to spark passionate debate among designers and theme users. However, almost everyone agrees the following are indicators of premium themes:

✔ **Very high-quality graphic design (beautiful, professional graphics) and CSS development.**

✔ **A theme structure with functions that make it easier for you to customize and adjust the theme to suit your needs.** This includes, but isn't limited to, altering the header graphic/logo and color scheme as well as changing images and icons.

✔ **Comprehensive documentation that provides the user with extensive instructions on how to use the theme.** This is especially useful if the theme has multiple features and customization options.

✔ **Full support by the designer who created the theme.** Typically, when you buy a premium theme, you get full support for that theme for as long as you use it.

✔ **Fee for use.** Premium themes cost money. Prices on premium themes range from $10 to $500.

This isn't to say that some free themes don't have some, or all, the features I just listed — it's just that, for the most part, they don't.

10

Working with the Default Theme: Twenty Thirteen

In This Chapter

▶ Discovering Twenty Thirteen's layout features

▶ Tweaking your header image

▶ Installing custom navigation menus

▶ Exploring widgets on your website

*B*undled with every WordPress installation is the default Twenty Thirteen theme, named for the year it was released to the public. Twenty Thirteen was created by the core WordPress team. It's a starter theme that gets new users up and running with their websites and lets them apply a clean-looking theme that utilizes many of the built-in display features standard to a basic WordPress install. These display features include the ability to use different header images (such as your own custom header graphics) and build custom navigation menus easily with the Custom Menus feature.

By working with the Twenty Thirteen theme, you gain an understanding of the features WordPress users are accustomed to seeing in themes. If you plan to create your own WordPress themes, you can find out a lot by exploring these common features so you can implement them in your own themes. The information provided in this chapter can be carried over into other themes, as well.

In this chapter, I introduce you to the Twenty Thirteen theme's built-in features, such as different layouts, headers, menus, and widgets.

Exploring the Layout and Structure

The Twenty Thirteen theme, shown in Figure 10-1, offers a clean design style that's highly customizable for the millions of WordPress users who want a simple but modern look that focuses on the content for their sites. As such, the font is sharp and easy to read. Many of the new built-in theme features allow you to make simple yet elegant tweaks to the theme, including uploading new feature images and adjusting the background colors.

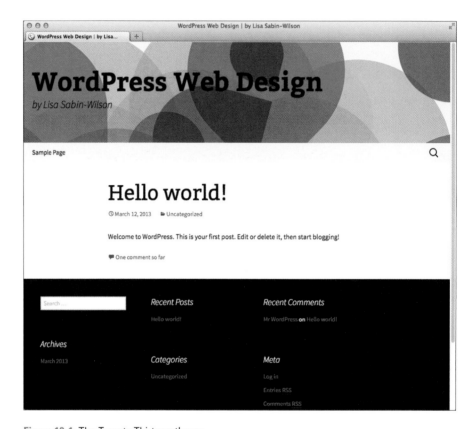

Figure 10-1: The Twenty Thirteen theme.

In Chapter 8, you find out how to plan a web design project that includes choosing how many columns you want to use for your design layout. The default Twenty Thirteen theme gives you two layout choices by using widget areas that come with it:

- **One-column default layout:** The one-column layout — a popular layout trend for websites and blogs — is the default view for the Twenty Thirteen theme, and it includes the header area (for the site name and menu navigation), a content area in the center of the site, and a widget-ready footer at the bottom of the site. (Refer to Figure 10-1.)

✔ **Two-column page layout:** The two-column layout, shown in Figure 10-2, is the more common layout that you may already be used to for websites and blogs. It provides all the layout options for the one-column (header, content, and footer) layout and adds a right sidebar that you can add widgets to.

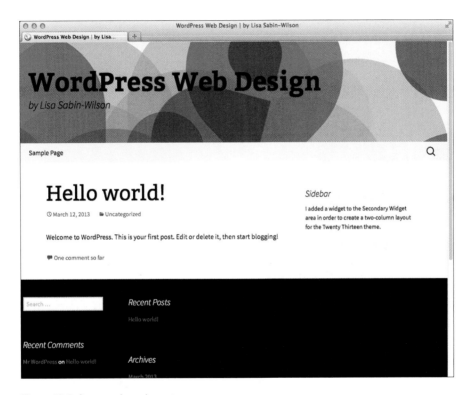

Figure 10-2: A two-column layout.

To apply Twenty Thirteen's two-column layout to a new WordPress page, simply add a widget or two (or more!) to the Secondary Widget area in the Widgets page in your Dashboard; see the "Enhancing your Website with Widgets" section for reference on how to use widgets.

The Twenty Thirteen theme has two widget areas: Main Widget Area and Secondary Widget Area. The widgets you add to the Main Widget Area appear in the footer area of your website, and the widgets you add to the Secondary Widget Area appear in the right sidebar of your site. Chapter 12 gives you lots more information on using the different widgets available in WordPress.

Customizing the Header Image

Most themes have a header image that appears at the top of the website. This image is generated by a graphic defined in the Cascading Style Sheet (CSS) value for the property that represents the header area or through the use of a custom header feature in WordPress. In the Twenty Thirteen theme, all the hard work's done for you, so including a custom header image on a site that uses that theme is pretty easy.

With the custom header feature that the Twenty Thirteen theme supports, you can choose one of three header images to display on your website, or you have the option to upload one of your own images. (For details on defining a background image for the header image using CSS, see Chapter 14.)

Selecting one of the available header images

To use one of the available header images on your site, follow these steps:

1. **On the WordPress Dashboard, choose Appearance⇨Header.**

   The Custom Header page appears in your browser window. Notice in the Preview section that one of the header images is selected by default and is already displayed on your website, as shown earlier in Figure 10-1.

2. **Scroll to the Default Images section, which shows the available header images, and select the header image you like.**

   Figure 10-3 shows the three available header images. The first one is already selected by default. You can also select the random option to have a different header image appear with each page view.

3. **Click the Save Changes button at the bottom of the page.**

   The Custom Header page refreshes and displays your chosen header image in the Preview section.

 You can easily switch between the different header images by revisiting the Custom Header page and applying one of the other header images on your site by following the preceding steps.

Figure 10-3: The Custom Header page shows the Twenty Thirteen theme's three default header images.

Uploading your own header image

Although the default header images are acceptable, you may want something unique for your site. You can choose a custom header image, such as a photograph you've taken or an image you've designed. (See Chapter 6 for the lowdown on different image types and formats.)

Follow these few steps to upload your own header image to your website:

1. **On the WordPress Dashboard, choose Appearance⊏⟩Header.**

   The Custom Header page loads in your browser window (refer to Figure 10-3).

2. **Scroll to the Select Image section, shown in Figure 10-4, and click the Browse button.**

   A dialog box pops up asking you to select an image from your computer's hard drive.

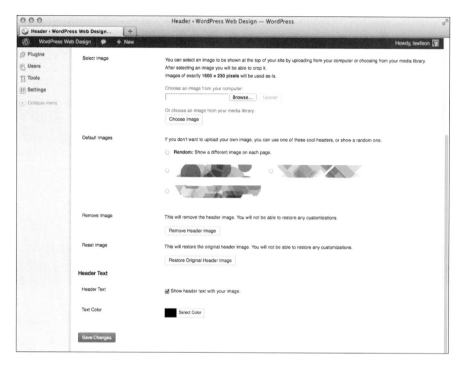

Figure 10-4: The Twenty Thirteen Select Image section.

3. **Select the image you want to use from your local computer, click the Open button, and then click the Upload button.**

   Your chosen image uploads to your web server, and the Crop Header Image page loads in your browser.

4. **(Optional) Use the image crop tool on the Crop Header Image page to resize your header image.**

   The Twenty Thirteen theme's default header size is 1600 x 230 pixels. Generally, it's best to upload a new header image already cropped in an image-editing program to that exact size. However, if your image is larger, you can use the built-in image crop tool to fit the image in the default space after you upload the header, as shown in Figure 10-5.

To resize and crop your larger image, simply drag one of the eight small *handles* located at the corners and in the middle of each side of the image, as shown in Figure 10-5. You can also click within the image and move the entire image up or down to get the optimal placement and cropping effect you want.

Handle

Figure 10-5: Cropping the header image in the Twenty Thirteen theme.

5. **Click the Crop and Publish button.**

   The Custom Header page loads on the Dashboard and displays your new header image.

6. **Click the Save Changes button.**

   The changes you've made are saved to the header image, and it publishes to your site.

Figure 10-6 displays the new header image I uploaded and added to my site using the Custom Header feature available in the Twenty Thirteen theme. Compare that with the display of my site shown earlier in Figure 10-1 and you can see that the header image has changed, making the website unique to me!

Figure 10-6: Displaying a unique header image.

Including Custom Navigation Menus

A *navigation menu* lists the links displayed on your site. These links can take you to pages, posts, or categories within your site, or to other sites. No matter what they link to, you can define navigation menus on your site through the built-in menus feature in WordPress.

I suggest you provide at least one navigation menu on your site so that readers can see everything your site has to offer. Providing visitors with a link — or several — to click is in keeping with the point-and-click spirit of the web.

Much like the drag-and-drop widgets feature (which I cover later in this chapter) that enables you to tweak areas of your site without knowing hardly any code, the menus feature offers an easy way to add and reorder a variety of navigational links to your site as well as create secondary menu bars (if your theme offers multiple menu areas).

The menus feature is already built in to the default Twenty Thirteen WordPress theme, so you don't have to worry about preparing your theme for it. Not all themes have this feature available though, because you have to add support for it in the theme functions file. I discuss how to enable this feature by using a functions file in Chapter 12.

To create a new navigation menu in Twenty Thirteen, follow these steps:

1. **Choose Appearance⇨Menus on your Dashboard.**

   The Menus page opens on your WordPress Dashboard.

2. **Type a name in the Menu Name box and click the Create Menu button.**

   The Menus page reloads with a message that your new menu has been created. I named my menu *Main,* as shown in Figure 10-7.

Click to expand module.   New menu items added

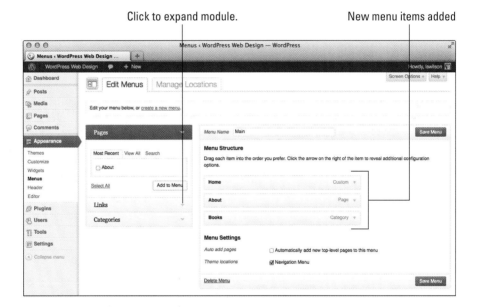

Figure 10-7: The Menus page on the Dashboard.

3. **Add new links to your newly created menu. WordPress allows you to add new links to the menu in three ways, as shown in Figure 10-7:**

   - *Pages:* Click the View All link to display a list of all the pages you have currently published on your site. Select the check box next to the page names you want to add to your menu and then click the Add to Menu button.

   - *Links:* Expand the Links module by clicking the arrow on the right, and then in the URL field, type the URL of the website that you want to add (for example, type **http://www.google.com**). Then type the name of the link that you want to display in your menu in the Text field (in this case, type **Google**). Then click the Add to Menu button.

- *Categories:* Expand the Categories module by clicking the arrow on the right, and then click the View All link to display a list of all the categories you've created on your site. Select the check box next to the category names you want to add to the menu and then click the Add to Menu button.

4. **Review your menu choices on the right side of the page.**

   When you add new menu items, the column on the right side of the Menus page populates with your menu choices. In Figure 10-7, I populated my menu with one link, one page, and one category (Home, About, and Books, respectively).

5. **(Optional) Edit your menu choices by clicking the down arrow to the right of the menu item name.**

6. **When you're satisfied with your menu choices, click the Save Menu button on the top-right of the Menus page.**

   A message confirming that the new menu has been saved appears.

You can create as many menus as you need for your website. Although the main navigation menu (which is determined in Appearance⟳Menus⟳Manage Locations⟳Navigation Menu) appears below the header image on the Twenty Thirteen theme (refer to Figure 10-1), menu widgets are available that allow you to display other menus you've created in different areas of your website, such as the sidebar or footer. (I cover widgets in the next section.)

After you save your navigation menu, you can customize it in the following ways:

✔ **Rearrange menu items:** Use the drag-and-drop interface on the Menus page to rearrange your menu items by clicking a menu item with your mouse, dragging it to the desired location, and then releasing your mouse to finalize its position (see Figure 10-8).

Figure 10-8: Dragging the About menu link to the top of the menu.

✔ **Create *subpages* under top-level menu items:** To create a subpage, move a menu item slightly to the right and below the top-level item, as shown in Figure 10-9. Subpages can be especially handy for sites with lots of page content because they enable you to avoid cluttering the navigation bar and to organize content logically. Click the Save Menu button to ensure that any changes you've made to the menu are saved and applied to your website.

Figure 10-9: Dragging the About menu link under the Home link to create a submenu item.

Figure 10-10 shows my site with the navigation menu displayed directly underneath the header image.

Figure 10-10: The navigation menu appears under the header image.

Enhancing Your Website with Widgets

WordPress *widgets* are very helpful tools built in to WordPress. They enable you to easily arrange how your content — such as your blogroll, recent posts, and monthly and category archive lists — appears in your website sidebar. With widgets, you can arrange and display the content in the sidebar without knowing PHP or HTML.

In the following sections, I introduce you to widgets, explain how to add one to your site, and describe in detail two popular widgets — the Text widget and the Recent Posts widget.

Understanding how widgets work

Widget areas are the editable regions defined in your theme that enable you to insert or arrange content, such as a list of your recent blog posts, links to your favorite sites, or new custom menus, by simply dragging and dropping (and editing) available widgets on the Dashboard's Widgets page into those corresponding areas.

Many of the available widgets offered by WordPress (and those added sometimes by WordPress themes and plugins) provide drag-and-drop ease of installation of more advanced functions that would typically be available only if you wrote code directly into your theme files.

To view the widgets available for use on your website, choose Appearance⇨ Widgets from the Dashboard. The Widgets page appears, displaying the available widgets on the left side of the page, as shown in Figure 10-11. This page enables you to control what features you use and where you place them — all without knowing a lick of code.

By default, the footer and sidebar in the Twenty Thirteen theme are *widgetized,* meaning the footer and sidebar areas expand to show any content you add to any of the two widget-ready areas. Figure 10-11 shows the widget areas displayed on the Widgets page on your Dashboard.

When you activate the Twenty Thirteen theme, the Widgets page on your Dashboard shows two widget areas:

- Main Widget Area
- Secondary Widget Area

Widgets in footer

Widgets in right sidebar

Figure 10-11: The Widgets page lists available widgets.

With the Twenty Thirteen theme activated on your site, the first widget area, Main Widget Area, displays widgets on your website in the footer area, as shown in Figure 10-12. The Secondary Widget Area displays widgets in the right sidebar of your website.

The number and appearance of widgets will vary depending on the theme you're currently using on your website. The Twenty Thirteen theme has two widget areas, but another theme may have more, to accommodate more content areas on your site.

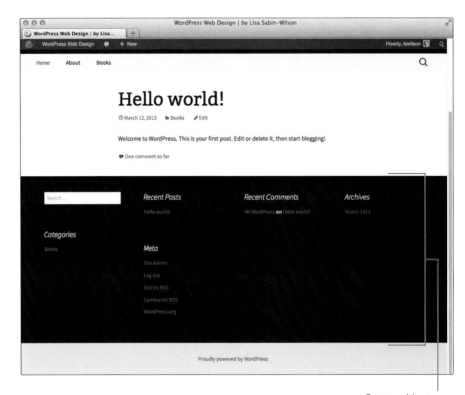

Footer widget area

Figure 10-12: The Twenty Thirteen theme's footer widget area.

Adding widgets to your sidebar or footer

The left side of the Widgets page lists all the available widgets for your WordPress site (refer to Figure 10-11). The right side of the page lists the widget areas designated in your theme. Drag your selected widget from the left side of the page into your chosen widget area on the right. For example, to add a search box to the right sidebar of the default layout of the Twenty Thirteen theme, drag the Search widget from the Available Widgets section to the Secondary Widget Area.

To add a new widget to your sidebar or footer, follow these steps:

1. **Choose Appearance⇨Widgets from the Dashboard.**

   The Widgets page appears (refer to Figure 10-11).

2. **Decide which widget you want to use from the Available Widgets section.**

   For the purpose of these steps, I chose the Recent Posts widget.

3. **Click the widget title and then drag and drop the widget into the Main Widget Area or Secondary Widget Area on the right side of the page.**

   I dragged the Recent Posts widget to the Secondary Widget Area.

4. **Configure options for the widget as desired and then click Save.**

   Each widget has different options that you can configure. Some widgets have a number of editable options; others simply let you write a title for the widget area. As shown in Figure 10-13, the Recent Posts widget has two options: one for editing the title of the widget and one to determine how many recent posts to display. Open the widget, by clicking the arrow to the right of the widget title, to explore the options available.

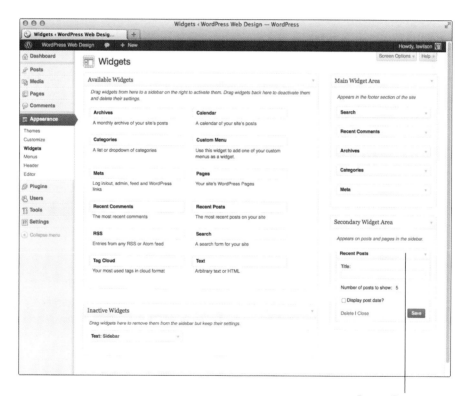

Recent Posts widget

Figure 10-13: Editing the Recent Posts widget options.

I discuss the options for the Text widget and RSS widget in more detail in the next two sections.

5. **(Optional) Repeat Steps 1 through 4 to add more widgets to your layout.**

6. **Arrange your widgets in the order you want them to appear on your site by clicking a widget and dragging it above or below another widget. Repeat this step until your widgets are arranged the way you want them.**

After you select and configure all your widgets, visit your website in your web browser and you can see that your site's sidebar matches the content (in the proper order) you've arranged in the Main Widget Area and Secondary Widget Area on the Widgets page on your Dashboard. How cool is that? You can go back to the Widgets page and rearrange, add, or remove items to your heart's content.

TIP

To remove a widget from your sidebar or footer, open the widget title's drop-down list and then click the Delete link. WordPress removes the widget from the widget area on the right side of this page and places it back in the Available Widgets section. If you want to remove a widget but want WordPress to remember the settings that you configured for it, instead of clicking the Delete link, simply drag the widget into the Inactive Widgets section on the left side, near the bottom of the page. This stores the widget, with all its settings, for future use.

Using the Text widget

The *Text widget* is one of the most useful WordPress widgets because it enables you to add text and HTML code into widget areas without editing the theme's template files. For that reason, the Text widget is the jack-of-all-trades widget; it enables you to include several types of information on your site by including your own text within it.

To illustrate this, here are some diverse examples for how I've used the Text widget and why it's such a popular feature:

- ✔ **Add an e-mail newsletter subscription form:** You can add a form that allows your site visitors to sign up for your e-mail newsletter. This often involves HTML, so the Text widget is especially helpful because it allows you to include basic HTML markup within it.

- ✔ **Display business hours of operation:** You can display the days and hours of your business operation where everyone can easily see them.

- ✔ **Post your updates from social networks:** Many social networking sites like Twitter and Facebook offer embed codes to display your updates on those sites directly on your website. They often include JavaScript, HTML, and CSS, and with the Text widget, you can easily embed the code provided.

- ✔ **Announce special events and notices:** If your organization has a special sale, an announcement about a new staff member, or an important notice about inclement weather closings, you can use the Text widget to quickly post these types of things in just a few seconds to your site.

WARNING!

The WordPress Text widget does not allow you to include PHP code of any kind, such as special WordPress template tags or functions like the ones you find in Chapter 12. However, a great plugin — the Advanced Text Widget — allows you to insert PHP code within it. If you need this feature, you can download the Advanced Text Widget from the WordPress Plugin Directory page at `http://wordpress.org/extend/plugins/advanced-text-widget`. (I discuss how to install plugins in Chapter 16.)

To add the Text widget to a sidebar or footer on your site, follow these steps:

1. **From the WordPress Dashboard, choose Appearance⇨Widgets.**

2. **Drag and drop the Text widget from the Available Widgets section to the desired widget area on the right. (See the preceding section for instructions on how to do this.)**

   The Text widget opens automatically to allow for editing.

3. **Add a widget title in the Title field and any desired text in the text area, as shown in Figure 10-14.**

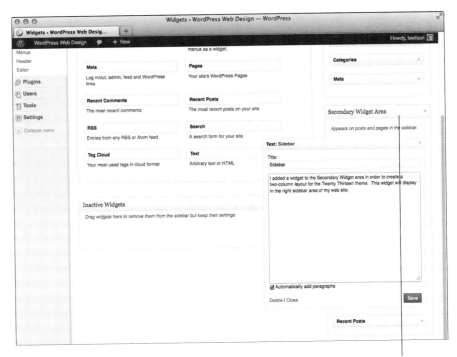

Text widget

Figure 10-14: The Text widget.

4. **Click the Save button and then click the Close link.**

The text widget closes, and you can view the content of the widget on your website.

Adding the RSS widget

The *RSS widget* allows you to pull headlines from almost any RSS (really simple syndication) feed, including recent headlines from your other WordPress blogs or sites, and headlines from news sites or other sources that offer RSS feeds. This is commonly referred to as *aggregation,* gathering information from a syndicated RSS-feed source to display on your site.

Follow these steps to add the RSS widget to your site:

1. **From the WordPress Dashboard, choose Appearance⇨Widgets.**

2. **Drag and drop the RSS widget from the Available Widgets section to the desired widget area on the right.**

See the section "Adding widgets to your sidebar or footer," earlier in this chapter, for instructions on how to do this.

3. **Open the RSS widget's drop-down list to display the options you can configure for the RSS widget, as shown in Figure 10-15.**

4. **In the Enter the RSS Feed URL Here text box, type the RSS URL of the blog (or site) you want to add.**

You can usually find the RSS feed URL of a blog (or a site) listed in its sidebar.

5. **(Optional) Type the title of the RSS widget.**

This title is what appears in your site above the links from the site. If I wanted to add the RSS feed from my personal site, for example, I'd type *Lisa's Site.*

6. **Select the number of items (from 1 to 20) from the RSS feed to display on your site.**

7. **(Optional) Select the following options as desired:**

   - *Display Item Content:* Select this check box if you want WordPress to also display the content of the feed (usually, the content of the post from the feed URL). If you want to display only the title, leave this check box deselected.

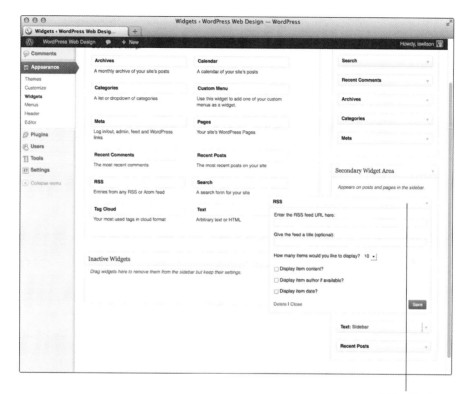

RSS widget

Figure 10-15: The RSS widget options.

- *Display Item Author If Available:* Select this option if you want to display the author's name along with the item's title.

- *Display Item Date:* Select this option if you want to display the date the item was published along with the item title.

8. **Click the Save button.**

   WordPress saves all the options you've just set and reloads the Widgets page with your RSS widget intact.

11

Dissecting Themes and Templates

*W*hen you start your journey in web design using the WordPress platform, your tasks often dip into the development and design sides of creating websites. Designing websites with WordPress is more than simply putting pretty graphics on display; it involves some knowledge of how to use WordPress templates and Cascading Style Sheets (CSS) to make the website function *and* look the way you want it to.

Before you take the big dive and dig in to the code and functions necessary to a WordPress theme for your website, you need at least a basic understanding of the programming languages in play. Many, if not all, of the function and template tags for WordPress use the Hypertext Preprocessor (PHP) language. When combined with the WordPress core code, these tags make things (such as displaying post content, categories, archives, links, and more) happen on your website.

One of the reasons WordPress is the most popular content management system (CMS) is that you don't really need to know PHP code to use it. That's to say, you can use WordPress easily without ever looking at any of the code or template files contained within it. However, if you want to tweak the settings of your WordPress theme (as described in Chapters 12, 13, and 14), you need to understand the basics of how PHP works. But don't worry; you don't need to be a PHP programmer.

This chapter introduces you to the very basics of PHP and *MySQL,* which is the database system that stores your WordPress data. You find out how PHP and MySQL work together with the WordPress platform to serve up your website in visitors' browsers. This chapter also introduces you to some basic WordPress theme concepts, such as a vital function referred to as *The Loop*. You gain an understanding of template parts and template tag parameters to prepare you for the upcoming chapters in this book that delve deep into WordPress themes, template files, and functions.

Understanding How PHP and MySQL Work Together

WordPress uses a PHP/MySQL platform, which provides everything you need to create your own site and publish your own content dynamically, without knowing how to program those pages. In short, all your content is stored in a MySQL database in your hosting account.

PHP is a server-side scripting language for creating dynamic web pages. When a visitor opens a page built in PHP, the server processes the PHP commands and then sends the results to the visitor's browser. *MySQL* is an open-source relational database management system (RDBMS) that uses *Structured Query Language (SQL),* the most popular language for adding, accessing, and processing data in a database. If all that sounds like Greek to you, just think of MySQL as a big filing cabinet where all the content on your site is stored.

Every time visitors go to your site to read your content, they make a request that's sent to a host server. The PHP programming language receives that request, makes a call to the MySQL database, obtains the requested information from the database, and then presents the requested information to your visitors through their web browsers.

Here *content* refers to the data stored in the MySQL database — that is, your blog posts, pages, comments, links, and options that you set up on the WordPress Dashboard. However, the *theme* (or design) you choose to use for your site — whether it's the default theme, one you create, or one you have custom-designed — isn't part of the content in this case. Theme files are part of the file system and aren't stored in the database. So creating and keeping a backup of any theme files that you're currently using are good ideas.

Chapter 8 covers important information about how to back up your WordPress website with the BackupBuddy plugin (`http://ithemes.com/purchase/backupbuddy`).

Exploring PHP Basics

WordPress requires PHP to work; therefore, your web-hosting provider must have PHP enabled on your web server. If you already have WordPress up and running on your website (as described in Chapter 3), you know PHP is running and working just fine. Currently, the PHP version required for the latest version of WordPress is PHP 5.2.4, or greater.

Before you play around with template tags (which I cover in Chapter 12) in your WordPress templates or plugin functions, you need to understand what makes up a template tag, as well as the correct syntax, or function, for a template tag as it relates to PHP. Additionally, take a look at the WordPress files contained within the download files. Many of the files end with the file extension `.php` — an extension required for PHP files, which separates them from other file types like JavaScript (`.js`) or CSS (`.css`).

This book doesn't turn you into a PHP programmer or MySQL database administrator, but it gives you a glimpse of how PHP and MySQL work together to help WordPress build your website. If you're interested in finding out how to program PHP or become a MySQL database administrator, check out *PHP & MySQL For Dummies* by Janet Valade (Wiley). You can also check out a very cool resource on the web called Codeacademy — `http://codeacademy.com` — a website where you can learn to code, for free, with interactive examples and lessons for HTML, CSS, PHP, JavaScript, jQuery, and more.

Examining the makeup of a template tag

As I state earlier, WordPress is based in *PHP* (a scripting language for creating web pages) and uses PHP commands to pull information from the MySQL database. Every tag begins with a function to start PHP and ends with a function to stop it. In the middle of those two commands lives the request to the database that tells WordPress to grab the data and display it.

A typical template tag, or function, looks like this:

```
<?php get_info(); ?>
```

This example tells WordPress to do three things:

- ✓ **<?php:** Start PHP.
- ✓ **get_info();:** Use PHP to get information from the MySQL database and deliver it to your site.
- ✓ **?>:** Stop PHP.

In this case, `get_info()` represents the tag function, which grabs information from the database to deliver it to your site. The information retrieved depends on what tag function appears between the two PHP commands.

Every PHP command you start requires a stop command. For every `<?php`, you must include the closing `?>` command somewhere later in the code. PHP commands structured improperly cause really ugly errors on your site, and they've been known to send programmers, developers, and hosting providers into loud screaming fits. You find a lot of starting and stopping of PHP throughout the WordPress templates and functions. The process seems as though it'd be resource-intensive, if not exhaustive — but it really isn't.

Always make sure the PHP start and stop commands are separated from the function with a single space. You must have a space after `<?php` and a space before `?>` — if not, the PHP function code doesn't work. So make sure the code looks like this: `<?php get_info(); ?>` — not like this: `<?phpget_info();?>`.

Trying out a little PHP

To make sure you understand the basics of PHP, including how to start and stop PHP within a file, try your hand at a little sample of PHP code. Follow these steps to create a simple HTML web page with an embedded PHP function:

1. **Open a new, blank file in your default text editor — Notepad (Windows) or TextMate (Mac) — then type** `<html>` **and press Enter.**

   The `<html>` tag tells the web browser that this is an HTML document and should be read as a web page.

2. **Type** `<head>` **and then press Enter.**

   The `<head>` HTML tag contains elements that tell the web browser about the document; this information is read by the browser but hidden from the web page visitor.

3. **Type** `<title>This is a Simple PHP Page</title>` **and then press Enter.**

   The `<title>` HTML tag tells the browser to display the text between the two tags as the title of the document in the browser title bar.

   All HTML tags need to be opened and then closed, just like PHP tags that I describe in the preceding section. In this case, the `<title>` tag opens the command, and the `</title>` tag closes it and tells the web browser that you're finished dealing with the title.

4. **Type** `</head>` **to close the `<head>` tag from Step 2 and then press Enter.**

5. **Type** `<body>` **to define the body of the web page and then press Enter.**

   Anything that appears after this tag appears in the web browser window.

6. **Type** `<?php` **to tell the web browser to start a PHP function and then press Enter.**

   See the preceding section on starting and stopping PHP functions.

7. **Type** `echo '<p>Testing my new PHP function</p>';` **and then press Enter.**

   This is the function that you want PHP to execute on your web page. This particular function echoes the text, "Testing my new PHP function" and displays it on your website.

8. **Type** `?>` **(be sure to insert a space before) to tell the web browser to end the PHP function and then press Enter.**

9. **Type** `</body>` **to close the** `<body>` **HTML tag from Step 5 and then press Enter.**

   This tells the web browser that you're done with the body of the web page.

10. **Type** `</html>` **to close the** `<html>` **tag from Step 1 and then press Enter.**

    This tells the web browser that you're at the end of the HTML document.

When you're done with Steps 1 through 10, double-check that the code in your text editor looks like this:

```
<html>
<head>
<title>This is a Simple PHP Page</title>
</head>
<body>
 <?php echo '<p>Testing my new PHP function</p>'; ?>
</body>
</html>
```

After you write your code, follow these steps to save and upload your file:

1. **Save the file to your local computer as** `testing.php`.

2. **Upload the** `testing.php` **file via File Transfer Protocol (FTP) to the root directory of your web server.**

   If you need details on how to use FTP to transfer files to your web server, check out Chapter 5.

3. **Open a web browser and type the address** `http://yourdomain.com/testing.php` **in the web browser's address bar.**

   In this example, *yourdomain.com* is your actual domain name.

   A single line of text displays `Testing my new PHP function`, as shown in Figure 11-1.

Figure 11-1: A basic PHP page in a browser.

If the `testing.php` file appears correctly in your browser, congratulations! You programmed PHP to work in a web browser.

If the `testing.php` file does not appear correctly in your browser, you see some common PHP error messages that indicate what errors exist in your code (usually it gives the error message plus the line number where the error exists in the file).

Managing Your MySQL Database

A lot of new WordPress users are pretty intimidated by the MySQL database, perhaps because it seems to be way above their technical skills or abilities. Truth be told, regular WordPress users — those who just use it to publish content — don't really ever have to dig into the database unless they want to. You need to explore the database only if you're dealing with theme or plugin development, or contributing code to the WordPress project. In this section, I give you a basic overview of the WordPress database stored in MySQL so that you have an understanding of the structure and know where items are stored.

Currently, WordPress requires MySQL version 5.0 (or greater) to work correctly. If your web-hosting provider doesn't have 5.0 (or greater) installed on your web server, kindly ask to upgrade.

After you install WordPress on your server (which I discuss in Chapter 3), the database gets populated with 11 tables that exist to store different types of data from your WordPress site. Figure 11-2 displays the structure of the tables, as follows:

- **wp_commentmeta:** This table stores every comment published to your site containing information, or *metadata,* that includes

    - A unique comment ID number.

    - A comment meta key, meta value, and meta ID — the meta information here are unique identifiers assigned to each comment left by you, or visitors, on your site.

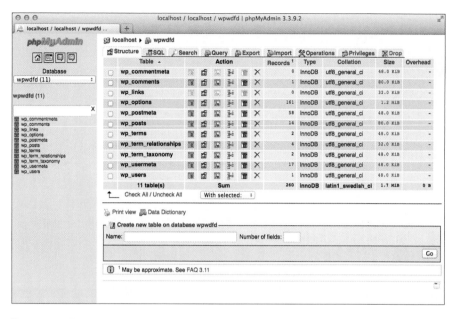

Figure 11-2: The WordPress database structure.

✔ **wp_comments:** This table stores the body of the comments published to your site, including

- A post ID that specifies which post the comment belongs to
- The comment content
- The comment author's name, URL, IP address, and e-mail address
- The comment date (day, month, year, and time)
- The comment status (approved, unapproved, or spam)

✔ **wp_links:** This stores the name, URL, and description of all links you create using the WordPress Link Manager; it also stores all the advanced options for the links you created, if any.

✔ **wp_options:** This stores all the option settings that you set for WordPress after you install it, including all theme and plugin option settings.

✔ **wp_postmeta:** This includes all posts or pages published to your site and contains metadata that includes

- The unique post ID number (each blog post has a unique ID number to set it apart from the others).
- The post meta key, meta id, and meta value — the meta information here are unique identifiers assigned to every post on your site and any custom fields you've created for the post.

✔ **wp_posts:** This table features the body of any post or page you've published, including autosaved revisions and post option settings, such as

- The post author, date, and time
- The post title, content, and excerpt
- The post status (published, draft, or private)
- The post comment status (open or closed)
- The post type (page, post, or custom post type)
- The post comment count

✔ **wp_terms:** This stores the categories you've created for posts and links as well as tags that have been created for your posts.

✔ **wp_term_relationships:** This stores the relationships among the posts as well as the categories and tags that have been assigned to them.

✔ **wp_term_taxonomy:** WordPress has three types of taxonomies by default: category, link, and tag. This table stores the taxonomy associated for the terms stored in the wp_terms table.

✔ **wp_usermeta:** This table features metadata from every user with an account on your WordPress website. This metadata includes

- A unique user ID
- A user meta key, meta value, and meta ID — the meta information here includes unique identifiers for each user on your site

✔ **wp_users:** The list of users with an account on your WordPress website is maintained within this table and includes information like

- The username, first name, last name, and nickname
- The user login
- The user password
- The user e-mail
- The registration date
- The user status and role (subscriber, contributor, author, editor, or administrator)

Most web-hosting providers provide you with a *utility,* or an interface, to view your MySQL database, and the most common one is phpMyAdmin, as shown in Figure 11-2. If you're unsure how you can view your database on your hosting account, get in touch with your hosting provider to find out.

Viewing the Template Files in a WordPress Theme

A WordPress theme is a collection of WordPress templates made up of WordPress template tags. When I refer to a WordPress *theme,* I'm talking about the group of templates that makes up the theme. When I talk about a WordPress *template,* I'm referring to only one of the template files that contains WordPress template tags. WordPress *template tags* make all the templates work together as a theme (more about this topic later in the chapter).

The rest of this chapter provides important information about the steps to take when building a WordPress theme, but here, I give you a brief overview of the templates that make up a WordPress theme and where you find them, both on your server and on your WordPress Dashboard. Follow these steps:

1. **Connect to your web server via FTP and look at the existing WordPress themes on your server in the folder `/wp-content/ themes`. See the left side of Figure 11-3.**

   When you open this folder, you find the `/twentythirteen` theme folder.

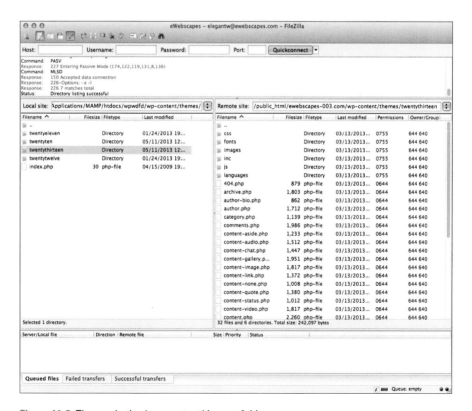

Figure 11-3: Themes in the /wp-content/themes folder.

If a theme is uploaded to any folder other than `/wp-content/themes`, it won't work.

2. **Open the folder for the Twenty Thirteen theme (`/wp-content/themes/twentythirteen`) and look at the template files inside, as shown in the right side of Figure 11-3.**

   When you open the Twenty Thirteen theme folder, you see several files. At a minimum, you find these five templates in any theme:

   - *Stylesheet* (`style.css`)
   - *Header template* (`header.php`)
   - *Main Index* (`index.php`)
   - *Sidebar template* (`sidebar.php`)
   - *Footer template* (`footer.php`)

   These files are the main WordPress template files, which I discuss in more detail in the next section. Take a peek inside these files and see the different template functions they contain. These filenames are the same in every WordPress theme. (Chapter 12 contains more information about these template files.)

3. **On your WordPress Dashboard, choose Appearance⇨Editor to look at the template files within a theme.**

   The Edit Themes page appears and lists the various templates available within the active theme. Figure 11-4 shows the templates in the default Twenty Thirteen theme. A text box in the center of the screen displays the contents of each template, and this box is also where you can edit the template file(s).

4. **To view and edit a template file, click the template name in the list on the right side of the page.**

The Edit Themes page also shows the template tags within the template file. These tags make all the magic happen in your site; they connect all the templates to form a theme. Chapter 12 provides steps for putting them all together to create your own theme (or to edit an existing theme).

Below the text box on the Edit Themes page is the Documentation drop-down list for every file you edit, except `style.css`. Click the arrow on the right side of the menu, and a list drops down that contains all the template tags used in the template you're currently viewing. This list is helpful when you edit templates and it gives you some insight into the different template tags used to create functions and features within your WordPress theme.

Figure 11-4: A list of templates available in the default Twenty Thirteen WordPress theme.

The template files don't work alone; for the theme to function, the files need one another. To tie these files together as one working entity, use template tags to pull the information from each template — Header, Sidebar, and Footer — into the Main Index. I refer to this procedure as *calling* one template into another.

Examining the Templates That Make Up a WordPress Theme

Creating themes requires you to step into the code of the templates, which can be a scary place sometimes — especially if you don't really know what you're looking at. A good place to start is by understanding the structure of a WordPress theme. A WordPress theme, in its very basic form, has four main areas that appear in the default theme that comes in every version of WordPress:

- ✔ **Header:** This area usually contains the name of the site along with the site tagline or slogan. Sometimes, the header also contains a graphic or image.

- ✔ **Body:** This area is where your content (such as blog posts, pages, and so on) appears in chronological order.

- ✔ **Sidebar:** This area is where you find lists of navigation elements such as the blogroll, the archives, and a list of recent posts.

- ✔ **Footer:** This area, at the bottom of the page, often contains links to further information about the site, such as who designed it, which company provides hosting for the site, and copyright information.

These four areas are the absolute bare bones of a *basic* WordPress site theme. You can extend these areas and create new sections that carry more information, of course, but for the purpose of this chapter, I focus on the basics.

The default WordPress theme is Twenty Thirteen (discussed in detail in Chapter 10), and in my opinion, it's a pretty doggone wonderful starting point for you, especially if you're just getting your feet wet. I don't cover all the tags and templates that the Twenty Thirteen theme includes; rather, I touch on the basics to get you on your way to understanding templates and template tags for WordPress.

To build a *basic* WordPress theme that covers the four basic areas of a site, you need these five templates:

- ✔ header.php (Header)
- ✔ index.php (Main Index)
- ✔ sidebar.php (Sidebar)
- ✔ footer.php (Footer)
- ✔ style.css (Stylesheet)

Each WordPress theme comes with a stylesheet (style.css), which drives the formatting and layout of your site theme in terms of where the elements are positioned on the page, what the font looks like, what colors your hyperlinks will be, and so on. As you may have already figured out, you don't use CSS to put content on your site; rather, you use CSS to style the content that's already there.

Chapter 14 provides information on tweaking the design of your theme by combining the template tags presented in this chapter with some CSS adjustments in your theme files.

In the following sections, I cover only the basic templates in a WordPress theme; in Chapter 12, however, I provide some ideas on how you can use various templates to further extend your website functionality — using templates for categories, archives, static pages, multiple sidebars, and so on. After you build the basics, you can spread your wings and step into more advanced themes.

The stylesheet

Every WordPress theme includes a `style.css` file. A browser uses this file, commonly known as the *stylesheet,* to provide style to the website design, such as font types, colors, and sizes; graphics; icons; background colors; borders; and other styling elements. The stylesheet targets areas of the site to style using CSS IDs and classes (covered in Chapter 14). CSS IDs and classes are simply a means of naming a particular element of the site. IDs are used for elements that appear only once on a page, whereas classes can be used as many times as you need. Although this file references *style,* it contains much more information about the theme.

At the very beginning of the `style.css` file, a comment block, or the *stylesheet header,* passes information about your theme to WordPress. *Comments* are code statements included only for programmers, developers, and others who read the code. Computers tend to ignore comment statements entirely, but WordPress uses the stylesheet header to get information about your theme. In CSS, comments always begin with a forward slash (/) followed by a star (*), and always end with a star followed by a forward slash (*/). The following code listing shows an example of the stylesheet header for the Twenty Thirteen theme:

```
/*
Theme Name: Twenty Thirteen
Theme URI: http://wordpress.org/extend/themes/twentythirteen
Author: the WordPress team
Author URI: http://wordpress.org/
Description: The 2013 theme for WordPress takes us back to the blog, featuring
            a full range of post formats, each displayed beautifully in their
            own unique way. Design details abound, starting with a gorgeous
            color scheme and matching header images, optional display fonts
            for beautiful typography, and a wide layout that looks great on
            large screens yet remains device-agnostic and is readable on any
            device.
Version: 0.1
```

```
License: GNU General Public License v2 or later
License URI: http://www.gnu.org/licenses/gpl-2.0.html
Tags: black, brown, orange, tan, white, yellow, light, one-column, two-columns,
             right-sidebar, flexible-width, custom-header, custom-menu, editor-
             style, featured-images, microformats, post-formats, rtl-language-
             support, sticky-post, translation-ready
Text Domain: twentythirteen

This theme, like WordPress, is licensed under the GPL.
Use it to make something cool, have fun, and share what you've learned with
             others.
*/
```

If you make modifications to the stylesheet comments, the changes are reflected on the WordPress Dashboard on the Themes page (choose Appearance⫯Themes).

Themes must provide this information, by way of comments, in the stylesheet header, and no two themes can have the same information. Two themes with the same name and details would conflict in the Manage Themes page. If you create your own theme based on another theme, make sure you change this information first.

Below the stylesheet header are the CSS styles that drive the formatting and styling of your theme. Chapter 14 goes into detail about CSS, including some examples you can use to tweak the style of your existing WordPress theme — check it out.

The Main Index and The Loop

Your theme is required to have only two files. The first is `style.css` (described in the preceding section). The other is a Main Index file, known in WordPress as `index.php`. The `index.php` file is the first file WordPress tries to load when someone visits your site. Extremely flexible, `index.php` can be used as a stand-alone file or can include other templates. The Main Index template drags your posts out of the MySQL database and inserts them into your site. This template is to your website what the dance floor is to a nightclub — where all the action happens.

The first template tag in the Main Index template *calls in* the Header template, meaning that it pulls the information from the Header template into the Main Index template, as follows:

```
<?php get_header(); ?>
```

Your theme can work without calling in the Header template, but it'll be missing several essential pieces — the CSS and the site name and tagline, for starters.

The Main Index template in the Twenty Thirteen theme calls in three other files in a similar fashion:

- ✔ **get_template_part(content, get_post_format());:** This function calls in the template `content.php` first, but if there are other content template files like `content-image.php` or `content-video.php`, the function will use one of the other template files, depending on what post format is being used. (See Chapter 15 for information about post formats.)

- ✔ **get_sidebar();:** This function calls in the template `sidebar.php` file.

- ✔ **get_footer();:** This function calls in the template `footer.php` file.

I cover each of these three functions and template files in upcoming sections of this chapter.

The concept of *calling in* a template file using a function or template tag is exactly what the Main Index template does with the four functions for the Header, Loop, Sidebar, and Footer templates explained later in this section.

Generally, one of the important functions of the Main Index is to contain *The Loop*. In WordPress, The Loop is a function that WordPress uses to display posts and pages on your site. Any PHP or HTML that you include in The Loop will repeat for each of your posts and pages that it displays. The Loop has a starting point and an ending point; anything placed in between is used to display each post or page, including any HTML, PHP, or CSS tags and codes.

Here's a look at what the WordPress Codex calls "The World's Simplest Index":

```php
<?php
get_header();
if (have_posts()) :
   while (have_posts()) :
     the_post();
     the_content();
   endwhile;
endif;
get_sidebar();
get_footer();
?>
```

First, the template starts by opening the `php` tag. Next, the template includes the header, meaning that it retrieves anything contained in the `header.php` file and displays it. Now the good stuff starts happening. The Loop begins with the `while (have_posts())` : bit. Anything between `while` and `endwhile` repeats for each post that appears. The number of posts that appears is determined in the Settings section of the WordPress Dashboard.

If your site has posts (and most do, even when you first install it), WordPress proceeds with The Loop, starting with the piece of code that looks like this:

```
if (have_posts()) :
    while (have_posts()) :
```

This code tells WordPress to grab the posts from the MySQL database and display them on your site.

Then The Loop closes with this tag:

```
    endwhile;
endif;
```

Near the beginning of the Loop template is a template tag that looks like this:

```
if (have_posts()) :
```

To read that template tag in plain English, it says: If [this site] has posts.

If your site meets that condition (that is, if it has posts), WordPress proceeds with The Loop and displays your posts; if it does not meet that condition (that is, it does not have posts), WordPress displays nothing.

When The Loop ends (at the endwhile), the index.php (Main Index) template executes the files for the sidebar and footer. Although it's simple, The Loop is one of the core functions of WordPress.

Misplacement of the while or endwhile statement causes The Loop to break. If you're having trouble with The Loop in an existing template, check your version against the original and see whether the while statements are misplaced.

In your travels as a WordPress user, you may run across plugins or scripts with instructions that say something like this: This must be placed within The Loop. That's The Loop that I discuss in this section, so pay particular attention. Understanding The Loop arms you with the knowledge you need for tackling and understanding your WordPress themes.

The Loop is no different from any other template tag; it must begin with a function to start PHP, and it must end with a function to stop PHP. The Loop begins with PHP and then makes a request: While there are posts in my blog, display them on this page. This PHP function tells WordPress to grab the post information from the database and return it to the site. The end of The Loop is like a traffic cop with a big red stop sign telling WordPress to stop the function completely.

You can set the number of posts displayed per page in the Reading Settings page (choose Settings⇨Reading) on the WordPress Dashboard. The Loop abides by this rule and displays only the number of posts per page that you've set.

The Header template

The *Header template* is the starting point for every WordPress theme because it tells web browsers the following information:

- ✓ The title of your site
- ✓ The location of the CSS
- ✓ The RSS feed URL
- ✓ The site URL
- ✓ The tagline (or description) of the site

In many themes, the first elements in the header are a main image and the navigation. These two elements are usually in the `header.php` file because they load on every page and rarely change. The following statement is the built-in WordPress function to call the Header template:

```
<?php get_header(); ?>
```

Every page on the web has to start with a few pieces of code. In every `header.php` file in any WordPress theme, you find these bits of code at the top:

- ✓ The **DOCTYPE** (*document type declaration*) tells the browser which type of XHTML *(Extensible Hypertext Markup Language)* standards you're using. The Twenty Thirteen theme uses `<!DOCTYPE html>`, which is a declaration for W3C (World Wide Web Consortium) standards compliance mode and covers all major browser systems (and is the markup doctype specifically for HTML5).
- ✓ The `<html>` **tag** (Hypertext Markup Language) tells the browser which language you're using to write your web pages.
- ✓ The `<head>` **tag** tells the browser that the information contained within the tag shouldn't be displayed on the site; rather, it's information about the document.

In the Header template of the Twenty Thirteen theme, these bits of code look like the following example, and you need to leave them intact:

```
<!DOCTYPE html>
<html <?php language_attributes(); ?>>
<head>
```

The WordPress body class

In WordPress, you want to use the body class template tag instead of the generic `<body>` HTML markup. WordPress provides us with the body class tag to dynamically generate classes that are dependent upon the page you're viewing within your site. The body class tag looks like `<body <?php body_class(); ?>>`, and it is the `<?php body_class(): ?>` portion of that code that tells WordPress to dynamically generate page-specific classes. For example, with the body class tag in place, when you are viewing a single post page on your site, the body tag dynamically changes the classes to `<body class="single single-post">`, enabling you to use CSS to create styles for different page views within your site. (Read more about CSS in Chapter 14.)

On the Edit Themes page (choose Appearance➪Editor on the WordPress Dashboard), click the Header template link to display the template code in the text box. Look closely, and you see that the `<!DOCTYPE html>` declaration, `<html>` tag, and `<head>` tag appear in the template.

The `<head>` tag needs to be closed at the end of the Header template, which looks like this: `</head>`. You also need to include a fourth tag, the `<body>` tag, which tells the browser where the information you want to display begins. Both the `<body>` and `<html>` tags need to be closed at the end of the template, like this: `</body></html>`.

There is one line of code that should exist in every Header template for any WordPress theme: `<?php wp_head(); ?>`. This tag serves as a hook in WordPress that plugin developers use to insert necessary code and functions. Without this tag, the majority of plugins for WordPress will not function correctly, so be sure your Header template includes the tag `<?php wp_head(); ?>` before the closing `</head>` HTML markup.

Using bloginfo parameters

The Header template makes much use of one WordPress template tag in particular: `bloginfo();`.

What differentiates the type of information that a tag pulls in is a parameter. *Parameters* are placed inside the parentheses of the tag, enclosed in single quotations. For the most part, these parameters pull information from the settings on your WordPress Dashboard. The template tag to get your blog title, for example, looks like this:

```
<?php bloginfo('name'); ?>
```

Table 11-1 lists the various parameters you need for the `bloginfo();` tag and shows you what the template tag looks like. Some of the parameters in

Table 11-1 are used in the Twenty Thirteen `header.php` template file and pertain only to the `bloginfo();` template tag.

Table 11-1	Tag Values for bloginfo();	
Parameter	*Information*	*Tag*
`charset`	Character settings, set in Settings/General	`<?php bloginfo ('charset'); ?>`
`name`	Site title, set in Settings/General	`<?php bloginfo ('name'); ?>`
`description`	Tagline for your site, set in Settings/General	`<?php bloginfo ('description'); ?>`
`url`	Your site's web address, set in Settings/General	`<?php bloginfo ('url'); ?>`
`stylesheet_ url`	URL of primary CSS file	`<?php bloginfo ('stylesheet_url'); ?>`
`pingback_url`	Displays the track-back URL for your site on single post pages	`<?php bloginfo ('pingback_url'); ?>`

Creating title tags

Here's a useful tip about your site's `<title>` tag: Search engines pick up the words used in the `<title>` tag as keywords to categorize your site in their search engine directories.

The `<title></title>` tags are HTML tags that tell the browser to display the title of your website in the title bar of a visitor's browser window.

Search engines love the title bar. The more you can tweak that title to provide detailed descriptions of your site (otherwise known as *search engine optimization,* or *SEO*), the more the search engines will love your site. Browsers will show that love by giving your site higher rankings in their results. (For more information and tips on SEO with WordPress, see Chapter 15.)

The site `<title>` tag is the code that lives in the Header template between these two tag markers: `<title></title>`. In the default Twenty Thirteen theme, this bit of code looks like this (don't let this code scare you — I promise I will break it down for you!):

```
<title><?php wp_title( '|', true, 'right' ); ?></title>
```

It may help to put this example into plain English. The way the Twenty Thirteen Header template displays the title is based on the type of page that appears — and it shrewdly uses SEO to help you with the browser powers that be.

The title bar of the browser window always displays your site name unless you're on a single post page. In that case, it displays your site title plus the title of the post on that page.

Within some of the WordPress template tags, such as the `<title>` tag in the earlier example, you may notice some weird characters that look like a foreign language. You may wonder what `&raquo;` is, for example; it isn't part of any PHP function or CSS style. Rather, `&raquo;` is a *character entity* — a kind of code that enables you to display a special character. The `&raquo;` character entity displays a double right-angle quotation mark.

Displaying your site name and tagline

The default Twenty Thirteen theme header displays your site name and tagline on the top of your site, on every page. You can use the `bloginfo();` tag plus a little HTML code to display your site name and tagline. Most sites have a clickable title, which is a site title that takes you back to the home page when it's clicked. No matter where your visitors are on your site, they can always go back home by clicking the title of your site in the header.

To create a clickable title, use the following code:

```
<a href="<?php bloginfo('url'); ?>"><?php bloginfo('name'); ?></a>
```

The `bloginfo('url');` tag is your main Internet address, and the `bloginfo('name');` tag is the name of your site (refer to Table 11-1). So the code creates a link that looks something like this:

```
<a href="http://yourdomain.com">Your Blog Name</a>
```

The tagline generally isn't linked back home. You can display it by using the following tag:

```
<?php bloginfo('description'); ?>
```

This tag pulls the tagline directly from the one that you've set up on the General Settings page on your WordPress Dashboard (choose Settings⇨ General).

This example shows how WordPress is intuitive and user-friendly; you can do things like change the site name and tagline with a few keystrokes on the Dashboard. Changing your options on the Dashboard creates the change on every page of your site — no coding experience required. Beautiful, isn't it?

In the Twenty Thirteen templates, these tags are surrounded by tags that look like these: `<h1></h1>` or `<h2></h2>`. These tags are `<header>` tags, which define the look and layout of the site name and tagline in the CSS of your theme. (I cover CSS and tackle basic HTML markup in Chapter 14.)

The Sidebar template

The Sidebar template in WordPress has the filename `sidebar.php`. The sidebar is usually found on the left or right side of the main content area of your WordPress theme. (In the Twenty Thirteen theme, the sidebar appears to the right of the main content area.) The sidebar is a good place to put useful information about your site, such as a site summary, advertisements, or testimonials.

Many themes use widget areas in the Sidebar template. This allows you to display content easily on your WordPress pages and posts. The following statement is the built-in WordPress function to call the Sidebar template:

```
<?php get_sidebar(); ?>
```

This code calls the Sidebar template and all the information it contains into your site. (For more information on widgets, see Chapter 10.)

The Footer template

The Footer template in WordPress has the filename `footer.php`. The footer is generally at the bottom of the page and contains brief reference information about the site. This usually includes copyright information, template design credits, and a mention of WordPress. Similar to the Header and Sidebar templates, the Footer template gets called into the Main Index template through this bit of code:

```
<?php get_footer(); ?>
```

This code calls the Footer template and all the information it contains into your site.

The default Twenty Thirteen theme shows a statement that says `Proudly powered by WordPress`. You can use the footer to include all sorts of information about your site, however; you don't have to restrict it to small bits of information.

There is one line of code that should exist in every Footer template for any WordPress theme: `<?php wp_footer(); ?>`. This tag serves as a hook in WordPress that plugin developers use to insert necessary code and functions. Without this tag, the majority of plugins for WordPress will not function correctly, so be sure your Footer template includes the tag `<?php wp_footer(); ?>` before the closing `</html>` HTML markup.

Other template files

To make your website work properly, WordPress uses all the theme files together. Some, such as the header and footer, are used on every page. Others, such as the Comments template (`comments.php`), are used only at specific times, to pull in specific functions. When someone visits your site, WordPress uses a series of queries to determine which templates to use.

You can include many more templates in your theme. Here are some of the other template files you may want to use:

- **Comments template (`comments.php`):** The Comments template is required if you plan to host comments on your blog; it provides all the template tags you need to display those comments. The template tag used to call the comments into the template is `<?php comments_template(); ?>`.

- **Single Post template (`single.php`):** When your visitors click the title or permalink of a post you've published, they're taken to that post's individual page. There, they can read the entire post, and if you have comments enabled, they see the comments form and can leave comments.

- **Page template (`page.php`):** You can use a Page template for static pages in your WordPress site.

- **Search Results template (`search.php`):** You can use this template to create a custom display of search results. When someone uses the search feature to search your site for specific keywords, this template formats the return of those results.

- **404 template (`404.php`):** Use this template to create a custom *404 page*, which is the page visitors get when the browser can't find the page requested and returns that ugly 404 Page Cannot Be Found error.

The templates in the preceding list are optional. If these templates don't exist in your WordPress `themes` folder, nothing breaks. The Main Index template handles the display of these items (the single post page, the search results page, and so on). The only exception is the Comments template. If you want to display comments on your site, you must have that template included in your theme.

Exploring Template Tags, Values, and Parameters

I cover a full breakdown and explanation of WordPress template tags in Chapter 12, introducing the concept of parameters and values, and how to use them, as well as the different types of parameters. You should have a primary grasp of these concepts before moving forward with using template tags within your WordPress theme files.

If every piece of content on your site were hard-coded, it wouldn't be easy to use and modify. Template tags allow you to add information and content dynamically to your site. One example of adding information using a template tag is the `the_category` tag. Rather than typing all the categories and links that each post belongs in, you can use the `the_category()` tag in your template to automatically display all the categories as links.

When you use a template tag, you're really telling WordPress to do something or retrieve some information. Often, template tags are used to fetch data from the MySQL database and display it on your website. More than 100 template tags are built in to WordPress, and the tags vary greatly in what they can accomplish. You can view a complete list of template tags in the WordPress Codex at `http://codex.wordpress.org/Template_Tags`.

Template tags can be used only inside PHP blocks. The PHP blocks can be opened and closed as many times as needed in a template file. Once opened, the server knows that anything contained in the block is to be translated as PHP.

The opening tag (`<?php`) must be followed, at some point, by the closing tag (`?>`). All blocks must contain these tags. A template tag is used in the same way that PHP functions are. The tag is always text with no spaces (may be separated by underscores or dashes), with opening and closing brackets, and with a semicolon. The following line of code shows you how it all looks:

```
<?php template_tag_name(); ?>
```

Because a template tag is a PHP function, you can pass parameters to the tag. A *parameter* is simply a variable that allows you to change or filter the output of a template tag. Here are the three types of template tags in WordPress:

- **Tags without parameters:** Some template tags don't require any options, so they don't need any parameters passed to them. For example, the `is_user_logged_in()` tag doesn't accept any parameters because it returns only `true` or `false`.

- **Tags with PHP function–style parameters:** Template tags with PHP function–style parameters accept parameters that are passed to them by placing one or more values inside the function's parentheses. For example, if you're using the `bloginfo();` tag, you can filter the output to just the description by using

  ```
  <?php bloginfo('description'); ?>
  ```

  If there are multiple parameters, the order you list them is very important. Each function sets the necessary order of its variables, so double-check the order of your parameters.

  Always place the value in single quotations and separate multiple parameters by commas.

✏ **Tags with query string–style parameters:** Template tags with query string–style parameters allow you to change the values of just the parameters you require. This is useful for template tags that have a large number of options. For example, the `wp_list_pages()` tag has 18 parameters. Rather than using the PHP function–style parameters, this function allows you to get to the source of what you need and give it a value. For example, if you want to list all your WordPress pages except for page 24, you'd use

```
<?php wp_list_pages('exclude=24'); ?>
```

Query string–style parameters can be the most difficult to work with because they generally deal with the template tags that have the most possible parameters.

Table 11-2 helps you understand the three variations of parameters used by WordPress.

Table 11-2	Three Variations of Template Parameters	
Variation	**Description**	**Example**
Tags without parameters	These tags have no additional options available. Tags without parameters have nothing within the parentheses.	`the_tag();`
Tags with PHP function–style parameters	These tags have a comma-separated list of values placed within the tag parentheses.	`the_tag('1,2,3');`
Tags with query-string parameters	These types of tags generally have several available parameters. This tag style enables you to change the value for each parameter without being required to provide values for all available parameters for the tag.	`the_tag('parameter=true);` Also accepts multiple parameters: `the_tag('parameter=true&parameter2=true');`

The WordPress Codex page, located at `http://codex.wordpress.org`, has every conceivable template tag and possible parameter known to the WordPress software; in addition, I go into greater depth on template tags and parameters you can use to create the features and content display that you

need for your website in Chapter 12. The tags and parameters that I share
with you in this chapter are the very basic ones most commonly used in just
about every WordPress theme available.

Customizing Your Blog Posts with Template Tags

This section covers the template tags that you use to display the body of
each blog post you publish. The body of a blog post includes information
such as the post date and time, title, author name, category, and content.
Table 11-3 lists the common template tags you can use for posts, available in
any WordPress theme template. The tags in Table 11-3 work only if you place
them within The Loop (which I cover earlier in this chapter and is found in
the `loop.php` template file).

Table 11-3	Template Tags for Blog Posts
Tag	*Function*
`get_the_date();`	Displays the date of the post.
`get_the_time();`	Displays the time of the post.
`the_title();`	Displays the title of the post.
`the_permalink();`	Displays the permalink (URL) of the post.
`get_the_author();`	Displays the post author's name.
`the_author_link();`	Displays the URL of the post author's site.
`the_content('Read More...');`	Displays the full content of the post.
`the_excerpt();`	Displays an excerpt (snippet) of the post.
`the_category();`	Displays the category (or categories) assigned to the post. If the post is assigned to multiple categories, they're separated by commas.
`comments_popup_link('No Comments', 'Comment (1)', 'Comments(%)');`	Displays a link to the comments, along with the comment count for the post in parentheses. (If no comments exist, a No Comments message displays.)
`next_posts_link('&laquo; Previous Entries')`	Displays a Previous Entries link that links to the previous page of blog entries.
`previous_posts_link('Next Entries &raquo;')`	Displays the Next Entries link that links to the next page of blog entries.

The last two tags in the table aren't like the others. You don't place these tags in The Loop; instead, you insert them after The Loop but before the if statement ends. Here's an example:

```
<?php endwhile; ?>
<?php next_posts_link('&laquo; Previous Entries') ?>
<?php previous_posts_link('Next Entries &raquo;') ?>
<?php endif; ?>
```

Putting It All Together

Template files can't do a whole lot by themselves — the real power comes when they're put together.

Connecting the templates

WordPress has built-in functions to include the main template files, such as header.php, sidebar.php, and footer.php, in other templates. An include function is a custom PHP function that's built in to WordPress allowing you to retrieve the content of one template file and display it along with the content of another template file. Table 11-4 shows the templates and the function to include them.

Table 11-4	Template Files and Include Functions
Template Name	**Include Function**
header.php	`<?php get_header(); ?>`
sidebar.php	`<?php get_sidebar(); ?>`
footer.php	`<?php get_footer(); ?>`
search.php	`<?php get_search_form(); ?>`
comments.php	`<?php comments_template(); ?>`

If you want to include a file that doesn't have a built-in include function, you need a different piece of code. For instance, if you want to add a unique sidebar (different from the default sidebar.php file within your existing theme) to a certain page template, you can name the sidebar file sidebar-page.php. To include that in another template, you use the following code:

```
<?php get_template_part('sidebar', 'page'); ?>
```

In this statement, the PHP `get_template_part` function looks through the main theme folder for the `sidebar-page.php` file and displays the content from the `sidebar-page.php` file. If it does not find that file, WordPress defaults to displaying the `sidebar.php` file.

In the following sections, you put together the guts of a basic Main Index template by using the information on templates and tags I provide in the previous sections of this chapter. There seem to be endless lines of code when you view the `loop.php` template file in the Twenty Thirteen theme, so I've simplified it for you. These steps give you a basic understanding of the WordPress Loop and the common template tags and functions you can use to create your own.

Creating basic WordPress templates

You create a new WordPress theme by using some of the basic WordPress templates. The first steps in pulling everything together are as follows:

1. **Connect to your web server via FTP, click the `/wp-content` folder, and then click the `/themes` folder.**

   This folder contains the themes currently installed in your WordPress site. (See Chapter 5 if you need more information on FTP.)

2. **Create a new folder and name it `mytheme`.**

   In most FTP programs, you can right-click and choose New Folder. (If you aren't sure how to create a folder, refer to your FTP program's help files.)

3. **In your favored text editor, such as Notepad (Windows) or TextMate (Mac), create the Header template with the code in Listing 11-1 and then save with the filename `header.php`.**

   When typing templates, be sure to use a text editor, such as Notepad or TextMate. Using a word processing program, such as Microsoft Word, opens a whole slew of problems in your code. Word processing programs insert hidden characters and format quotation marks in a way that WordPress can't read.

Listing 11-1:   header.php

```
<!DOCTYPE html>
<html <?php language_attributes(); ?> />
<head profile="http://gmpg.org/xfn/11">
<meta http-equiv="Content-Type" content="<?php bloginfo('html_type'); ?>;
charset=<?php bloginfo('charset'); ?>" />
<title><?php bloginfo( 'name' ); ?> <?php if ( is_single() ) { ?> &raquo; Blog
          Archive <?php } ?>
```

(continued)

Listing 11-1 *(continued)*

```
<?php wp_title(); ?></title>

<link rel="stylesheet" href="<?php bloginfo( 'stylesheet_url' ); ?>" type="text/
        css" media="screen" />
<link rel="pingback" href="<?php bloginfo( 'pingback_url' ); ?>" />

<?php if ( is_singular() ) wp_enqueue_script( 'comment-reply' ); ?>
<?php wp_head(); ?>
</head>
<body <?php body_class() ?>>
<div id="page">
<header id="header">
<h1><a href="<?php bloginfo('url'); ?>"><?php bloginfo('name'); ?></a></h1>
<h2><?php bloginfo('description'); ?></h2>
</header>
<section>
```

4. **Create a theme functions file with the code in Listing 11-2 and then save with the filename `functions.php`.**

   The theme functions file registers the widget area for your site so that you can add widgets to your sidebar using the available WordPress widgets on the Widgets page on the Dashboard.

Listing 11-2: functions.php

```
<?php
if ( function_exists('register_sidebar') ) register_sidebar(array('name'=>'Side
        bar',
));
?>
```

5. **Create a Sidebar template file with the code in Listing 11-3 and then save with the filename `sidebar.php`.**

   The code here tells WordPress where you want the WordPress widgets to appear in your theme; in this case, widgets appear in the sidebar of your site.

Listing 11-3: sidebar.php

```
<aside id="side" class="sidebar">
<ul>
<?php if ( !function_exists('dynamic_sidebar') || !dynamic_sidebar('Sidebar') )
            : ?>
<?php endif; ?>
</ul>
</aside>
```

6. **Create the Footer template file with the code in Listing 11-4 and then save it with the filename `footer.php`.**

Listing 11-4:   footer.php

```
</div>
<footer id="footer">
<p>&copy; Copyright <a href="<?php bloginfo('url'); ?>"><?php bloginfo('name');
            ?></a>. All Rights Reserved</p>
</footer>
<?php wp_footer(); ?>
</body>
</html>
```

7. **Create the stylesheet file with the code in Listing 11-5 and then save it with the filename `style.css`.**

   I cover CSS in more detail in Chapter 14 — this example gives you just some very basic styling to create your sample theme.

Listing 11-5:   style.css

```
/*
Theme Name: My Theme
Description: Basic Theme from WordPress Web Design For Dummies example
Author: Lisa Sabin-Wilson
Author URI: http://lisasabin-wilson.com
*/

body {
font-family: verdana, arial, helvetica, sans-serif;
font-size:16px;
color: #555;
background: #eee;
}

#page {
width: 960px;
margin: 0 auto;
background: white;
border: 1px solid silver;
}

#header {
width: 950px;
height: 100px;
background: black;
color: white;
padding: 5px;
```

(continued)

Listing 11-5 *(continued)*

```
}

#header h1 a {
color: white;
font-size: 22px;
font-family: Georgia;
text-decoration: none;
}

#header h2 {
font-size: 16px;
font-family: Georgia;
color: #eee;
}

section {
width: 600px;
float:left;
}

#side {
width: 220px;
margin: 0 15px;
float:left;
}

#footer {
clear:both;
width: 960px;
height: 50px;
background: black;
color: white;
}

#footer p {
text-align:center;
padding: 15px 0;
}

#footer a {
color:white;
}
```

Creating the Main Index template and activating the theme

Using the tags provided earlier in Table 11-3, along with the information on The Loop and the calls to the Header, Sidebar, and Footer templates provided in earlier sections, you can follow the next steps for a bare-bones example of what the Main Index template looks like when you put the tags together.

To create a Main Index template to work with the other templates in your WordPress theme, follow these steps:

1. **Open a new window in a text editor program, enter the code in Listing 11-6, and save the file as `index.php`.**

   I describe the lines in the `index.php` file in more detail immediately following this step list.

Listing 11-6: index.php

```
<?php get_header(); ?>                                              → 1
<?php if (have_posts()) : ?>                                        → 2
<?php while (have_posts()) : the_post(); ?>                         → 3
<article <?php post_class() ?> id="post-<?php the_ID(); ?>">        → 4
        <a href="<?php the_permalink(); ?>"><?php the_title(); ?></a>  → 5
        Posted on: <?php echo get_the_date(); ?> at <?php echo get_the_time();
            ?>                                                      → 6
        Posted in: <?php the_category(','); ?>                      → 7

        <?php the_content('Read More..'); ?>                        → 8
        Posted by: <?php the_author(); ?> | <?php comments_popup_link('No
            Comments', '1 Comment', '% Comments'); ?>               → 9
</article>                                                          → 10

<?php endwhile; ?>                                                  → 11
<?php next_posts_link('&laquo; Previous Entries') ?>               → 12
<?php previous_posts_link('Next Entries &raquo;') ?>              → 13
<?php else : ?>                                                     → 14
<p>Not Found</p>                                                    → 15
<p>Sorry, but you are looking for something that isn't here.</p>
<?php endif; ?>                                                     → 17
</section>
<?php get_sidebar(); ?>                                             → 18
<?php get_footer(); ?>                                              → 19
```

2. **Activate the theme on the WordPress Dashboard and then view your site to see your handiwork in action.**

Here's a closer look at each of the lines in `index.php` in Listing 11-6:

→ **1**   This template tag pulls the information in the Header template of your WordPress theme.

→ **2**   This template tag is an `if` statement that asks, "Does this blog have posts?" If the answer is yes, it grabs the post content information from your MySQL database and displays the posts in your site.

→ **3**   This template tag starts The Loop.

→ **4**   This tag helps you create some interesting styles in your template using CSS, so check out Chapter 14 to find out all about it.

→ **5**   This tag tells your blog to display the title of a post that's clickable (or linked) to the URL of the post.

→ **6**   This template tag displays the date and time when the post was made. With these template tags, the date and time format are determined by the format you set on the Dashboard.

→ **7**   This template tag displays a comma-separated list of the categories to which you've assigned the post — *Posted in: category 1, category 2,* for example.

→ **8**   This template tag displays the actual content of the post. The `'Read More..'` portion of this tag tells WordPress to display the words *Read More,* which are clickable (hyperlinked) to the post's permalink, where the reader can read the rest of the post in its entirety. This tag applies when you're displaying a post excerpt, as determined by the actual post configuration on the Dashboard.

→ **9**   The template tag `Posted by: <?php the_author(); ?>` displays the author of the post in this manner: *Posted by: Lisa Sabin-Wilson.* The template tag `<?php comments_popup_link('No Comments', '1 Comment', '% Comments'); ?>` displays the link to the comments for this post, along with the number of comments.

→ **10**   This is the HTML markup that closes the <div> tag that was opened in Line 4.

→ **11**   This template tag ends The Loop and tells WordPress to stop displaying blog posts here. WordPress knows exactly how many times The Loop needs to work, based on the setting on the WordPress Dashboard. That's exactly how many times WordPress will execute The Loop.

→ **12**   This template tag displays a clickable link to the previous page of posts, if any.

→ **13**   This template tag displays a clickable link to the next page of posts, if any.

→ **14**   This template tag refers to the `if` question asked in Line 2. If the answer to that question is no, this step provides the `else` statement — IF this blog has posts, THEN list them here (Line 2 and Line 3), or ELSE display the following message.

→ **15**   This is the message followed by the template tag that appears after the `else` statement from Line 14. You can reword this statement to have it say whatever you want.

→ **17**   This template tag ends the `if` statement from Line 2.

→ **18**   This template tag calls in the Sidebar template and pulls that information into the Main Index template.

→ **19**   This template tag calls in the Footer template and pulls that information into the Main Index template. ***Note:*** The code in the `footer.php` template ends the `<body>` and the `<html>` tags that were started in the Header template (`header.php`).

This very simple Main Index template that you just built does not have the standard HTML markup in it, so the visual display of your site differs somewhat from the default Twenty Thirteen theme. This example gives you the bare-bones basics of the Main Index template and The Loop in action. Chapter 14 of this book goes into detail about the use of HTML and CSS to create nice styling and formatting for your posts and pages.

Using additional stylesheets

Often, a theme uses multiple stylesheets for browser compatibility or consistent organization. If you use multiple stylesheets, the process for including them in the template is the same as any other stylesheet.

To add a new stylesheet, create a `css` directory in the root theme folder. Next, create a new `mystyle.css` file within the `css` folder. To include the file, you must edit the `header.php` file. The following example shows the code you need to include in the new CSS file.

```
<link rel="stylesheet" href="<?php bloginfo('stylesheet_directory');
?>/css/mystyle.css" type="text/css" media="screen" />
```

12

Displaying Content with Widgets and Template Tags

In This Chapter

▷ Looking at the common template tags

▷ Adding new widget areas to a theme

▷ Creating templates to handle specific content display

▷ Adding theme support for specific features

This chapter gives you the lowdown on ways you can control how content appears on your site. When you create a WordPress theme, you use a combination of template tags to display certain types of content such as blog posts, navigation menus, page content, archive links, and so on. This chapter takes a look at common template tags that tell WordPress what information you want to show on your site.

As WordPress becomes more intuitive and user-friendly, I find that in several areas you don't really need to use template tags or code to get the results you need; instead, you can add new widget areas to your theme, which enables you to use the drag-and-drop widget feature to include different types of content and/or navigation on your website. If your theme doesn't have widget areas in all the places where you need them, this chapter shows you how to add new widget areas so that you can take full advantage of the ease of the widget interface.

WordPress also lets you create different templates that handle specific types of content such as categories, archives, search results, author pages, and more. This chapter explores the methods of creating content-specific templates to drive the content delivery and visual look of your site.

And, finally, you find out how to add some of the great tools in the WordPress core to your theme to give you more customization options, including popular built-in features such as custom navigation menus, post types, post formats, and post thumbnails or featured images.

Exploring Common Template Tags

In this section, I describe the template tags for the items commonly placed in the sidebar of a site. I say *commonly placed* because it's possible to get creative with these template tags and place them in other locations, such as the Footer template. To keep this introduction to sidebar template tags simple, I stick with the most common use, leaving the creative and uncommon uses for you to try when you're comfortable with the basics.

Most of the functions and sidebar template tags I cover in this chapter can be accomplished through widgets (see Chapter 10), without having to code them into the template at all. I present them to you in this chapter to make sure you understand and are comfortable with template tags and their associated parameters.

This section also discusses the tag parameters that you can include in the tag to control some of its display properties. You need to know these three types of parameters:

 ✔ **String:** A line of text that can be anything from a single letter to a long list of words. A string is placed between single quotation marks and sets an option for the parameter or is displayed as text.

 ✔ **Integer:** A positive or negative number. Integers are placed within the parentheses and either inside or outside single quotation marks. Either way, they're processed correctly.

 ✔ **Boolean:** Sets the parameter options to `true` or `false`. This parameter can be numeric (0 = `false` and 1 = `true`) or textual. Boolean parameters aren't placed within quotation marks.

You place tag parameters inside the parentheses of the tag. Information in Chapter 11 helps you understand the three variations of parameters used in template tags. Keep in mind that not all template tags have parameters.

The WordPress Codex page at `http://codex.wordpress.org` has every conceivable template tag and possible parameter known to the WordPress software. The tags and parameters I share with you in this chapter are the ones used most often.

Calendar

The calendar template tag displays a calendar that highlights each day of the week on which you've created a blog post. Those days are also hyperlinked to the original blog post. Here's the tag to use to display the calendar:

```
<?php get_calendar(); ?>
```

The `get_calendar();` tag has only one parameter, and it's Boolean. Set this parameter to `true`, and it displays the day of the week with one letter (Friday = F, for example). Set this parameter to `false`, and it displays the day of the week as a three-letter abbreviation (Friday = Fri., for example). Here are examples of the template tag used to display the calendar on your WordPress site:

```
<?php get_calendar(true); ?>
<?php get_calendar(false); ?>
```

List pages

The `<?php wp_list_pages(); ?>` tag displays a list of the static pages, such as About Me or Contact, that you can create on your WordPress site. Displaying links to the static pages allows readers to click the links and read the content you've provided.

WordPress has a handy Custom Menus feature that I cover in Chapter 10. If you like the navigation tool, you may never need to use the `wp_list_pages();` template tag. Still, I discuss this tag here because you may want to use it if you want complete control over how the list of pages appears on your website.

This tag uses the string style parameters. Table 12-1 lists the most common parameters used for the `wp_list_pages();` template tag.

Table 12-1		Most Common Parameters (Query-String) for wp_list_pages();
Parameter	*Type*	*Description and Values*
`child_ of`	Integer	Displays only the *subpages* of the page (pages with a parent page set in the Page Attributes section of the Edit Page page on your Dashboard); uses the numeric ID for a page as the value. Defaults to 0 (display all pages).
`exclude`	String	Lists the numeric page ID numbers, separated by commas, that you want to exclude from the page list display (for example, `'exclude=10, 20, 30'`). There is no default value.

(continued)

Table 12-1 *(continued)*

Parameter	Type	Description and Values
sort_ column	String	Sorts pages with one of the following options: `'post_title'` sorts alphabetically by page title (default). `'menu_order'` sorts by *page order* (that is, the order in which pages appear in the Manage tab and Pages subtab of the Dashboard). `'post_date'` sorts by the date on which pages were created. `'post_modified'` sorts by the time when the page was last modified. `'post_author'` sorts by author, according to the author ID #. `'post_name'` sorts alphabetically by the post slug.
depth	Integer	Uses a numeric value for how many levels of pages appear in the list of pages. Possible options: `0` displays all pages, including main and subpages (default). `-1` shows subpages but doesn't indent them in the list display. `1` shows only main pages, no subpages.
show_ date	String	Displays the date when the page was created or last modified. Possible options: `' '` displays no date (default). `'modified'` displays the date when the page was last modified. `'created'` displays the date when the page was created.
date_ format	String	Sets the format of the date to be displayed. Defaults to the date format configured in the Options tab and General subtab of the Dashboard.
title_li	String	Types text for the heading of the page list. Defaults to display the text: `"Pages"`. If the value is empty (`' '`), no heading appears; for example, `'title_li=My Pages'` displays the heading My Pages above the page list.

Page lists appear in an *unordered list* (or *bulleted list*). Whichever term you use, an unordered list is a list with a bullet point in front of every page link.

The following tag and query string displays a list of pages without the text heading *Pages.* In other words, this tag displays no title at the top of the page's link list:

```
<?php wp_list_pages('title_li='); ?>
```

The following tag and query string displays the list of pages sorted by the date when they were created; the date also appears along with the page name:

```
<?php wp_list_pages('sort_column=post_date&show_date='created'); ?>
```

Take a look at the way query-string parameters are written:

```
'parameter1=value&parameter2=value&parameter3=value'
```

The entire string is surrounded by single quotation marks, and there is no white space within the query string. Each parameter is joined to its value by the = character. When you use multiple parameters/values, separate them with the & character. You can think of the string like this: `parameter1=value`**AND**`parameter2=value`**AND**`parameter3=value`. Keep this convention in mind for the remaining template tags and parameters in this chapter.

Post archives

The `<?php wp_get_archives(); ?>` template tag displays the blog post archives in a number of ways, using the parameters and values shown in Table 12-2. Values that appear in bold are the default values set by WordPress. Here are just a few examples of what you can produce with this template tag:

- ✔ Display the titles of the last 15 posts you've made to your blog.
- ✔ Display the titles of the posts you've made in the past ten days.
- ✔ Display a monthly list of archives.

Table 12-2	Most Common Parameters (Query-String) for wp_get_archives();	
Parameter and Type	**Possible Values**	**Example**
type (string) Determines the type of archive to display.	**monthly**; daily; weekly; post bypost	`<?php wp_get_ archives('type= postbypost'); ?>` Displays the titles of the most recent blog posts.
format (string) Formats the display of the links in the archive list.	**html** (surrounds links with `<li>` `</li>` tags); option (places archive list in drop-down list format); link (surrounds links with `<link>` `</link>` tags); custom (use your own HTML tags with before and after parameters)	`<?php wp_get_ archives ('format= html'); ?>` Displays the list of archive links in which each link is surrounded by the `<li>` `</li>` HTML tags.
limit (integer) Limits the number of archives to display.	If no value, all display	`<?php wp_get_ archives ('limit=10'); ?>` Displays the last ten archives in a list.
before (string) Places text or formatting before the link in the archive list when using the custom parameter.	No default	`<?php wp_get_ archives ('before= <strong>'); ?>` Inserts the `<strong>` HTML tag before each link in the archive link list.
after (string) Inserts text or formatting after the link in the archive list when using the custom parameter.	No default	`<?php wp_get_ archives('after= </strong>'); ?>` Inserts the `</strong>` HTML tag after each link in the archive link list.
show_post_count (Boolean) Displays the number of posts in the archive. You'd use this if you use the 'type' of monthly.	true or 1; false or 0	`<? wp_get_ archives ('show_post_ count=1'); ?>` Displays the number of posts in each archive after each archive link.

Here are a couple examples of tags used to display blog post archives.

This tag displays a linked list of monthly archives (for example, January 2011, February 2011, and so on):

```
<?php wp_get_archives('type=monthly'); ?>
```

This tag displays a linked list of the 15 most recent blog posts:

```
<?php wp_get_archives('type=postbypost&limit=15'); ?>
```

Categories

WordPress lets you create categories and assign posts to a specific category (or multiple categories). *Categories* provide an organized navigation system that helps you and your visitors find posts you've made on certain topics.

The `<?php wp_list_categories(); ?>` template tag lets you display a list of your categories by using the available parameters and values. Table 12-3 shows some of the most popular parameters. Each category is linked to the appropriate category page that lists all the posts you've assigned to it. Again, the values that appear in bold are the default values set by WordPress.

Table 12-3	Most Common Parameters (Query-String) for wp_list_categories();	
Parameter and Type	*Possible Values*	*Example*
`orderby` (string) Determines how the category list will be ordered.	**id**; name; slug; count	`<?php wp_list_categories('orderby=name'); ?>` Displays the list of categories by name, alphabetically, as they appear on the Dashboard.
`order` (string) Determines the order of category list.	**ASC** (ascending); DESC (descending)	`<?php wp_list_categories('order=DESC'); ?>` Displays categories in descending order.

(continued)

Table 12-3 *(continued)*

Parameter and Type	Possible Values	Example

`style` (string)
 	
Determines the format of the category list display.
	`list`; `none`	`<?php wp_\list_ categories ('style=list'); ?>`
		
		Displays the list of category links in which each link is surrounded by the `<li>` `</li>` HTML tags.
		
		`<?php wp_ list_categories ('style=none'); ?>`
		
		Displays the list of category links with a simple line break after each link.

`show_count` (Boolean) Determines whether to display the post count for each listed category.	`true` or `1`; **`false`** or **`0`**	`<?php wp_ list_categories ('show_count=1'); ?>` Displays the post count, in parentheses, after each category list. `Espresso (10)`, for example, means that there are ten posts in the Espresso category.
`hide_empty` (Boolean) Determines whether categories with no posts assigned to them should appear in the list.	**`true`** or **`1`**; `false` or `0`	`<?php wp_ list_categories ('hide_empty=0'); ?>` Displays all categories – even ones that currently have no posts assigned to them.
`feed` (string) Determines whether the RSS feed should display for each category in the list.	`rss`; **default is no feeds display**	`<?php wp_ list_categories ('feed=rss'); ?>` Displays category titles with an RSS link next to each one.

Parameter and Type	Possible Values	Example
feed_image (string) Provides the path/filename for an image for the feed.	No default	`<?php wp_list_categories('feed_image=/wp-content/images/feed.gif'); ?>` Displays the feed.gif image for each category title. This image is linked to the RSS feed for that category.
hierarchical (Boolean) Determines whether the child categories should appear after each parent category in the category link list.	**true** or **1**; false or 0	`<?php wp_list_categories('hierarchical=0'); ?>` Doesn't display the child categories after each parent category in the category list.

Here are a couple of examples of tags used to display a list of your categories.

This example, with its parameters, displays a list of categories sorted by name without showing the number of posts made in each category; it also displays the RSS feed for each category title:

```
<?php wp_list_categories('orderby=name&show_count=0&feed=RSS'); ?>
```

This example, with its parameters, displays a list of categories sorted by name with the post count showing; it also shows the subcategories of every parent category:

```
<?php wp_list_categories('orderby=name&show_count=1&hierarchical=1'); '>
```

Content types (WP_Query tag)

WordPress makes it possible to pull in very specific types of content on your website through the WP_Query(); template class. Place this template tag before The Loop (described in Chapter 11), and it lets you specify which category you want to pull information from. If you have a category called WordPress, and you want to display the last three posts from that category on your front page, in your blog sidebar, or somewhere else on your site, you can use this template tag.

Looking at some of the parameters

The `WP_Query();` template class has several parameters that let you display different types of content such as posts in specific categories, content from specific pages/posts, or dates in your blog archives. Here's an example of two parameters you can use with the `WP_Query();` tag:

- **posts_per_page=X:** This parameter tells WordPress how many posts you want to display. If you want to display only three posts, for example, enter **posts_per_page=3**.

- **category_name=X:** This parameter tells WordPress that you want to pull posts from the category with this specific slug. If the category slug is `books-i-read`, for example, enter **category_name=books-i-read**.

The parameter `category_name` is slightly misleading because you don't use the category name, but rather the category slug, which is different, as I explain in the "Exploring content-specific standard templates" section, later in this chapter.

The `WP_Query();` class lets you pass many variables and parameters; it's not just limited to categories either. You can use it for pages, posts, tags, and more. Visit the WordPress Codex at `http://codex.wordpress.org/Class_Reference/WP_Query` and read about this feature.

Adding the WP_Query (); tag

Choose which category you want to list posts from and locate the slug that belongs to the category. After you do that, you're ready to add the `WP_Query();` tag to your template. The category slug is usually the same as the category name, except in lowercase with words separated by dashes; for example, the Books category on my site has a `books` slug. To double-check, visit the Categories page on your Dashboard by choosing Posts⇨Categories, click the name of the category you want to use, and find the category slug listed. The line of code to display five posts from the Books category looks like this:

```
<?php $the_query = new WP_Query('posts_per_page=5&category_name=books;); ?>
```

It's not enough just to add that one line of code, however; you need to use the `WP_Query();` class within The Loop in WordPress (see Chapter 11 to review the WordPress Loop). Follow these steps to include a WP_Query within The Loop in your template:

1. **On your Dashboard, choose Appearance⇨Editor.**

   The Edit Themes page opens.

2. **In the Templates list on the right side of the page, click the template in which you want to display the content.**

   For example, if you want to display content in a sidebar, choose the Sidebar template: `sidebar.php`.

   The template you select appears in the editor in the middle of the page.

3. **Locate the first closing `</ul>` or `</div>` tag in the Sidebar template for the theme you're using.**

   If you're using the Twenty Thirteen theme, for example, the ending `</div>` looks like this: `</div><!-- .widget-area -->`

4. **Type the following code directly above the ending `</div>` tag:**

   ```php
   <?php $the_query = WP_Query('posts_per_page=5&category_name=books;); ?>
   <?php while ($the_query->have_posts()) : $the_query->the_post(); ?>
   <strong><a href="<?php the_permalink() ?>" rel="bookmark" title="Permanent
           Link to
   <?php the_title_attribute(); ?>"><?php the_title(); ?></a></strong>
   <?php the_excerpt(); endwhile; ?>
   ```

   In the first line, I indicate the following: `posts_per_page=5&` `category_name=books`. You can change these numbers to suit your specific needs. Just change 5 to whatever number of posts you want to appear (there's no limit!), and change `books` to the specific category slug that you want to use.

5. **Click the Update File button to save the changes to your template.**

Miscellaneous but useful template tags

In this chapter, I've picked the most common template tags to get you started. You can find the rest of the template tags in the WordPress Codex at `http://codex.wordpress.org/Template_Tags`.

A few miscellaneous tags aren't included in the preceding sections, but I want to mention them here briefly because they're helpful and sometimes fun. Table 12-4 lists some of these tags, their locations in the templates where they're commonly used, and their purposes.

Table 12-4	Some Useful Template Tags for WordPress

Tags Used in the Comments Template (`comments.php`)

Tag	Function
`<?php comment_ author(); ?>`	Displays the comment author's name.
`<?php comment_ author_link(); ?>`	Displays the comment author's name, linked to the author's website if a URL was provided in the comment form.
`<?php comment_ text(); ?>`	Displays the text of a comment.
`<?php comment_ date() ?>`	Displays the date when a comment was published.
`<?php comment_ time(); ?>`	Displays the time when a comment was published.
`<?php echo get_ avatar(); ?>`	Displays the *gravatar* (globally recognized avatar) of the comment author.
`<?php previous_ comments_link() ?>`	Displays navigation links to the previous page of comments (if you're using paged comments).
`<?php next_ comments_link() ?>`	Displays navigation links to the next page of comments (if you're using paged comments).

Tags Used to Display RSS Feeds

Tag	Function
`<?php bloginfo ('rss2_url'); ?>`	Displays the URL of the RSS feed for your site. Usually surrounded by the `a href` HTML tag to provide a hyperlink to the RSS feed: `<a href=" <?php bloginfo('rss2_ url'); ?>">RSS Feed</a>`.
`<?php bloginfo ('comments_rss2_ url'); ?>`	Displays the URL of the RSS feed for your comments. Usually surrounded by the `a href` HTML tag to provide a hyperlink to the comments RSS feed: `<a href=" ="<?php bloginfo('comments_rss2_url'); ?>">Comments RSS</a>`.

Tags Used to Display Author Information

Tag	Function
`<?php the_author_ description(); ?>`	Pulls the information from the author bio located in the About Yourself section of the author profile on the Dashboard and displays that information.
`<?php the_author_ email(); ?>`	Pulls the author's e-mail address from the author profile on the Dashboard.

Adding New Widget Areas to Your Theme

About 99.99 percent of the WordPress themes available are coded with *widgetized sidebars*. This coding means that you can use the widgets within WordPress to populate your sidebar area with content, navigation menus, and lists. In Chapter 10, I go into detail about what widgets are and how you can use them to dress up your sidebar — so check out that chapter if you need more information about widgets.

With widgets in place, generally you don't need to mess around with the code in the `sidebar.php` template file because most of the content you want to add to your sidebar can be accomplished with widgets.

In the following sections, you discover how to register new widget areas and then add those widget areas to your template file so you can use WordPress widgets on your site.

Registering your widget areas

In a WordPress theme, you can create widget areas to use literally anywhere within your theme. The sidebar is the most common place widgets are used, but many people also use widgets in the footer, header, and main content areas of their websites. Sidebars and widgets can appear anywhere you want them to. For this example, I use the Sidebar template (`sidebar.php`).

First, you have to define the sidebar in your theme. Therefore, you need to alert WordPress that this theme can handle widgets, also referred to as *registering* a widget with the WordPress software. To register a widget, you need to add the `register_sidebar` function to the Theme Functions template (`functions.php`). In the `functions.php` file in the Twenty Thirteen theme (choose Appearance➪Editor and then click the theme functions [`functions.php`] file), the code for registering a widget looks like this:

```
register_sidebar( array (
'name' => __( 'Primary Widget Area'),
'id' => 'widget-name',
'description' => __( 'The primary widget area'),
'before_widget' => '<li id="%1$s" class="widget-container %2$s">',
'after_widget' => "</li>",
'before_title' => '<h3 class="widget-title">',
'after_title' => '</h3>',
) );
```

This code contains seven arrays. An *array* is a set of values similar to a query string that tells a function what variables to use. In this case, it tells WordPress how you want your sidebar and its widgets handled and displayed:

✔ **name:** This name is unique to the widget and appears on the Widgets page on the Dashboard; this name is helpful if you register several widgetized areas on your site.

✔ **id:** This is the unique ID given to the widget.

✔ **description:** This is a text description of the widget. The text appears on the Widgets page on the Dashboard.

✔ **before_widget:** This is the HTML markup that gets inserted directly before the widget; it's helpful for Cascading Style Sheets (CSS) styling purposes.

✔ **after_widget:** This is the HTML markup that gets inserted directly after the widget.

✔ **before_title:** This is the HTML markup that gets inserted directly before the widget title.

✔ **after_title:** This is the HTML markup that gets inserted directly after the widget title.

The preceding code snippet registers a widget — Primary Widget Area — on the WordPress Dashboard. Additionally, the code places the sidebar's content in an element that has the CSS `widget` class (and is styled as an unordered list) and puts <h3> tags around the widget's title. You can insert this code directly below the first opening PHP tag (<?php). (See Chapter 14 for more on CSS and HTML.)

Pressing Enter to add a few extra lines when you enter code can be helpful. The browser ignores the extra empty lines around your code, but they can greatly increase readability.

With that code in your theme functions (`functions.php`) file, WordPress recognizes that you've registered a widget area for your theme and makes the widget area available for you to drag and drop widgets into from the Widgets page on the Dashboard. All that's left to do now is to call that widget into your `sidebar.php` file, as described next. By doing so, you allow the widgets to appear on your site.

Adding widget areas to your template files

Follow these steps to call widgets to your site (these steps assume the widget code isn't already in the Sidebar template):

1. **On your Dashboard, choose Appearance⇨Editor.**

   The Edit Themes page opens.

2. **Click the Sidebar (`sidebar.php`) template in the list on the right side of the page.**

   The Sidebar template opens in the text box in the middle of the page.

3. **Type the following code in the Sidebar (`sidebar.php`) template:**

```
<ul id="sidebar">
<?php if ( ! dynamic_sidebar( 'Primary Widget Area' ) ) : ?>
<?php endif; ?>
</ul>
```

The parameter within the `dynamic_sidebar` template tag corresponds to the name that you provided in the `'name'` widget array earlier in this section. For this example, I used `'Primary Widget Area'`. The name you use must be the same one that you used earlier; otherwise, it won't appear on your website.

4. **Click the Update File button.**

The changes you've made to the Sidebar (`sidebar.php`) template file are saved.

You can register an unlimited number of widgets for your theme. This flexibility allows you to create several widgetized areas and widget features in different areas of your site.

Using Template Files

In Chapter 11, I introduce the concept of template files and give you an overview of the basic template files that make up a standard WordPress theme: `index.php`, `header.php`, `footer.php`, `sidebar.php`, and `style.css`. The WordPress theme engine is flexible and gives you several ways of using templates and tags to pull different types of content from your database to appear on your website.

In Chapter 11, you find out how to create a very simple theme using the standard templates. In the following sections, I discuss the options to extend the standard functionality of WordPress so that you have the flexibility to quickly address specific needs for your website.

Creating named templates

WordPress recognizes three special areas of a theme: header, footer, and sidebar. The `get_header`, `get_footer`, and `get_sidebar` functions default to loading `header.php`, `footer.php`, and `sidebar.php`, respectively. Each of these functions also supports a name parameter that allows you to load an alternative version of the file. For example, running `get_header('main')` causes WordPress to load `header-main.php`.

You may wonder why you'd use the name parameter when you can just create a template file named whatever you like and load it directly. The following are reasons for using the `get_header`, `get_footer`, or `get_sidebar` functions with a name parameter:

✔ You use a standard naming convention that users can easily recognize and understand.

✔ You can load specialized template files easily and quickly.

✔ You offer a fallback that loads the unnamed template file if the named one doesn't exist. For example, if you use the tag `get_header('main');` in your template, but for some reason the `header-main.php` template file does not exist, WordPress defaults to `header.php`, which saves the integrity of your website display until you can load the `header-main.php` file correctly.

In short, use the name parameter feature if you have multiple, specialized Header, Footer, or Sidebar template files.

Creating and using template parts

Template parts are relatively new (they were added in version 3.0 in June 2010). A *template part* is very similar to the Header, Footer, and Sidebar templates except that you aren't limited to just these. You can branch out and create any number of template parts to call into your WordPress theme to provide specific functions, such as displaying posts from a specific category or displaying a gallery of photos you've uploaded to your website.

The `get_header`, `get_footer`, and `get_sidebar` functions allow for code that was once duplicated in many of the template files to be placed in a single file and loaded using a standard process. The purpose of template parts is to offer a new standardized function that can be used to load sections of code specific to an individual theme. Using the concept of template parts, sections of code that add a specialized section of header widgets or display a block of ads can be placed in individual files and easily loaded as a template part.

Template parts are loaded via the `get_template_part` function. The `get_template_part` function accepts two parameters:

✔ **Slug:** The slug parameter is required and describes the generic type of template part to be loaded, such as `content`.

✔ **Name:** The name parameter is optional and selects a specialized template part, such as `post`.

A call to `get_template_part` with just the slug parameter tries to load a template file with the *slug*.php filename. Thus, a call to `get_template_part('content')` tries to load `content.php`. And a call to `get_template_part('header', 'widgets')` tries to load `header-widgets.php`. See a pattern here? When I refer to a *slug,* I mean the name of the template file, minus the `.php` extension, because WordPress already assumes that it's a PHP file.

A call to `get_template_part` with both the slug and name parameters tries to load a template file with a *slug-name*.php filename. If a template file with a *slug-name*.php filename doesn't exist, WordPress tries to load a template file with a *slug*.php filename. Thus, a call to `get_template_part` (`'content'`, `'post'`) first tries to load `content-post.php` followed by `content.php` if `content-post.php` doesn't exist. A call to `get_template_part('header-widgets', 'post')` first tries to load `header-widgets-post.php` followed by `header-widgets.php` if `header-widgets-post.php` doesn't exist.

The Twenty Thirteen theme offers a good example of the template part feature in use; it uses a `loop` template part to allow The Loop to be pulled into individual template files.

The Loop is the section of code found in most theme template files that uses a PHP `while` loop to literally loop through the set of content (such as post, page, archive, and so on) and then display it. The presence of The Loop in a template file is crucial for a theme to function properly. Chapter 11 has a more detailed examination of The Loop.

Twenty Thirteen's `index.php` template file shows a template part for The Loop in action in line 7 of the following code using the `get_template_part();` template tag:

```php
<?php get_header(); ?>
<div id="primary" class="content-area">
<div id="content" class="site-content" role="main">
<?php if ( have_posts() ) : ?>
<?php /* The loop */ ?>
<?php while ( have_posts() ) : the_post(); ?>
<?php get_template_part( 'content', get_post_format() ); ?>
<?php endwhile; ?>
<?php twentythirteen_paging_nav(); ?>
<?php else : ?>
<?php get_template_part( 'content', 'none' ); ?>
<?php endif; ?>
</div><!-- #content -->
</div><!-- #primary -->
<?php get_sidebar(); ?>
<?php get_footer(); ?>
```

Loading The Loop by using a template part, Twenty Thirteen cleans up the `index.php` code considerably when compared with other themes. This cleanup of the template file code is just the icing on the cake. The true benefits are the improvements to theme development.

Twenty Thirteen's `index.php` template file calls for a template part with a slug of `content` and the `get_post_format();` tag. The `get_post_format();` refers to post formats that are in use in the theme. Post formats are covered later in this chapter in the "Adding support for post formats" section, which refers to different types of post formats such as audio, video, and image. If you look at the other template files in Twenty Thirteen, you'll see files with the `content` slug:

- content-aside.php
- content-audio.php
- content-chat.php
- content-gallery.php
- content-image.php
- content-link.php
- content-none.php
- content-quote.php
- content-status.php
- content-video.php
- content.php

The `get_post_format();` tag within the `get_template_part();` automatically picks up the type of post format defined for the post and uses the corresponding template file. For example, if the post format is image, the `content-image.php` is used. Alternatively, if no post format is defined, WordPress simply uses `content.php`.

Before template parts, the full Loop code, which can have up to ten lines of code (or more), would be duplicated in each of the template files, over and over. This means that a modification to the `index.php` file's Loop code would also require the same modification to the `single.php` file. Imagine if you had to make the same modification to five template files; repeatedly making the same modifications would quickly become tiring, and each modification would increase your chance of making mistakes. Using a template part means that the modifications to The Loop need to be made only once, so it's applied to all templates using The Loop code via the `get_template_part();` function, cutting down your overall development time.

The `get_template_part` call allows for easily creating as many customized templates as needed without having to duplicate the multiple lines of The Loop code over and over again. Without the duplicate code, the code for The Loop can be easily modified in one place.

When you duplicate sections of code in numerous template files, place the code in a separate file and use the `get_template_part` function to load it where needed.

Exploring content-specific standard templates

The template files discussed so far in this book span a wide scope of site views specific to the view, not the content. For example, the `category.php` template file applies to all category archive views but not to a specific category, and the `page.php` template file applies to all page views but not to a specific page. However, you can create template files for specific content and not just the view.

Four content-specific template types are available: author, category, page, and tag. Each allows you to refer to specific content by the term's ID (an individual author's ID, for instance) or by the *slug*.

The slug I discuss in this section differs from the slug parameter of the `get_template_part` function described in the preceding section. For this section, *slug* refers to a post, page, category, or so on — for example, a Press Releases category having a `press-releases` slug or a Hello World post with a `hello-world` slug.

Imagine that you have an About Us page with a `138` id and an `about-us` slug. You can create a template for this specific page by creating either a `page-138.php` or a `page-about-us.php` file. In the same way, if you want to create a template specific to an awesome author named Lisa with a `7` id and a `lisa` slug, you can create an `author-7.php` or an `author-lisa.php` file.

Creating a template using the slug can be extremely helpful for sites that you don't manage. If you want to share a theme that you created, you can create a `category-featured.php` template. This template would automatically apply to any category view that has a `featured` slug.

Using categories as the example, the file-naming conventions are as follows:

- ✔ A template with the filename `category.php` is a catch-all (default) for the display for all categories. (Alternatively, a template with the `archives.php` filename is used to display categories if a `category.php` file does not exist.)

- ✔ You can add a dash and the category ID number to the end of the filename, as shown in Table 12-5, to specify a template for an individual category.

  Alternatively, you can add a dash and the category slug to the end of the filename, as shown in Table 12-5, to define it as a template for that particular category. For example, if you have a `Books` category, the category slug is `books`; the individual category template file is `category-books.php`.

- ✔ If you don't have a `category.php`, an `archives.php`, or a `category-#.php` file, the category display pulls from the Main Index template (`index.php`).

Table 12-5 gives you some examples of file-naming conventions for category templates, specifically.

Table 12-5	Category Template File-Naming Conventions
If the Category ID or Slug Is . . .	*The Category Template Filename Is . . .*
1	`category-1.php`
2	`category-2.php`
3	`category-3.php`
books	`category-books.php`
movies	`category-movies.php`
music	`category-music.php`

Because creating a template using slugs is so useful (and because an `id` is relevant to only a specific site), you may wonder why the `id` option exists. The short answer is that the `id` option existed before the slug option; however, it is still valuable in specific instances. You can use the `id` option for a content-specific template without worrying about the customization breaking when the slug changes. This is especially helpful if you set up the site for someone and can't trust that he'll leave the slugs alone (such as a category with a `news` slug changing to `press-releases`).

Using Page templates

Although the `page-slug.php` feature is very helpful, sometimes requiring the theme's user to use the name you chose for a feature is too difficult or unnecessary. Page templates allow you to create a stand-alone template (just like `page.php` or `single.php`) that users can use on any specific page they choose. As opposed to the `page-slug.php` feature, a Page template can be used on more than one page. The combined features of user selection and multiple uses make Page templates a much more powerful theme tool than `page-slug.php` templates.

To make a template a Page template, simply add `Template Name: Descriptive Name` to a comment section at the top of the template file. For example, this is the beginning of a `onecolumn-page.php` Page template:

```php
<?php
/**
 * Template Name: One column, no sidebar
 *
 * A custom Page template without sidebar.
 *
 * The "Template Name:" bit above allows this to be selectable
 * from a dropdown menu on the edit page screen.
 *
 * @package WordPress
 * @subpackage Twenty_Thirteen
 * @since Twenty Thirteen 1.0
 */
```

This code registers the template file with WordPress as a Page template and adds One Column, No Sidebar to the Template drop-down list found under Page Attributes in the Add New Page (or Edit Page) screen, as shown in Figure 12-1. Using a template on a static page is a two-step process: Upload the template and then tell WordPress to assign the template by tweaking the page's code.

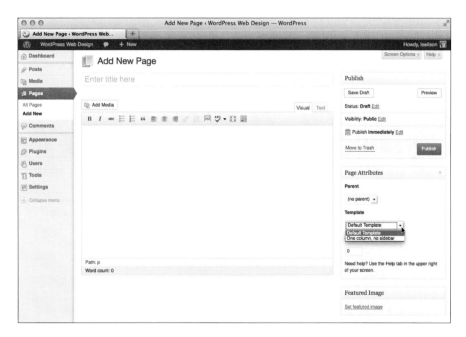

Figure 12-1: The Add New Page screen on the Dashboard showing page attributes for template assignment.

The preceding code sample demonstrates how the WordPress developers created the One Column, No Sidebar Page template in the Twenty Thirteen theme; however, in reality, you need only three lines to make it happen. Here is the code that appears at the top of the static-page template I use for my About page at http://webdevstudios.com/about:

```php
<?php
/*
Template Name: About Page
*/
?>
```

The important part is defining the Template Name between the starting and ending PHP function calls. This tells WordPress to recognize this as a unique template and then include it in the list of available templates within the Page Attributes on the Add New Page screen, as shown in Figure 12-1 (it also appears on the Add New Page page).

By providing a robust set of Page templates, you can offer your theme users easy-to-use options for formatting different pages within their websites.

Adding Theme Support for Built-In Features

The WordPress core offers a number of great tools that you can easily add to a theme to give it more customization options. WordPress provides you with several built-in features that let you enhance your site and theme. This section covers four of the most popular features:

- Custom navigation menus
- Custom post types
- Post formats
- Post thumbnails (or featured images)

These features are part of the WordPress core; however, they aren't activated by default. By *adding theme support,* I really mean that you're activating a built-in feature in your theme. When you're traveling around the WordPress community — whether on a support forum or at a WordCamp event — and hear folks say, "That theme supports *a certain feature,*" you can smile because you know exactly what they're talking about.

You need to activate support for these features in the theme you're using:

- **Core function:** Add support for the feature in your theme by including the core function in the theme functions (functions.php) file in your theme.

- **Template function:** Add the necessary function tags in your theme template(s) to display the features on your website.

- **Templates:** In some cases, you can create feature-specific templates to create additional enhancement to display and include on your site.

The following sections take you through each feature, in this order: First, add the core function to your theme; second, add the function tags to your templates; and last, if indicated, create a feature-specific template in your theme that handles added features.

Adding support for custom navigation menus

I think the WordPress menu-building feature is the single greatest tool WordPress offers to theme developers. Before this tool, each theme developer implemented his own menu solution, creating a huge number of themes that had little navigation customization that didn't require coding and a small set of themes that had very different ways of handling navigation. Now creating complex, multilevel menus on your WordPress site takes just a few steps, as I outline in the upcoming sections.

Exploring the Custom Menus feature in Twenty Thirteen

The Twenty Thirteen theme already supports menus. Looking at Twenty Thirteen's `functions.php` file, you can see that the following lines of code handle registering the theme's menu:

```
// This theme uses wp_nav_menu() in one location.
        register_nav_menu( 'primary', __( 'Navigation Menu',
        'twentythirteen' ) );
```

This code registers a single navigation area with a `primary` theme location name and a `Navigation Menu` human-readable name. With the Twenty Thirteen theme active, choose Appearance⇨Menus and then flip to Chapter 10 for steps on how to create menus using the Custom Menus feature on your Dashboard.

Adding the Custom Menus feature to a theme

The Custom Menus feature is already built in to the default Twenty Thirteen theme, so you don't have to worry about preparing your theme for it. However, if you're using a different theme, or creating your own, follow these steps to add this functionality:

1. **On the Dashboard, choose Appearance⇨Editor.**

   The Edit Themes page appears.

2. **Click the Theme Functions (`functions.php`) template.**

   The Theme Functions template opens in the text editor in the center of the Edit Themes page.

3. **Type the following function on a new line anywhere above the closing `?>` in the Theme Functions template:**

   ```
   // ADD MENU SUPPORT
   add_theme_support( 'nav-menus' );
   ```

   This template tag tells WordPress that your theme can use the Custom Menus feature.

4. **Click the Update File button to save the changes to the template.**

   A Menus link appears in the Appearance menu.

   Next, you want to add the menus template tag to the Header template (`header.php`).

5. **On the Edit Themes page, open the Header template (`header.php`).**

   The Header template opens in the text editor in the middle of the Edit Themes page.

6. **Add the following template tag by typing it on a new line anywhere in the Header template (`header.php`):**

```
<?php wp_nav_menu(); ?>
```

This template tag is needed so that the menu you build using the Custom Menus feature appears at the top of your website. Table 12-6 gives the details on the different parameters you can use with the `wp_nav_menu();` template tag to customize the display to suit your needs.

7. Click the Update File button to save the changes you've made to the Header template.

The navigation menu that you build on the Menus page on your Dashboard (choose Appearance⟳Menus) now appears in the header area of your website.

Table 12-6   Common Tag Parameters for wp_nav_menu();

Parameter	Information	Default	Tag Example
id	Unique ID of the menu (because you can create several menus, each has a unique ID number)	Blank	wp_nav_ menu(array ('id' => '1'));
slug	Menu name in slug form (for example, nav-menu)	Blank	wp_nav_menu (array('slug' => 'nav-menu'));
menu	Menu name	Blank	wp_nav_menu (array('menu' => 'Nav Menu')); or wp_nav_menu ('Nav Menu');
menu_ class	CSS class used to style the menu list	Menu	wp_nav_menu(array('menu_class' => 'mymenu'));
format	HTML markup used to style the list, either an unordered list (ul/ li) or div class	div	wp_nav_menu(array('format' => 'ul'));

Parameter	Information	Default	Tag Example
`fall-back_cb`	Parameter that creates a fallback if a custom menu doesn't exist	`wp_page_ menu` (a default list of page links)	`wp_nav_menu ( array( ' fallback_cb' => 'wp_page_ menu') );`
`before`	Text that displays before the link text	None	`wp_nav_menu ( array( 'before' => 'Click Here' ) );`
`after`	Text that displays after the link text	None	`wp_nav_menu ( array( 'after' => '&raquo;' ) );`

Figure 12-2 shows the default Twenty Thirteen theme with a navigation menu displayed below the header graphic (you see the links Home, Blog, and About).

Navigation menu

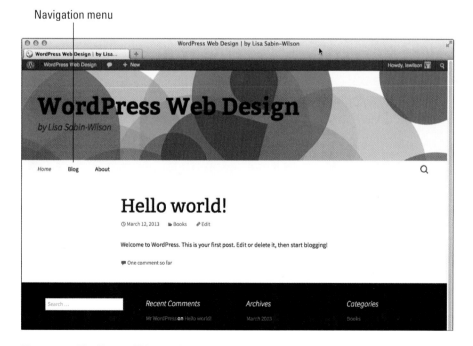

Figure 12-2: The Twenty Thirteen theme displayed with a navigation menu below the header.

I created a Main menu on the WordPress Dashboard. (See Chapter 10 for steps to create new and multiple menus on the WordPress Dashboard.) The template tag used in the theme to display that menu looks like this:

```
<?php wp_nav_menu('Main'); ?>
```

The HTML markup for the menu is generated as an unordered list, by default, and looks like this:

```
<ul id="menu-main" class="menu">
<li id="menu-item-53" class="menu-item menu-item-type-custom menu-item-object-
        custom menu-item-53"><a href="/">Home</a></li>
<li id="menu-item-51" class="menu-item menu-item-type-post_type menu-item-
        object-page menu-item-51"><a href="http://localhost/wpdemo/
        blog/">Blog</a></li>
<li id="menu-item-52" class="menu-item menu-item-type-post_type menu-item-
        object-page menu-item-52"><a href="http://localhost/wpdemo/
        about/">About</a></li>
</ul>
```

Notice in the HTML markup that the first line defines the CSS ID and class:

```
<ul id="menu-main" class="menu">
```

The ID in that line reflects the name that you gave your menu. Because I gave my menu the name Main when I created it on the Dashboard, the CSS ID is 'menu-main'. If I had named the menu Foo, the ID would be 'menu-foo'. This assignment of menu names in the CSS and HTML markup allows you to use CSS to create different styles and formats for your menus.

When developing themes for yourself or others, make sure that the CSS you define for the menus accounts for subpages by creating *drop-down list effects,* or links that drop down from the menu when you hover your mouse pointer over the main parent link. You can accomplish this in several ways, and Listing 12-1 gives you one example of a block of CSS that you can use to create a nice style for your menu.

Listing 12-1:   Sample CSS for Drop-Down List Navigation

```
#menu-main {
    width: 960px;
    font-family: Georgia, Times New Roman, Trebuchet MS;
    font-size: 16px;
    color: #FFFFFF;
    margin: 0 auto 0;
    clear: both;
    overflow: hidden;
}


#menu-main ul {
    width: 100%;
```

```css
    float: left;
    list-style: none;
    margin: 0;
    padding: 0;
    }

#menu-main li {
    float: left;
    list-style: none;
    }

#menu-main li a {
    color: #FFF;
    display: block;
    font-size: 16px;
    margin: 0;
    padding: 12px 15px;
    text-decoration: none;
    position: relative;
    }

#menu-main li a:hover, #menu-main li a:active, #menu-main .current_page_item a,
            #menu-main .current-cat a, #menu-main .current-menu-item {
    color: #CCC;
    }

#menu-main li li a, #menu-main li li a:link, #menu-main li li a:visited {
    background: #555;
    color: #FFF;
    width: 138px;
    font-size: 12px;
    margin: 0;
    padding: 5px 10px;
    border-left: 1px solid #FFF;
    border-right: 1px solid #FFF;
    border-bottom: 1px solid #FFF;
    position: relative;
    }

#menu-main li li a:hover, #menu-main li li a:active {
    background: #333;
    color: #FFF;
    }

#menu-main li ul {
    z-index: 9999;
    position: absolute;
    left: -999em;
    height: auto;
    width: 160px;
    }
```

(continued)

Listing 12-1 *(continued)*

```
#menu-main li ul a {
    width: 140px;
    }

#menu-main li ul ul {
    margin: -31px 0 0 159px;
    }

#menu-main li:hover ul ul, #menu-main li:hover ul ul ul{
    left: -999em;
    }

#menu-main li:hover ul, #menu-main li li:hover ul, #menu-main li li li:hover ul{
    left: auto;
    }

#menu-main li:hover {
    position: static;
    }
```

The CSS you use to customize the display of your menus differs; the example that I provide in Listing 12-1 is just that — an example. After you get the hang of using CSS, you can try different methods, colors, and styling to create a custom look of your own. You can find additional information about basic HTML and CSS in Chapter 14.

Displaying custom menus using widgets

You don't have to use the `wp_nav_menu();` template tag to display the menus on your site because WordPress also provides you with a Custom Menu widget that you can add to your theme, allowing you to use widgets, instead of template tags, to display the navigation menus on your site. This is especially helpful if you've created multiple menus for use in and around your site in various places. (See Chapter 10 for more information on using WordPress widgets.)

Your first step is to register a special widget area for your theme to handle the Custom Menu widget display. To do this, open your theme's `function.php` file and add the following lines of code anywhere before the closing `?>`:

```
// ADD MENU WIDGET
if ( function_exists('register_sidebars') )
            register_sidebar(array('name'=>'Menu',));
```

These few lines of code create a new Menu Widget Area on the Widgets page on your Dashboard. At this point, you can drag the Custom Menu widget into the Menu Widget Area to indicate that you wish to display a custom menu in that area. If you have more than one menu, you can select which menu to display from the Select Menu drop-down list. The Menu Widget Area with the Custom Menu widget added is shown in Figure 12-3.

To add the Menu Widget Area to your theme, head over to the Edit Themes page (choose Appearance⇨Editor), click the Header template (`header.php`) file, and add these lines of code in the area you want the Menu Widget Area displayed:

```
<ul>
<?php if ( !function_exists('dynamic_sidebar') || !dynamic_sidebar('Menu') ) :
            ?>
<?php endif; ?>
</ul>
```

These lines of code tell WordPress that you want information contained in the Menu Widget Area displayed on your site.

New menu widget area

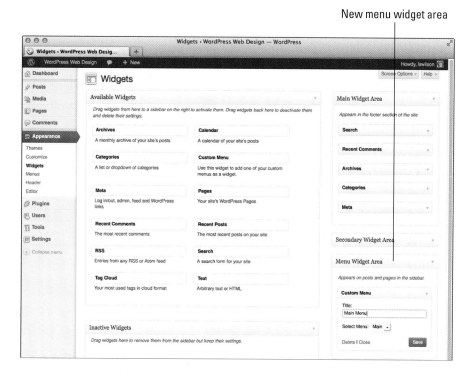

Figure 12-3: On the Widgets page, add the Custom Menu widget to the Menu Widget Area.

Adding support for custom post types

Custom post types and custom taxonomies have expanded the content management system (CMS) capabilities of WordPress and are likely to be a big part of plugin and theme features as more developers become familiar with their use. *Custom post types* allow developers to create new content types separate from posts and pages, such as movie reviews or recipes. *Custom taxonomies* allow developers to create new types of content groupings separate from categories and tags, such as genres for movie reviews or seasons for recipes (for example, fall, spring, or winter recipes).

Posts and pages are nice, generic containers of content. A *page* is timeless content that has a hierarchal structure because a page can have a parent (forming a nested, or hierarchal, structure of pages). A *post* is content listed in linear (not hierarchal) order based on when it was published and can be organized into categories and tags. What happens when you want a hybrid of these features? What if you want content that doesn't appear in the post listings, doesn't have either categories or tags, but displays the posting date? Custom post types satisfy this desire to customize content types.

By default, WordPress already has different post types built in to the software, ready for you to use. These default post types include

- Blog posts
- Pages
- Menus
- Attachments
- Revisions

Custom post types let you create new and useful types of content on your website, including a smart and easy way to publish those content types to your site.

The possibilities for using custom post types are endless, but here are a few ideas that may help kick-start your imagination; these are also some of the more popular and useful ideas that others have implemented on sites:

- Photo galleries
- Podcasts or videos
- Book reviews
- Coupons and special offers
- Events calendars

Creating a custom post type

To create and use custom post types on your site, you need to be sure that your WordPress theme contains the correct code and functions. In the following steps, you create a basic and generic custom post type called "Generic Content," and later in this section, you find detailed information on the different parameters you can use with custom post types to suit your needs:

1. **On your Dashboard, choose Appearance⇨Editor.**

   The Edit Themes page opens.

2. **Click the Theme Functions template link to open the `functions.php` file.**

   The Theme Functions template opens in the text editor in the middle of the page.

3. **Add the custom post type code to the bottom of the Theme Functions template.**

   Scroll down to the bottom of the `functions.php` file and include the following code to add a Generic Content custom post type to your site:

```
// ADD CUSTOM POST TYPE
add_action( 'init', 'create_post_type' );
function create_post_type() {
 register_post_type( 'generic-content',
  array(
    'labels' => array(
    'name' => __( 'Generic Content' ),
    'singular_name' => __( 'Generic Content' )
    ),
    'public' => true
  )
 );
}
```

   The function `register_post_type();` can accept several arguments and parameters, which I detail in Table 12-7. You can use a variety and a combination of arguments and parameters to create a specific post type. You can find more information on custom post types and using the `register_post_type();` function on the WordPress Codex page at `http://codex.wordpress.org/Function_Reference/register_post_type`.

4. **Click the Update File button to save the changes made to the `functions.php` file.**

Table 12-7 **Arguments and Parameters for register_post_type();**

Parameter	Information	Parameters	Example
label	The name of the post type.	None	'label' => __('Generic Content'),
labels	Same as label, but in singular, not plural format (Posts become Post, for example).	None	'singular_label' => __('Generic Content'),
description	The description of the post type; displayed on the Dashboard to represent the post type.	None	'description' => __('This is a description of the Generic Content type'),
public show_ui publicly_queryable exclude_from_search show_in_nav_menus	public sets whether the post type is public. show_ui either shows admin screens or doesn't. publicly_queryable allows this post type to be included in public queries within template code. exclude_from_search either shows post type in search results or doesn't.	true or false (default)	'public' => true, 'show_ui' => true, 'publicly_queryable' => true, 'exclude_from_search' => false, 'show_in_nav_menus' => true
menu_position	Sets the position of the post type menu item on the Dashboard navigation menu; by default, custom post types appear after the Comments menu on the Dashboard.	Default: 20; sets integers in intervals of 5	'menu_position' => 25,

Parameter	Information	Parameters	Example
menu_icon	Defines a custom icon (or graphic) to the post type menu item on the Dashboard navigation menu; creates and uploads the image into the images directory of your theme folder.	None	'menu_icon' => get_stylesheet_directory_uri() . '/images/generic-content.png',
hierarchical	Tells WordPress whether to display the post type content list in a hierarchical manner.	true or false; default is true	'hierarchical' => true,
query_var	Controls whether this post type can be used with a query variable, such as query_posts.	true or false (default)	'query_var' => true,
capability_type	Defines permissions for users to edit, create, or read the custom post type.	post (default); gives the same capabilities for those who can edit, create, and read blog posts	'query_var' => post,
capabilities	Tells WordPress what capabilities are accepted for this post type.	Default: empty, the capability_type value is used. edit_post: allows post type to be edited read_post: allows post type to be read delete_post: allows post type to be deleted	'capabilities' => edit_post,
map_meta_cap	Tells WordPress whether to use the default internal meta capabilities.	true or false; Default is false	'map_meta_cap' => true,

(continued)

Table 12-7 (continued)

Parameter	Information	Parameters	Example
supports	Defines what meta boxes, or *modules*, are available for this post type on the Dashboard.	title (text box for title); editor (text box for content); comments (check boxes to toggle comments); trackbacks (check boxes to toggle trackbacks); revisions (allows revisions); author (drop-down box to define author); excerpt (text box for excerpt); thumbnail (featured image selection); custom-fields (custom fields input area); page-attributes (page parent and Page template drop-down lists)	`'supports' => array ( 'title', 'editor', 'excerpt', 'custom-fields', 'thumbnail' ),`
rewrite	Rewrites the permalink structure for the post type.	true or false; slug (permalink slug to prepend custom post types); with_front (if you've set permalink structure with a specific prefix)	`'rewrite' => array( 'slug' => 'my-content', 'with_front' => false ),`
taxonomies	Uses existing WordPress taxonomies (category and tag).	Category post_tag	`'taxonomies' => array( 'post_tag', 'category'),`

If you don't feel up to writing all this code in the Theme Functions file, the Custom Post Type UI plugin from WebDevStudios (`http://webdevstudios. com`) provides you with an easy interface on your WordPress Dashboard. This plugin also simplifies the creation of custom post types on your site and bypasses the need to create the code in the theme functions (`functions. php`) file. You can find the free plugin at `http://wordpress.org/extend/ plugins/custom-post-type-ui`.

After you complete the steps to add the Generic Content post type to your site, it's added to the left navigation menu on the Dashboard, as shown in Figure 12-4.

New post type added

Figure 12-4: The Generic Content post type is added to the Dashboard.

You add and publish new content using the new custom post type just as you would when you write and publish blog posts. The published content isn't added to the chronological listing of blog posts, but is instead treated as separate content, just like static pages.

View the permalink for the custom post type, and you see that it adopts the post type name, Generic Content, and uses it as part of the permalink structure. The permalink looks like `http://yourdomain.com/generic-content/new-article`.

Listing 12-2 gives you a real-life example that I used on the No Rules Theatre Company site I developed, which you can see at `http://norulestheatre. org`. This site uses a Shows custom post type to create custom content for the shows that the theatre produces each season. Reference the parameters and information in the preceding Table 12-7 while you read through the lines of code in Listing 12-2 to see how the custom post types for the No Rules Theatre Company site were created and applied.

Listing 12-2: Custom Post Types from the No Rules Theatre Company Site

```
// ADD CUSTOM POST TYPE: SHOWS
add_action( 'init', 'create_my_post_types' );
function create_my_post_types() {
        register_post_type( 'shows',
        array(
        'labels' => array(
        'name' => __( 'Shows' ),
        'singular_name' => __( 'Show' ),
        'add_new' => __( 'Add New Show' ),
        'add_new_item' => __( 'Add New Show' ),


        'edit' => __( 'Edit' ),
        'edit_item' => __( 'Edit Show' ),
        'new_item' => __( 'New Show' ),
        'view' => __( 'View Show' ),
        'view_item' => __( 'View Show' ),
        'search_items' => __( 'Search Shows' ),
        'not_found' => __( 'No shows found' ),
        'not_found_in_trash' => __( 'No shows found in Trash' ),
        'parent' => __( 'Parent Show' ),
            ),

        'public' => true,
        'show_ui' => true,
        'publicly_queryable' => true,
        'exclude_from_search' => false,
        'menu_position' => 10,
        'menu_icon' => get_stylesheet_directory_uri() . '/img/nrt-shows.
          png',
        'hierarchical' => true,
        'query_var' => true,
        'rewrite' => array( 'slug' => 'shows', 'with_front' => false ),
        'taxonomies' => array( 'post_tag', 'category'),
        'can_export' => true,
        'supports' => array(
        'post-thumbnails',
        'excerpts',
        'comments',
        'revisions',
        'title',
        'editor',
        'page-attributes',
        'custom-fields')
        )
        );
}
```

To add custom post types to the Menus options on the Menus page accessible from the Dashboard (choose Appearance➪Menus), click the Screen Options tab at the top right of that page. You see a check box next to Post Types that you can select to enable your custom post types in the menus you create. The Post Types appear in the Screen Options only if you have custom post types enabled in your theme.

Building a template for a custom post type

By default, custom post types use the `single.php` template in your theme — that is, unless you create a specific template for your custom post type. You may find the regular WordPress `single.php` template limiting for your post type. This depends on the type of content you want to include and whether you want to apply different formats and styles for your custom post type with HTML and CSS markup.

In the preceding section, I share the code to build a simple Generic Content custom post. After you add that, the Generic Content menu on the WordPress Dashboard appears (refer to Figure 12-4). Choose Generic Content➪Add New, and then publish a new post with some content for testing. For example, add a new Generic Content type with a `Test` title and a `test` slug. Because the Generic Content type doesn't have a specific template yet, it uses the `single.php` template, and resulting posts look no different from the standard.

If a Not Found page appears when you try to access a new custom post type entry, reset your permalink settings. Choose Settings➪Permalinks on the Dashboard and then click the Save Changes button. This forces WordPress to reset the permalinks for your site and add the new custom post type permalink formats. (See Chapter 4 for more on permalinks.)

To build a template specific for the Generic Content post type, add a new `single-posttype.php` template (*posttype* is the first argument passed to the `register_post_type` function from the preceding section). For this example, the template file specific to the Generic Content post type is `single-generic-content.php`. Any modifications made to this template file are shown only for instances of the Generic Content post type.

Tying this together with the section "Creating and using template parts," earlier in this chapter, a basic structure for `single-generic-content.php` for the Twenty Thirteen theme is

```php
<?php get_header(); ?>
<div id="container">
  <div id="content" role="main">
    <?php get_template_part('loop', 'generic-content'); ?>
  </div>
</div>
<?php get_sidebar(); ?>
<?php get_footer(); ?>
```

By using the template part, creating a `loop-generic-content.php` file allows for easy customization of The Loop for the Generic Content post type entry.

Adding support for post formats

Including the post formats in your theme allows you to designate a different content display and styling for certain types of designated posts. Unlike custom post types (which I describe earlier in this chapter), you can't create different post formats because WordPress has already assigned them for you — it's up to you which post format, if any, you want to use in your theme. You can, however, use one or all of them, depending on your needs.

Hopefully, this doesn't sound too confusing. Here are examples of the post formats that are currently designated in WordPress:

- **Aside:** This format is a very short post to share a random thought or idea. Typically, an Aside is shared without a post title or category/tag designations. An Aside is simply a random, one-off thought shared on your blog, but is not a full post.

- **Audio:** The Audio post format is for sharing audio files, or podcasts. Usually, Audio posts have very little text included and instead include items, such as a built-in audio player, that visitors can click and listen to audio files from.

- **Chat:** This post format is a transcript of an online chat conversation that can be formatted to look just like a chat or instant messaging window.

- **Gallery:** This is a gallery of images in which you can click each image to access a larger version. Often these post formats don't contain text and display only a gallery (but they may have a title).

- **Image:** This post format is used for displaying one image, such as in a photo blog. The image may, or may not, have text or a caption to go along with the post.

- **Link:** Use this to display a quick post that provides a link that you want to share with your readers. These post formats often contain a title and sometimes a short bit of text that describes the link you're sharing.

- **Quote:** Display a quotation on your blog with this post format. Often, users include the quotation along with a byline for its source.

- **Status:** This provides a short status update, usually limited to 140 characters or less (think Twitter!).

- **Video:** This format allows you to display a video, usually embedded within a handy video player (á la YouTube), so your readers can simply click to play the video without leaving your site.

- **Standard:** This displays your blog posts in the default manner, meaning it's just an ordinary blog post without special formats applied to it.

You can find a good, real-world example of post formats on my website at `http://lisasabin-wilson.com`, as shown in Figure 12-5. My site separates the formats I've chosen through the use of individual post styling to designate the different formats. In Figure 12-5, you see that I use different colors for specific post formats; for example the quote format appears on my site in blue.

If your site needs a different type of post format than is currently available, consider adding it as a custom post type instead. (See the earlier sections for details.)

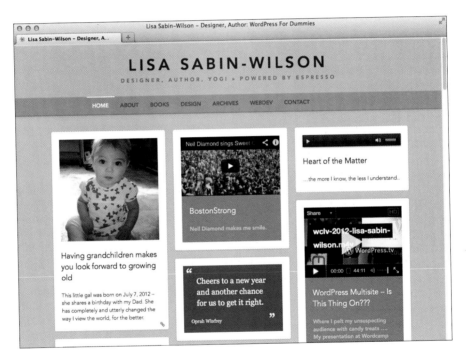

Figure 12-5: Post formats in use.

Adding post formats to a theme

To add support for post formats in your theme, you first need to add the function call to your Theme Functions (`functions.php`) template. After you follow these few steps, I show you the magic that occurs on the Add New Post page on your WordPress Dashboard. But first, follow the steps to add post formats support in your theme:

1. **From your Dashboard, choose Appearance⇨Editor.**

2. **Click the theme functions (`functions.php`) file in the Templates list on the right to open it.**

3. **In the text editor box, add the following function on a new line prior to the closing ?> tag:**

```
add_theme_support( 'post-formats', array( 'aside', 'chat', 'gallery',
           'image', 'link', 'quote', 'status', 'video', 'audio' ) );
```

The preceding code sample adds all nine of the available post formats to the theme. You don't have to use all nine; you can simply include only those formats that you think you'll use in your theme and leave out the rest.

4. **Click the Update File button to save the changes made to the functions.php file.**

You won't notice an immediate change to your site when you save your new theme functions file with the post formats support added. To see what WordPress has added to your site, visit the Add New Post page by choosing Posts⇨Add New on the Dashboard. Icons for each of the post formats appear across the top of the screen, as shown in Figure 12-6. Because I added all nine post format options, in the figure they're all listed as available formats that I can select. You also see a tenth format option — *Standard* — which is the format used if you don't select a specific format for your post.

Post format options

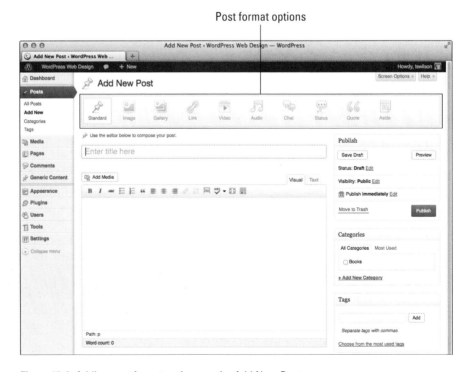

Figure 12-6: Adding post format options on the Add New Post page.

Using template tags for post formats

Adding post format support to your theme isn't enough. If you go through the hassle of adding post format support, you really should provide some unique styling for each type of format. If not, your different post formats will look just like the rest of your blog posts, and the point of adding them to your theme will be lost.

You can provide a unique display for your post formats in two ways:

- **Content:** For each format, you can designate what content you want to display. For example, if you don't want to display a title for an Aside, leave out the template tag that calls it but leave in the template tag that calls the title for your Video post format.

- **Style:** Have a look at the nearby sidebar "Post class defined." In the sidebar, I discuss using the HTML markup that's provided by the post_ class(); tag. Your formats each have their own CSS class assigned to them. Use those CSS classes to provide unique styles for fonts, colors, backgrounds, and borders to your different post formats.

Post class defined

In the default Twenty Thirteen theme, look at the content.php template by clicking it on the Edit Themes page. About three-fourths of the way into that template is this line of code:

```
<article id="post-<?php the_ID(); ?>"
         <?php post_class(); ?>>
```

The post_class(); section is the cool part of the template tag. This tag tells WordPress to insert specific HTML markup in your template. This HTML markup allows you to use CSS to make custom styles for sticky posts, categories, tags, and post formats.

For example, you can set the following options for a post:

- Stick this post to the front page.
- File in a category called WordPress.
- Tag with News.

For the preceding example, WordPress inserts the following HTML markup:

```
<article class="post sticky category-
         wordpress tag-news">
```

Likewise, for post formats, if you publish a post using the images post format, the post_ class() tag in the template contains the following HTML markup, indicating that this post should be formatted for an image display:

```
<article class="post type-post format-
         image">
```

Combine this information with the CSS and HTML information in Chapter 14, and you see how you can use CSS along with the post_ class(); tag to provide custom styles for each of the post types, categories, and tags you've set up on your site.

Adding unique styles for your post formats starts with creating the content designations you wish to display for each format. Earlier in this chapter, I describe the nine possible post formats and give you some ideas on what you can do to display them on your site. The possibilities are endless, and it's really up to you. See Chapter 11 for more information on the different content-related template tags you can use in these areas.

In the following steps, you create a simple, stripped-down Main Index (index. php) file to use on your site and include post format support. This is just a sample template for you to follow and refer to when you create your custom display for your post formats. No time like the present; follow these steps:

1. **Open your favorite text editor, such as Notepad (Windows) or TextMate (Mac).**

2. **Enter the code in Listing 12-3 to create a simple template for post formats.**

   I describe the various lines of code following the listing.

3. **Save your file as `index.php` on your local computer.**

4. **Upload the file into your theme folder (located in the `/wp-content/ themes` directory), replacing your existing `index.php` file.**

   See Chapter 5 for details on transferring files with FTP.

Listing 12-3:   A Simple Template for Post Formats

```
<?php get_header(); ?>                                              → 1
<?php if (have_posts()) : ?>                                        → 2
<?php while (have_posts()) : the_post(); ?>
<article id="post-<?php the_ID(); ?>" <?php post_class(); ?>>       → 4
<?php                                                              → 5

if ( has_post_format( 'aside' )) {                                → 6
        echo the_content();
}

elseif ( has_post_format( 'chat' )) {                             → 9
        echo '<h3>';
        echo the_title();
        echo '</h3>';
        echo the_content();
}

elseif ( has_post_format( 'gallery' )) {                          → 15
        echo '<h3>';
        echo the_title();
        echo '</h3>';
        echo the_content();
}
```

```
elseif ( has_post_format( 'image' )) {                          → 21
          echo '<h3>';
          echo the_title();
          echo '</h3>';
          echo the_post_thumbnail('image-format');
          echo the_content();
}

elseif ( has_post_format( 'link' )) {                           → 28
          echo '<h3>';
          echo the_title();
          echo '</h3>';
          echo the_content();
}

elseif ( has_post_format( 'quote' )) {                          → 34
          echo the_content();
}

elseif ( has_post_format( 'status' )) {                         → 37
          echo the_content();
}

elseif ( has_post_format( 'video' )) {                          → 40
          echo '<h3>';
          echo the_title();
          echo '</h3>';
          echo the_content();
}

elseif ( has_post_format( 'audio' )) {                          → 46
          echo '<h3>';
          echo the_title();
          echo '</h3>';
          echo the_content();
}

else {                                                          → 52
          echo '<h3>';
          echo the_title();
          echo '</h3>';
          echo the_content();
}

?>                                                              → 58
</article>                                                      → 59
<?php endwhile; else: ?>                                        → 60
<?php endif; ?>
<?php get_sidebar(); ?>                                         → 62
<?php get_footer(); ?>                                          → 63
```

Here's a breakdown of the lines of code in Listing 12-3:

→ **1**   This function includes all the code from the `header.php` file of your theme.

→ **2**   Indicates the beginning of The Loop (see Chapter 11).

→ **4**   Provides HTML and CSS markup using the `post_class();` function that provides you with unique CSS classes for each of your post formats (see the earlier sidebar "Post class defined").

→ **5**   Initiates the start of a PHP function.

→ **6**   Provides content for the Asides post format.

→ **9**   Provides content for the Chat post format.

→ **15**   Provides content for the Gallery post format.

→ **21**   Provides content for the Image post format.

→ **28**   Provides content for the Link post format.

→ **34**   Provides content for the Quote post format.

→ **37**   Provides content for the Status post format.

→ **40**   Provides content for the Video post format.

→ **46**   Provides content for the Audio post format.

→ **52**   Provides content for all other Default posts.

→ **58**   Ends the PHP function.

→ **59**   Closes the HTML article tag that was opened in line 4.

→ **60**   Closes the `endwhile` and `if` statements that were opened in Lines 2–3.

→ **62**   This function calls in the code included in the `sidebar.php` file of your theme.

→ **63**   This function calls in the code included in the `footer.php` file of your theme.

Listing 12-3 is a simple example and does not include a lot of HTML markup or CSS classes. I did that on purpose to focus on the code bits required to designate and define different content displays for your post formats. You can see in Listing 12-3 that some of the formats contain the template tag to display the title — `the_title();` — and others do not. However, they all contain the template tag to display the content of the post: `the_content();`. As I mention earlier, you can play with different content types and markup that you want to add to your post formats.

Couple your template additions for post formats with the `post_class();`, which adds special CSS classes and markup for each post format type. You can really customize the display of each individual post format to your heart's content.

Adding support for post thumbnails

Post thumbnails (or featured images) take a lot of the work out of associating an image with a post and using the correct size each time. A popular way to display content in WordPress themes includes a thumbnail image with a short snippet (or excerpt) of text — the thumbnail images are all the same size and placement within your theme.

Prior to the inclusion of post thumbnails in WordPress, users had to open their images in an image-editing program (such as Photoshop) and crop and resize them. Or users had to write fancy scripts that would resize images on the fly; however, these scripts tended to be resource-intensive on web servers, so they weren't an optimal solution. How about a content management system that crops and resizes your images to the exact dimensions that you specify? Yep — WordPress does that for you, with just a few adjustments.

By default, when you upload an image in WordPress, it creates three versions of your image based on dimensions set on your Dashboard's Media Settings page (choose Settings⇨Media):

- **Thumbnail size:** Default dimensions are 150px x 150px.
- **Medium size:** Default dimensions are 300px x 300px.
- **Large size:** Default dimensions are 1024px x 1024px.

So, when you upload one image, you actually end up with four sizes of that same image stored on your web server: thumbnail, medium, large, and the original (full size) image you uploaded. Images are cropped and resized proportionally, and typically when you use them in your posts, you can designate which size you want to use in the image options of the uploader (which I describe in Chapter 16). You can find the uploader on the Add New Post, Add New Page, and Add New Media pages on your WordPress Dashboard.

Within the WordPress image uploader, you can designate a particular image as the featured image of the post, and then, using the Featured Images function that you add to your theme, you can include some template tags to display your chosen featured image with your post. This is helpful for creating Magazine or News Style themes that are so popular with WordPress sites. Figure 12-7 displays my business website where we use post thumbnails and featured images to display a thumbnail associated with each post excerpt on the blog at http://webdevstudios.com.

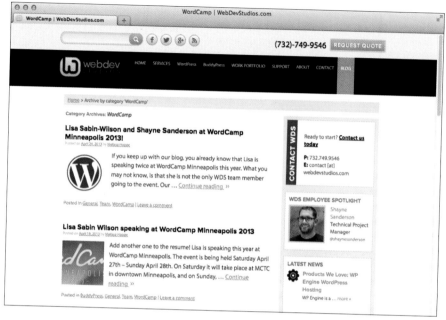

Figure 12-7: Post thumbnails on WebDevStudios.com.

In the section "Adding custom image sizes for post thumbnails," later in this chapter, I also cover adding support for different image sizes other than the default image sizes that are set on the Media Settings page on your Dashboard. This is helpful when you have sections of your site in which you want to display a much smaller thumbnail, or a larger version of the medium size but not as big as the large size.

Adding post thumbnails to a theme

To add support for post thumbnails, add one line of code to your theme functions (`functions.php`) file anywhere before the closing `?>`:

```
add_theme_support( 'post-thumbnails' );
```

After you add this line of code, you can use the featured image for your posts because it requires the Post Thumbnails function to be activated. You can then start designating images as featured using the built-in featured image found in the WordPress image uploader and on the Add New Post page, where you write and publish your posts.

After you start adding featured images to your posts, make sure you add the correct tag in your template(s) so the featured image appears on your site in the area you want it to. Open your `index.php` template, for example, and add the following line of code anywhere to include the default thumbnail-size version of your chosen featured image in your posts:

```
<?php if ( has_post_thumbnail() ) { the_post_thumbnail('thumbnail'); ?>
```

The first part of that line of code checks whether a featured image is associated with the post; if there is one, the image appears. If a featured image does not exist for the post, nothing returns. You can also include the other default image sizes — set in the Media Settings page on the Dashboard, as shown in Figure 12-8 — for medium, large, and full-sized images by using these tags:

```
<?php if ( has_post_thumbnail() ) { the_post_thumbnail('medium'); ?>
<?php if ( has_post_thumbnail() ) { the_post_thumbnail('large'); ?>
<?php if ( has_post_thumbnail() ) { the_post_thumbnail('full'); ?>
```

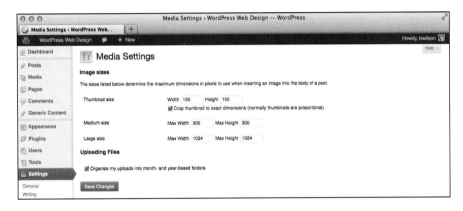

Figure 12-8: The Media Settings page on the Dashboard.

Adding custom image sizes for post thumbnails

If the predefined, default image sizes in WordPress (thumbnail, medium, large, and full) don't satisfy you and you have an area on your site that you want to display images with dimensions that vary from the default, WordPress makes it relatively easy to add custom image sizes in your theme functions file. You then use the the_post_thumbnail function to display the featured image in your theme.

You aren't limited on what sizes you can add for your images, and this example shows you how to add a new image size of 600px x 300px. Add the following line to your theme functions file (functions.php) below the previous function — add_theme_support('post-thumbnails') — covered in the "Adding the post thumbnails to a theme" section, earlier in this chapter:

```
add_image_size('custom', 600, 300, true);
```

This code tells WordPress that it needs to create an additional version of the images you upload and to crop and resize them to 600px in width and 300px in height. Notice the four parameters in the add_image_size function:

- **Name ($name):** Give the image size a unique name that you can use later in your template tag. In my example, I give the new image size the name 'custom'.

- **Width ($width):** Give the image size a width dimension in numbers. In my example, I define the width as 600.

- **Height ($height):** Give the image size a height dimension in numbers. In my example, I define the height as 300.

- **Crop ($crop):** This parameter is optional and tells WordPress whether it should crop the image to exact dimension, or do a soft proportional resizing of the image. In my example, I set this to true (the accepted arguments are true or false).

Adding the custom image size to your template to display the image you've designated as featured is the same as adding default image sizes, except the name of the image is set in the parentheses of the template tag. To add in my example custom image size, use the following tag:

```php
<?php if ( has_post_thumbnail() ) { the_post_thumbnail('custom'); ?>
```

13

Understanding Parent and Child Themes

*U*sing a theme exactly as a theme author released it is great. If a new version is released that fixes a browser compatibility issue or adds features offered by a new version of WordPress, a quick theme upgrade is very easy to do.

However, there's a good chance you'll want to tinker with the design, add new features, or modify the theme structure. If you modify the theme, you can't upgrade to a newly released version without modifying the theme again.

If only you could upgrade customized versions of themes with new features when they're released. Fortunately, child themes give you this best-of-both-worlds theme solution. This chapter explores what child themes are, how to create a child theme–ready parent theme, and how to get the most out of using child themes.

Customizing Theme Style with Child Themes

A WordPress *theme* consists of a collection of template files, stylesheets, images, and JavaScript files. The theme controls the layout and design that your visitors see on the site. When such a theme is properly set up as a parent theme, it allows a *child theme,* or a subset of instructions, to override its files. This ensures a child theme can selectively modify the layout, styling, and functionality of the parent theme.

The quickest way to understand child themes is by example. In this section, I show you how to create a simple child theme that modifies the style of the parent theme. Currently, the default WordPress theme is Twenty Thirteen (which I discuss in detail in Chapter 10). Figure 13-1 shows how the Twenty Thirteen theme appears on a sample site.

Figure 13-1: The Twenty Thirteen theme.

You likely have Twenty Thirteen on your WordPress site, and Twenty Thirteen is child theme–ready; therefore, it's a great candidate for creating an example child theme. To keep the names simple, I call the new child theme TwentyThirteen Child (original, I know).

Creating a child theme

Like regular themes, a child theme needs to reside in a directory inside the `/wp-content/themes` directory. The first step to creating a child theme is to add the directory that will hold it. For this example, create a new `twenty thirteen-child` directory inside the `/wp-content/themes` directory.

To register the twentythirteen-child directory as a theme and to make it a child of the Twenty Thirteen theme, create a style.css file and add the appropriate theme headers. To do this, type the following code into your favorite code or plain text editor, such as Notepad (Windows) or TextMate (Mac), and save the file as style.css:

```
/*
Theme Name: TwentyThirteen Child
Description: My fabulous child theme
Author: Lisa Sabin-Wilson
Version: 1.0
Template: twentythirteen
*/
```

Typically, you find the following headers in a WordPress theme:

- ✓ **Theme Name:** The theme user sees this name in the back end of WordPress.

- ✓ **Description:** This header provides the user any additional information about the theme. Currently, this header appears only on the Manage Themes page (choose Appearance➪Themes).

- ✓ **Author:** This header lists one or more theme authors. Currently, this header is shown only on the Manage Themes page (choose Appearance➪Themes).

- ✓ **Version:** The version number is very useful for keeping track of outdated versions of the theme. Updating the version number when modifying a theme is always a good idea.

- ✓ **Template:** This header changes a theme into a child theme. The value of this header tells WordPress the directory name of the parent theme. Because your example child theme uses Twenty Thirteen as the parent, your style.css needs to have a Template header with a value of twentythirteen (the directory name of the Twenty Thirteen theme).

Activate the new TwentyThirteen Child theme as your active theme. (See Chapter 9 for details on how to activate a theme.) You see a site layout similar to the one shown in Figure 13-2.

Figure 13-2 shows that the new theme doesn't look quite right. The problem is the new child theme replaced the style.css file of the parent theme, yet the new child theme's style.css file is empty. You could just copy and paste the contents of the parent theme's style.css file, but that'd waste some of the potential of child themes. Instead, you want to tweak only those styles and/or features that you want to modify and leave the rest alone, as I describe in the next section.

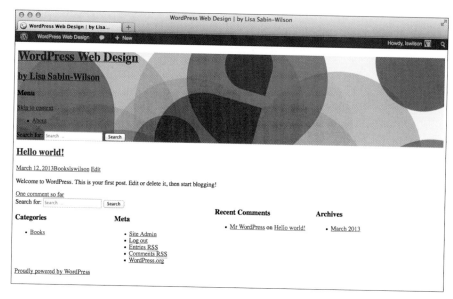

Figure 13-2: The TwentyThirteen Child theme.

Loading a parent theme's style

One of the great things about Cascading Style Sheets (CSS) is how rules can override one another. If you list the same rule twice in your CSS, the rule that comes last takes precedence. (I describe CSS in more detail in Chapter 14.)

For example:

```
a {
color: blue;
}

a {
color: red;
}
```

This example is overly simple, but it shows what I'm talking about nicely. The first rule says that all links (a tags) should be blue, whereas the second one says that links should be red. Because CSS says that the last instruction takes precedence, the links will be red.

Using this feature of CSS, you can inherit all the styling of the parent theme and selectively modify it by overriding the rules of the parent theme. But how can you load the child theme's style.css file so that it inherits the parent theme's styling?

Fortunately, CSS has another great feature that helps you do this with ease. Just add one line to the TwentyThirteen Child theme's `style.css` file at the end of the following listing:

```
/*
Theme Name: TwentyThirteen Child
Description: My fabulous child theme
Author: Lisa Sabin-Wilson
Version: 1.0
Template: twentythirteen
*/

@import url('../twentythirteen/style.css');
```

A number of things are going on here, so let me break it down piece by piece:

- ✓ **@import:** This tells the browser to load another stylesheet. Using this allows you to pull in the parent stylesheet quickly and easily.

- ✓ **url('...'):** This indicates that the value is a location and not a normal value.

- ✓ **('../twentythirteen/style.css');:** This is the location of the parent stylesheet. Notice the `/twentythirteen` directory name. This needs to be changed to match the `Template:` value in the header of the CSS so that the appropriate stylesheet is loaded.

After you refresh your site, you see that the child theme's design and layout match the original Twenty Thirteen theme. The updated child theme now looks like Figure 13-1, shown earlier.

Customizing the parent theme's styling

Your TwentyThirteen Child theme is set up to match the parent Twenty Thirteen theme. Now you can add new styling to the TwentyThirteen Child theme's `style.css` file. A simple example of how customizing works is adding a style that converts all h1, h2, and h3 headings to uppercase.

```
/*
Theme Name: TwentyThirteen Child
Description: My fabulous child theme
Author: Lisa Sabin-Wilson
Version: 1.0
Template: twentythirteen
*/

@import url('../twentythirteen/style.css');

h1, h2, h3 {
text-transform: uppercase;
}
```

Figure 13-3 shows how the child theme looks with the CSS style additions applied — getting better, isn't it?

As you can see, with just a few lines in a `style.css` file, you can create a new child theme that adds specific customizations to an existing theme. Not only is it quick and easy to do, but you don't have to modify anything in the parent theme to make it work. Therefore, when upgrades to the parent theme are available, you can upgrade the parent to get the additional features without making your modifications again.

More complex customizations work the same way. Simply add the new rules after the import rule that adds the parent stylesheet.

Figure 13-3: The updated child theme with uppercase headings.

Using images in child theme designs

Many themes use images to add nice touches to the design. Typically, you add these images to the `images` directory inside the theme. Just as a parent theme may refer to images in its `style.css` file, your child themes can have their own images directory. The following are examples of how these images can be used.

Using a child theme image in a child theme stylesheet

Including a child theme image in a child theme stylesheet is common. To do so, simply add the new image to the child theme's `images` directory and refer to it in the child theme's `style.css` file. To get a feel for the mechanics of this process, follow these steps:

1. **Create an `images` directory inside the child theme's directory** `/wp-content/themes/twentythirteen-child/images`.

2. **Add an image to the directory.**

   For this example, I added the `body-bg.png` image, which is a simple white-and-tan striped image that I created in Photoshop.

3. **Add the necessary styling to the child theme's `style.css` file, as follows:**

```
/*
Theme Name: TwentyThirteen Child
Description: My fabulous child theme
Author: Lisa Sabin-Wilson
Version: 1.0
Template: twentythirteen
*/

@import url('../twentythirteen/style.css');
body {
background: url('images/body-bg.png') repeat-x;
}
```

With a quick refresh of the site, it now has a new background, as shown in Figure 13-4. You can see how the background changed from plain white to a white-and-tan striped image.

Using a parent theme image in a child theme stylesheet

Child theme images are acceptable for most purposes. Sometimes, however, you're better off using images supplied by the parent theme. You could just copy the parent theme image folder, with all its images, to the child theme, but that'd prevent the child theme from matching the parent theme if the parent theme image ever changes, such as after an upgrade. Fortunately, you can refer to an image in the parent theme with the `@import` rule the same way you can reference the parent theme's `style.css` file.

In the navigation menu area of the Twenty Thirteen design, a magnifying glass icon shown in Figure 13-5 appears on the right side that designates the search area — users click it to display the search form. This is a parent theme image.

Figure 13-4: The TwentyThirteen Child theme after editing the background image.

Figure 13-5: Magnifying glass in the TwentyThirteen navigation menu area.

In this example, you add the magnifying glass icon in front of the post title. Because the icon image already exists inside the parent theme, you can simply add a customization to the child theme's `style.css` file to make this change, as follows:

```
/*
Theme Name: TwentyThirteen Child
Description: My fabulous child theme
Author: Lisa Sabin-Wilson
Version: 1.0
Template: twentythirteen
*/

@import url('../twentythirteen/style.css');

.entry-title {
background: url('../twentythirteen/images/search-icon.png') left center
            no-repeat;
padding-left: 30px;
}
```

Save the file and refresh your website to show the magnifying glass before the entry title. See Figure 13-6.

Using a child theme image in a parent theme stylesheet

In the earlier examples, you may wonder whether replacing an image used in the parent's stylesheet with one found in the child theme's directory is possible. Doing so would require a change to the parent theme's stylesheet; the very idea behind a child theme is to avoid changes to the parent, so no, that isn't possible. However, you can override the parent theme's rule to refer to the child theme's new image by simply creating an overriding rule in the child theme's stylesheet that points to the new image.

In the preceding example, you place the magnifying glass icon to the left of the entry title. Take that a step further; the magnifying glass icon next to the entry title (refer to Figure 13-6) is small. You can do better with a larger icon. For this example, use a different magnifying glass icon that you can download from: `http://lisasabin-wilson.com/magnifying-glass.jpg`. Right-click the image in your browser to save it to your local computer. (Be sure to remember where you saved it!)

After you add the desired image to your child theme's images directory as `magnifying-glass.jpg`, the following `style.css` file replaces the magnifying glass icon from the parent theme with the new one you just downloaded:

```
/*
Theme Name: TwentyThirteen Child
Description: My fabulous child theme
Author: Lisa Sabin-Wilson
Version: 1.0
Template: twentythirteen
*/

@import url('../twentythirteen/style.css');

.entry-title {
background: url(images/magnifying-glass.jpg) left center no-repeat;
padding-left: 50px;
}
```

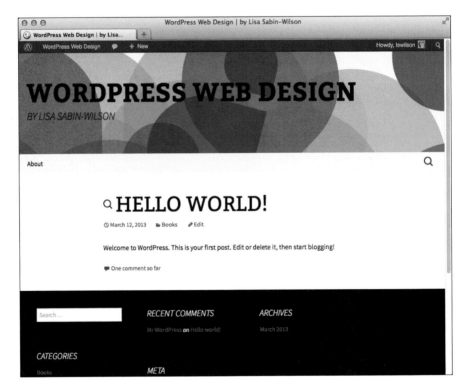

Figure 13-6: Showing the magnifying glass before the entry title.

Notice how some rules beyond just the background are modified to override parent theme styling that doesn't work well with the new icon, like the addition of the `padding-left: 50px` — that is put in place to provide correct spacing for the magnifying glass. Now your child theme shows the new magnifying glass to the left of the entry title. The new look, shown in Figure 13-7, is quite nice if you ask me.

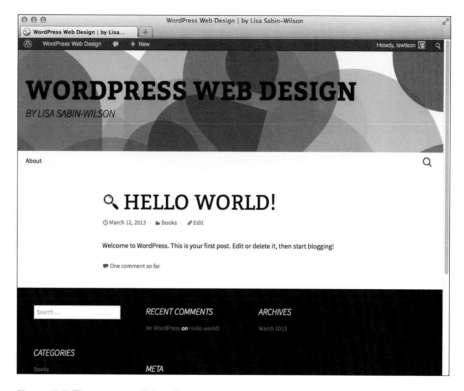

Figure 13-7: The new magnifying glass icon.

You can't directly replace parent theme images. Rather, you must provide a new image in the child theme and override the parent's styling to refer to this new image.

Modifying Theme Structure with Child Themes

The preceding section shows how to use a child theme to modify the stylesheet of an existing theme. This is a tremendously powerful capability. A talented CSS developer can use this technique to create a variety of layouts and designs.

However, this is just the beginning of the power of child themes. Although every child theme overrides the parent theme's `style.css` file, the child theme can override the parent theme's template files, too. And child themes aren't limited to just overriding template files; when needed, child themes can also supply their own template files.

Template files are PHP files that WordPress runs to render different views of the site. (See Chapter 11 for more on PHP.) A *site view* is the type of content being looked at in your web browser. Examples of different views are:

- ✔ **Home:** The home page of your website
- ✔ **Category archive:** A page that displays the archives within a particular category
- ✔ **Individual post:** A page that displays a single post from your blog
- ✔ **Page content:** A page that displays the content of a static page from your site

Some examples of common template files are `index.php`, `archive.php`, `single.php`, `page.php`, `attachment.php`, and `search.php`. (You can read more about available template files, including how to use them, in Chapter 11.)

You may wonder what purpose modifying template files of a parent theme serves. Although modifying the stylesheet of a parent theme can allow for some very powerful control over the design, it can't add new content, modify the underlying site structure, or change how the theme functions. To get that level of control, you need to modify the template files.

Overriding parent template files

When both the child theme and parent theme supply the same template file, the child theme file is used. *Overriding* is the process of replacing the original parent template file.

Although overriding every single one of the theme's template files can defeat the purpose of using a child theme — because if you're going to rewrite every single template file to make it different from the parent theme, you may as well create an entirely new theme that does not depend on a parent theme — sometimes, producing a desired result makes tweaking one or two of the template files necessary.

The easiest way to customize a specific template file in a child theme is to copy the template file from the parent theme folder to the child theme folder. After you copy the file, you can customize it as needed, and the changes will reflect in the child theme.

A good example of a template file that can you can typically override is the `footer.php` file. Customizing the footer enables you to add site-specific branding.

Adding new template files

A child theme can override existing parent template files, but it can supply template files that don't exist in the parent, too. Although you may never need your child themes to do this, this option can open possibilities for your designs.

For example, this technique proves most valuable with page templates. (Figure 13-8 shows the default page template in Twenty Thirteen.) The Twenty Thirteen theme does not have a One Column, No Sidebar page template because with Twenty Thirteen, all you need to do is omit widgets from the Secondary Widget Area (see Chapter 12), and WordPress removes the right sidebar. But what if you're using the Secondary Widget Area throughout your site and you want to omit the sidebar on just one page to display it full width? In a child theme, you can create a new page template, which still uses the styles and functions from the parent, but introduces a new layout in the child theme, in this case, a page template that omits the sidebar.

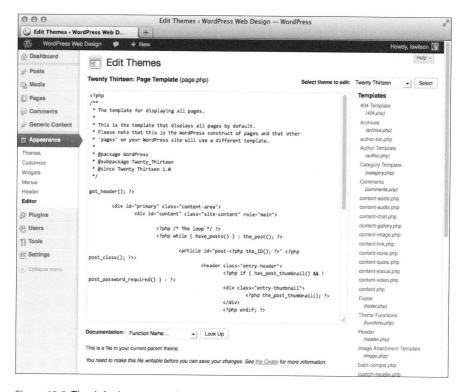

Figure 13-8: The default page template in Twenty Thirteen.

This isn't a design flaw. The layout was intentionally set up this way to make it easy for users to include, or not include, a right sidebar on their sites. I like to use the right sidebar, but sometimes need to have a full-width layout option so that I can embed a video, add a forum, or add other content that works well with full width. To add this feature to your child theme, simply add a new page template and the necessary styling to the `style.css` file.

A good way to create a new theme page template is to copy an existing one and modify it as needed. In this case, copying the page.php file of the parent theme to a new page-full.php file is a good start. After a few customizations, the page-full.php file looks like this:

```php
<?php
/**
 * Template Name: Full Width
 * The template for displaying full width.
 */

get_header(); ?>

<div id="primary" class="content-area">
<div id="content" class="site-content" role="main">
<?php /* The loop */ ?>
<?php while ( have_posts() ) : the_post(); ?>
<article id="post-<?php the_ID(); ?>" <?php post_class(); ?>>
<header class="entry-header">
<?php if ( has_post_thumbnail() && ! post_password_required() ) : ?>
<div class="entry-thumbnail">
<?php the_post_thumbnail(); ?>
</div>
<?php endif; ?>

<h1 class="entry-title"><?php the_title(); ?></h1>
</header><!-- .entry-header -->

<div class="entry-content">
<?php the_content(); ?>
<?php wp_link_pages( array( 'before' => '<div class="page-links"><span
            class="page-links-title">' . __( 'Pages:', 'twentythirteen' ) .
            '</span>', 'after' => '</div>', 'link_before' => '<span>', 'link_
            after' => '</span>' ) ); ?>
</div><!-- .entry-content -->

<footer class="entry-meta">
<?php edit_post_link( __( 'Edit', 'twentythirteen' ), '<span class="edit-
            link">', '</span>' ); ?>
</footer><!-- .entry-meta -->
</article><!-- #post -->

<?php comments_template(); ?>
<?php endwhile; ?>

</div><!-- #content -->
</div><!-- #primary -->
<?php get_footer(); ?>
```

The key modification here is the removal of the get_sidebar(); code, so the template does not call the sidebar widgets when this page template is assigned to a page on the site.

You need to make a small styling change in the child theme stylesheet to ensure the content of the full-width page spans the width of the site. By looking in the parent stylesheet, I can see that the content area width is defined by these lines:

```
.sidebar .entry-header,
.sidebar .entry-content,
.sidebar .entry-summary,
.sidebar .entry-meta {
  max-width: 1040px;
  padding: 0 376px 0 60px;
}
```

The padding in that style designates the right-side padding at 376px. You need to reduce the right side padding to allow for the content to extend farther to the right side of the browser window. Simply add the following lines after the @import rule in the child theme's `style.css` file to reduce the right side padding to 60px (more information about CSS is found in Chapter 14):

```
.sidebar .entry-header,
.sidebar .entry-content,
.sidebar .entry-summary,
.sidebar .entry-meta {
  max-width: 1040px;
  padding: 0 60px 0 60px;
}
```

Switching to the Full Width page template produces the layout shown in Figure 13-9.

Removing template files

You may be wondering why you'd want to remove a parent's template file. Unfortunately, the Twenty Thirteen theme doesn't provide a good example of why you'd want to do this. Therefore, for future reference, you must use your imagination a bit here to understand the mechanics of removing a file from the parent theme.

Imagine that you're creating a child theme built off an Example Parent parent theme. Example Parent is well designed, and the child theme looks and works exactly the way you want it to, but you have a problem.

The Example Parent theme has a home.php template file that provides a highly customized page template for use as the home page of your site. This works very well, but it isn't what you want for the site if you want a standard blog home page. If the home.php file didn't exist in Example Parent, everything would work perfectly.

Figure 13-9: The Full Width, No Sidebar page template.

You can't remove the `home.php` file from Example Parent without modifying the parent theme (which you never, ever want to do), so you have to use a trick. Instead of removing the file, override the `home.php` file and have it emulate `index.php`.

You may think that simply copying and pasting the Example Parent `index.php` code into the child theme's `home.php` file would be a good approach. Although this would work, I have a better way: You can tell WordPress to run the `index.php` file so that changes to `index.php` are respected. This single line of code inside the child theme's `home.php` file is all you need to replace `home.php` with `index.php`:

```
<?php locate_template( array( 'index.php' ), true ); ?>
```

The `locate_template` function does a bit of magic. If the child theme supplies an `index.php` file, it is used. If not, the parent `index.php` file is used.

This produces the same result that removing the parent theme's `home.php` file would have. The `home.php` code is ignored, and the changes to `index.php` are respected.

Modifying the theme functions file

Like template files, child themes can also provide a theme functions file, or a `functions.php` file. Unlike template files, the `functions.php` file of a child theme does not override the file of the parent theme.

When a parent theme and a child theme each have a `functions.php` file, WordPress runs both the parent and child `functions.php` files simultaneously. The child theme's `functions.php` file runs first, and the parent theme's `functions.php` file runs second. This is intentional because the child theme can replace functions defined in the parent theme's `functions.php` file.

However, this works only if the functions are set up to allow this.

The Twenty Thirteen `functions.php` file defines a `twentythirteen_setup` function. This function handles the configuration of many theme options and activates some additional features. Child themes can replace this function to change the default configuration and features of the theme, too.

The following lines of code summarize how the `functions.php` file allows this to happen:

```
function twentythirteen_setup()
```

Wrapping the function declaration in the `if` statement protects the site from breaking in the event of a code conflict and allows a child theme to define its own version of the function.

In the TwentyThirteen Child theme, you can see how modifying this function affects the theme. Add a new `twentythirteen_setup` function that adds post thumbnails support (see Chapter 12) to the TwentyThirteen Child theme's `functions.php` file:

```
<?php
function twentythirteen_setup() {
add_theme_support( 'post-thumbnails' );
}
```

The result of this change is that the child theme no longer supports other special WordPress features, such as custom editor styling, automatic feed link generation, internationalization and location, and so on.

The takeaway from this example is that a child theme can provide its own custom version of the function only because the parent theme wraps the function declaration in an `if` block that checks for the function first.

Preparing a Parent Theme

WordPress makes it easy for theme developers to make parent themes. WordPress does most of the hard work; however, a theme developer must follow some rules for a parent theme to function properly.

The terms *stylesheet* and *template* have been used numerous times in many contexts. Typically, *stylesheet* refers to a CSS file in a theme, and *template* refers to a template file in the theme. However, these words also have specific meanings when working with parent and child themes. You must understand the difference between a stylesheet and a template when working with parent and child themes.

In WordPress, the active theme is the *stylesheet,* and the active theme's parent is the *template.* If the theme doesn't have a parent, the active theme is both the stylesheet and the template.

Originally, child themes could replace only the `style.css` file of a theme. The parent provided all the template files and `functions.php` code. Thus, the child theme provided style and design, whereas the parent theme provided the template files. The capabilities of child themes expanded in future versions of WordPress, making the usage of these terms for parent and child themes somewhat confusing.

Imagine two themes: parent and child. The following code is in the parent theme's `header.php` file and loads an additional stylesheet provided by the theme:

```
<link type="text/css" rel="stylesheet" media="all" href="<?php
bloginfo('stylesheet_directory') ?>/reset.css" />
```

The `bloginfo()` function prints information about the site configuration or settings. This example uses the function to print the URL location of the stylesheet directory. The site is hosted at `http://example.com`, and the parent is the active theme. The preceding code produces the following output:

```
<link type="text/css" rel="stylesheet" media="all"
href="http://example.com/wp-content/themes/Parent/reset.css" />
```

If the child theme is activated, the output is

```
<link type="text/css" rel="stylesheet" media="all"
href="http://example.com/wp-content/themes/Child/reset.css" />
```

The location now refers to the `reset.css` file in the child theme. This can work if every child theme copies the `reset.css` file of the parent theme, but requiring child themes to add files to function isn't good design. The solution is simple: Rather than using the `stylesheet_directory()` in the `bloginfo()` call earlier, use `template_directory()`. The code looks like this:

```
<link type="text/css" rel="stylesheet" media="all" href="<?php
bloginfo('template_directory') ?>/reset.css" />
```

Now, all child themes properly load the parent `reset.css` file.

When developing, use `template_directory` in stand-alone parent themes and use `stylesheet_directory` in child themes.

Part IV
Building Your Custom Website

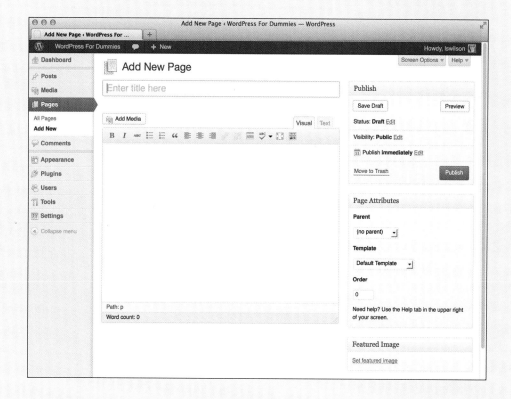

What good is having a great website if no one can find it? See how to optimize your WordPress website for search engines to make your site easier to find, at www.dummies.com/extras/wordpresswebdesign.

In this part . . .

- ✔ Discover the basics of CSS styling and HTML markup to provide the foundation for the style and layout of your WordPress web design.

- ✔ Step through the basics of CSS, including information about classes, IDs, properties, and values.

- ✔ Learn about styling background and header images, colors, and menus.

- ✔ Discover basic HTML techniques, including basic markup, inserting images and hyperlinks, and tying together CSS and HTML to create a dynamic style for your website project.

- ✔ Take an in-depth look at using WordPress as a full-blown content management system (CMS) via the use of static pages, page and category templates, built-in CSS classes, and custom styles.

- ✔ Explore the addition of complex features such as e-commerce shops, photo galleries, social communities, and popular social media integration.

14

Using Basic CSS and HTML to Customize Your Site Design

In This Chapter

▶ Understanding key CSS concepts

▶ Adjusting the background of a theme

▶ Adding your own header image to a theme

▶ Changing the look and feel of your site design

▶ Looking at basic HTML

*T*weaking is the practice of changing a few elements of an existing WordPress theme. Thousands of WordPress website owners tweak their existing themes regularly. This chapter provides information on some of the most common tweaks you can make to your theme, such as changing the header image, the color of the background or the text links, and font styles — and these changes are pretty easy to make, too. You'll be tweaking your own theme in no time flat.

This chapter introduces you to the basics of CSS and HTML markup that you use to provide style and structure to your WordPress theme. When combined with the functions and template tags that I cover in Chapters 11 and 12, CSS styling and HTML markup provide the finishing touches for a pleasing look and format for your website.

Before you go too wild with tweaking templates, make a backup of your theme so that you have the original files from which you can easily restore if you need to. You can back up your theme files by connecting to your web server via FTP (described in Chapter 5) and downloading your theme folder to your computer. When you have the original theme files safe and secure on your hard drive, feel free to tweak away, comfortable in the knowledge that you have a backup.

Styling with CSS: The Basics

Knowing some key Cascading Style Sheets (CSS) concepts can help you personalize your theme's stylesheet. *CSS* is simply a set of commands that allow you to customize the look and feel of your HTML markup. Some common commands and tools that I discuss here are selectors, IDs and classes, properties and values, and more. Together, you can use these commands to modify HTML to display your design customizations. (You can find out more about HTML in the section "Understanding Basic HTML Techniques to Use on Your Site," later in this chapter.)

Introducing CSS

A *Cascading Style Sheet* is a stylesheet that controls the appearance of content on a website. Every WordPress theme you use in your site uses CSS. CSS provides style and design flair to the template tags in your templates. (See Chapters 11 and 12 for information about WordPress template tags.) The CSS for your WordPress theme is pulled in through the Header template (`header.php`), and the file is named `style.css`.

On your Dashboard, choose Appearance➪Editor to open the Edit Themes page shown in Figure 14-1. Look at the far right side of the page under the Templates heading, scroll down to find the Header link, and click it to open the Header template. You find the following line of code, which pulls the CSS (`style.css`) into the page to provide the formatting of the elements of your site:

```
<link rel="stylesheet" type="text/css" media="all" href="<?php bloginfo(
          'stylesheet_url' ); ?>" />
```

Don't tweak the line of code that pulls in the `style.css` file; otherwise, CSS won't work for your site.

On the Edit Themes page, you can also explore your theme's stylesheet. When you first open this page, your theme's main stylesheet (`style.css`) appears by default, as shown in Figure 14-1. If not, under the Templates heading on the far right, scroll down to find the Styles heading and click the Stylesheet link to view the `style.css` file.

With CSS changes to your theme's stylesheet, you can apply unique styling such as fonts, sizes, and colors to headlines, text, links, and borders, and adjust the spacing between them, too. With all the CSS options available, you can fine-tune the look and feel of different elements with simple tweaks.

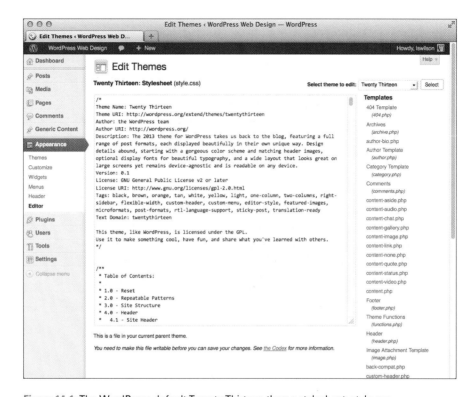

Figure 14-1: The WordPress default Twenty Thirteen theme stylesheet, style.css.

Making changes to the stylesheet or any other theme file can cause your site to load the theme improperly. Be careful what you change here. When you make changes, ensure you're on a playground or sandbox site so that you can easily restore your original file and don't permanently affect a live or important site. (See Chapter 8 for details on setting up a sandbox environment.) I also recommend saving a copy of the original stylesheet in a text program, such as Notepad (Windows) or TextMate (Mac), so if needed, you can find the original CSS and copy and paste it back into your stylesheet.

CSS selectors

With CSS, you can provide style (such as size, color, and placement) to the display of elements (such as text links, header images, font size and colors, paragraph margins, and line spacing) on your site. *CSS selectors* contain names, properties, and values to define which HTML elements in the templates you'll style with CSS. Table 14-1 provides some examples of CSS selectors and their uses.

Table 14-1		Basic CSS Selectors	
CSS Selector	**Description**	**HTML**	**CSS**
body	Sets the style for the overall body of the site, such as the background color and default fonts.	`<body>`	`body {background-color: white}` The background color on all pages is white.
p	Defines how paragraphs are formatted.	`<p>This is a paragraph</p>`	`p {color:black}` The color of the fonts used in all paragraphs is black.
h1, h2, h3, h4	Provides bold headers for different sections of your site.	`<h1>This is a site title</h1>`	`h1 {font-weight: bold;}` The fonts surrounded by the `<h1>...</h1>` HTML tags will be bold.
a	Defines how text links appear in your site.	`<a href="http://wiley.com">Wiley</a>`	`a {color: red}` All text links appear in red.

Classes and IDs

You can find the stylesheet (`style.css`) for the default Twenty Thirteen theme on the Edit Themes page on your Dashboard (refer to Figure 14-1). Everything in it may look foreign to you right now, but I want to bring your attention to two items you see when you scroll down through that template:

- **#container:** This is one type of CSS selector. The hash mark (#) indicates that it's a CSS *ID* and can be used only once per page.

- **.onecolumn:** This is another type of CSS selector. The period (.) indicates that it's a CSS *class* and can be used multiple times on a page to automate changes that are made more than once.

IDs and classes define styling properties for different sections of your WordPress theme. Table 14-2 shows examples of IDs and classes from the `header.php` template in the Twenty Thirteen WordPress theme. Armed with this information, you know where to look in the stylesheet when you want to change the styling for a particular area of your theme.

Table 14-2	Connecting HTML with CSS Selectors	
HTML	**CSS Selector**	**Description**
`<div id="wrapper">`	`#wrapper`	Styles the elements for the `wrapper` ID in your template(s)
`<div id="header">`	`#header`	Styles the elements for the `header` ID in your template(s)
`<div id="masthead">`	`#masthead`	Styles the elements for the `masthead` ID in your template(s)
`<h1 id="site-title">`	`#site-title`	Styles the elements for your `site-title` ID in your template(s), but also follows rules for the `h1` values set in the CSS
`<div id="site-description">`	`#site-description`	Styles the elements for your `site-description` ID in your template(s)
`<div class="skip-link screen-reader-text">`	`.skip-link` and `.screen-reader`	Styles the elements for your `skip-link` and `screen-reader` classes in your template(s)

If you find an element in the template code that says `id` (such as `div id=` or `p id=`), look for the hash symbol in the stylesheet. If you find an element in the template code that says `class` (such as `div class=` or `p class=`), look for the period in the stylesheet followed by the selector name.

CSS properties and values

CSS properties are assigned to the CSS selector name. You also need to provide values for the CSS properties to define the style elements for the particular CSS selector you're working with.

In the default Twenty Thirteen WordPress theme, for example, the first piece of markup in the Header template (`header.php`) is `<div id="wrapper">`. This ID, with the name `wrapper`, provides styling for the site page.

In the default Twenty Thirteen WordPress theme stylesheet, the CSS defined for the `site` class is as follows:

```
.site {
background-color: #fff;
border-left: 1px solid #f2f2f2;
border-right: 1px solid #f2f2f2;
margin: 0 auto;
max-width: 1600px;
width: 100%;
}
```

Every CSS property needs to be followed by a colon (:), and each CSS value needs to be followed by a semicolon (;).

The CSS selector is `.site`, which has six properties:

- ✔ The first CSS property is `background-color`, which has the value of `#fff` (or white).

- ✔ The second CSS property is `border-left`, which has the value `1px solid #f2f2f2` (a light gray border that is 1 pixel in width).

- ✔ The third CSS property is `border-right`, which has the value `1px solid #f2f2f2` (a light gray border that is 1 pixel in width).

- ✔ The fourth CSS property is `margin`, which has the value `0 auto`.

- ✔ The fifth CSS property is `max-width`, which has the value of `1600px` (the maximum width).

- ✔ The sixth, and final, CSS property is `width`, which has the value `100%` (uses 100% of the available width of the browser window).

Table 14-3 provides some examples of commonly used CSS properties and values.

Table 14-3	Common CSS Properties and Values	
CSS Property	**CSS Value**	**Examples**
background-color	Defines the color of the background (such as red, black, or white)	**Markup:** `<div class="site">` **CSS:** `.site {background-color: white}`
background	Defines a background image and/or color	**Markup:** `<header>` **CSS:** `header {background: url(images/header.jpg) no-repeat;}`

CSS Property	CSS Value	Examples
font-family*	Defines the fonts used for the selector	**Markup:** `<body>` **CSS:** `body {font-family: 'Lucida Grande', Verdana, Arial, Sans-Serif;}`
color	Defines the color of the text	**Markup:** `<h1>Website Title</h1>` **CSS:** `h1 {color: blue}`
font-size**	Defines the size of the text	**Markup:** `<h1>Website Title</h1>` **CSS:** `h1 {font-size: 18px;}`
text-align	Defines the alignment of the text (left, center, right, or justified)	**Markup:** `<div class="site">…</div>` **CSS:** `.site {text-align: left;}`

* *W3Schools has a good resource on the font-family property at* `http://w3schools.com/cssref/pr_font_font-family.asp`.

** *W3Schools has a good resource on the font-size property at* `http://w3schools.com/cssref/pr_font_font-size.asp`.

Changing the Background Image or Color Used in Your Theme

In the following sections, I show you how to add the custom background feature to your theme so that you can easily tweak the background color or image through the Dashboard. Alternatively, you can use the `<body>` tag in a Header template to change the background color or image of your website. (I discuss the Header template [`header.php`] in more detail in Chapter 12.)

Adding the custom background feature to a theme

The Twenty Thirteen WordPress theme is not packaged with an available feature in WordPress that allows you to change the background to a different color or use an image for your background. There is, however, a nifty feature you can add to your WordPress `functions.php` file to allow your theme to support the custom background feature, enabling you to change the background image and/or color for your site.

You can add the custom background feature to any theme with just one line of code. Follow these steps:

1. **From the Dashboard, choose Appearance⮑Editor.**

   The Edit Themes page appears.

2. **Click the Theme Functions (`functions.php`) template on the right side of the page.**

   The Theme Functions template opens in the text editor in the middle of the page.

3. **Add the following line of code to the Theme Functions template before the closing `?>` tag:**

   ```
   add_custom_background();
   ```

   This line of code tells WordPress that your theme has added the custom background feature.

4. **Click the Save File button.**

   The Theme Functions template is saved, along with your changes. The Background link now appears below the Appearance menu on your Dashboard.

Customizing the background

Any theme that has the custom background feature allows you to change the background to a different color or use an image for it. To change the background for your website, follow these steps:

1. **Choose Appearance⮑Background.**

   The Custom Background page loads on the Dashboard. By default, the background color is set to white.

2a. **To change the background color, click the Select Color button and then type the hexadecimal color code in the Color text box and then skip to Step 4.**

   If you don't know what hex code you want to use, click the Select a Color button and then, in the color selector that appears, click a color, as shown in Figure 14-2. (Note that when you click the *Select Color* button, the text changes to *Current Color.*)

   A hexadecimal (or *hex*) code represents a certain color. Hex codes always start with a hash symbol (#) and have six letters and/or numbers to represent a particular color, such as #d5d6d7 (light gray). I talk more about hexadecimal values in Chapter 7.

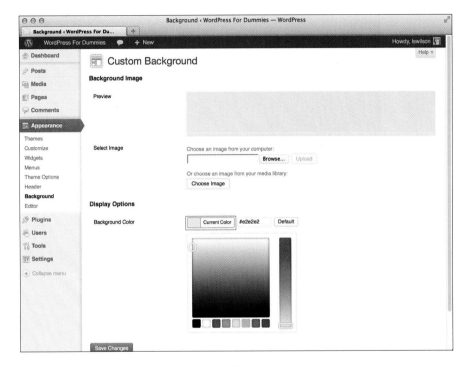

Figure 14-2: The color selector on the Custom Background page.

2b. To use an image file for the background, upload an image from your computer:

> *a. Click the Browse button in the Select Image section and then select a file from your computer.*

> *b. Click the Upload button.*

> The Custom Background page refreshes and gives you several display options.

3. Change the display options for your new background image:

> • *Position:* Select Left, Center, or Right to set the screen position of the background image on your website.

> • *Repeat:* Choose No Repeat, Tile, Tile Horizontally, or Tile Vertically in this drop-down list to set the image on your website.

> • *Attachment:* Select Scroll to set the background image to scroll down the page, or select Fixed to set the background image in a static position so that it doesn't scroll down the page.

4. Click the Save Changes button.

Be sure to click the Save Changes button before navigating away from the Custom Background page; otherwise, your new settings aren't saved.

Because all themes are not created equal, themes that don't have the custom header and background features enabled make it a little more challenging to change these elements. Without these features, you have to make tweaks via the theme CSS (`style.css`), covered in the next section.

Changing the background using CSS

The `<body>` tag is simple HTML markup. Every theme has this tag, which defines the overall default content for each page of your website — the site's *body*.

In the stylesheet (`style.css`), the background for the body is defined like this:

```
body {
  background: #f1f1f1;
}
```

The background for the `<body>` tag uses a hexadecimal color code of `#f1f1f1`, which gives the background a light gray color.

You can use a color or an image to style the background of your website. You can also use a combination of colors and images in your backgrounds.

Using an image as the site's background

You can easily use an image as a background for your site by uploading the image to the `images` folder in your theme directory. That value looks like this:

```
background: url(images/yourimage.jpg)
```

The `url` portion of this code automatically pulls in the URL of your site, so you don't have to change the `url` part to your URL.

Changing the background color

If you want to change the background color of your theme, follow these steps:

1. On the WordPress Dashboard, choose Appearance⇨Editor.

The Edit Themes page opens.

2. From the Select Theme to Edit drop-down list, choose the theme you want to change.

3. **Click the Stylesheet link in the list of templates.**

   The `style.css` template opens in the text editor in the middle of the Edit Themes page (refer to Figure 14-1).

4. **Scroll down in the text editor until you find the CSS selector body.**

   If you're tweaking the default theme, this section is what you're looking for:

   ```
   body {
     background: #f1f1f1;
   }
   ```

   If you're tweaking a different template, the CSS selector body looks similar.

5. **Edit the `background` property's values.**

   For example, in the default template, if you want to change the background color to black, you can enter either

   ```
   background: #000000;
   ```

   or

   ```
   background: black;
   ```

   In the case of some basic colors, you don't have to use the hex code. For colors like white, black, red, blue, and silver, you can just use their names — `background: black`, for example.

   The W3Schools website has a great resource on hex codes at `http://w3schools.com/HTML/html_colornames.asp`.

6. **Click the Update File button near the bottom of the page.**

   Your changes are saved and applied to your theme.

7. **Visit your site in your web browser.**

   The background color of your theme has changed.

Defining and Positioning Your Header Image with CSS

Most themes have a header image that appears at the top of the page. This image is generated by a graphic defined either in the CSS value for the property that represents the header area or through the use of a custom header feature in WordPress.

Defining a background image to use as a header

In the WordPress default Twenty Thirteen theme, including a custom header image on a site that uses the Twenty Thirteen theme is pretty darn easy, as I describe in Chapter 10. All the hard work's been done for you.

In themes that don't have the custom header image feature, you can easily define a background image for the header image using CSS. For purposes of this example, the HTML markup for the header in the template is

```
<div id="header"></div>
```

In the CSS (`style.css`) file, you can use a background image by defining it in the CSS properties for `#header`. Use this code:

```
#header {
background: url(/images/header-image.jpg) no-repeat;
width: 980px;
height: 100px;
}
```

The background value indicates a `header-image.jpg` image. For that image to appear on your site, you need to create the image and upload it to your web server in the `/images/` directory.

When working with graphics on the web, I recommend using GIF, JPG, or PNG image formats. For images with a small number of colors (such as charts, line art, logos, and so on), GIF format works best. For other image types (screen-shots with text and images, blended transparency, and so on), use JPG or PNG. I discuss graphics in more detail in Chapter 6.

Positioning, repeating, or scrolling your background image

After you upload a graphic to use in your theme, you can use CSS background properties to position it. The main CSS properties — `background-position`, `background-repeat`, and `background-attachment` — help you achieve the desired effect. Table 14-4 describes the CSS background properties and their available values for changing them in your theme stylesheet.

Table 14-4	CSS Background Properties		
Property	*Description*	*Values*	*Example*
background-position	Determines the starting point of your background image on your web page	bottom center bottom right left center right center center center	background-position: bottom center;
background-repeat	Determines whether your background image will repeat or tile	repeat (repeats infinitely) repeat-y (repeats vertically) repeat-x (repeats horizontally) no-repeat (does not repeat)	background-repeat: repeat-y;
background-attachment	Determines whether your background image is fixed or scrolls with the browser window	fixed scroll	background-attachment: scroll;

In the preceding section, the code example uploads a new background graphic named header-image.jpg. You can explore the positioning of this graphic with some of the values provided in Table 14-4. If you're a visual person like me, you'll enjoy testing and tweaking values to see the effects on your site.

Say your goal is to *tile,* or repeat, the background image *horizontally,* or across the browser screen from left to right so that it scales with the width of the browser on any computer. You also want to change the background color to a different color (like white, as in the following sample). To achieve this, open the stylesheet again and change:

```
background: #f1f1f1;
```

to

```
background: #FFFFFF;
background-image: url(images/header-image.jpg);
background-repeat: repeat-x;
```

or you can use

```
background: #FFFFFF url(images/header-image.jpg) repeat-x;
```

Changing Basic Elements to Create a Unique Look for Your Site

When you understand the basic concepts about personalizing your site with graphics and CSS, you begin to see how easy it is to change the look and feel of your site with these tools. The next few sections explore some of my favorite ways to accomplish an interesting design presentation or a unique and creative look.

Adding background colors and image effects

Earlier in this chapter, I provide you with a few examples of how you can change your background colors and image, as well as the image and/or background color for your header graphic, by adjusting the CSS and HTML. Changing the background image can completely change the feel of your site. However, you can also use background colors and images for other elements in your theme.

Background techniques include using solid colors and repeating gradients or patterns to achieve a subtle yet polished effect.

Use colors that accent the colors of your logo and don't hamper text readability.

You can add CSS background colors and image effects to the following areas of your theme:

- Post and page content sections
- Sidebar widgets
- Comment blocks
- The footer area

Choosing a font family, color, and size

You can change the fonts in your theme for style or readability purposes. I've seen typographic (or font) design experts use simple font variations to achieve amazing design results. You can use fonts to separate headlines from body text (or widget headlines and text from the main content) to be less distracting. Table 14-5 lists some examples of often-used font properties.

Table 14-5	Fonts	
Font Properties	*Common Values*	*CSS Examples*
`font-family`	`Georgia, Times, serif`	`body {font-family: Georgia; serif;}`
`font-size`	`px, %, em`	`body {font-size: 14px;}`
`font-style`	`italic, underline`	`body {font-style: italic;}`
`font-weight`	`bold, bolder, normal`	`body {font-weight: normal}`

Font family

The web is actually kind of picky about how it displays fonts, as well as what kind of fonts you can use in the `font-family` property. Not all fonts appear correctly on the web. To be safe, here are some commonly used font families that appear correctly in most browsers:

- **Serif fonts:** Times New Roman, Georgia, Garamond, and Bookman Old Style
- **Sans-serif fonts:** Verdana, Arial, Tahoma, and Trebuchet MS

Serif fonts have little tails, or curlicues, at the edges of letters. (This text is in a serif font.) *Sans-serif* fonts have straight edges and are devoid of any fancy styling. (The heading in Table 14-5 uses a sans-serif font . . . no tails!)

When you want to change a font family in your CSS, open the stylesheet (`style.css`), search for `property: font-family`, change the values for that property, and save your changes.

In the default template CSS, the font is defined in the `<body>` tag like this:

```
font-family: Georgia, "Bitstream Charter", serif;
```

Font color

With more than 16 million HTML color combinations available, you can find just the right shade of color for your project. After some time, you'll memorize your favorite color codes. I find that knowing codes for different shades of gray helps me quickly add an extra design touch. For example, I often use the shades of gray listed in Table 14-6 for backgrounds, borders on design elements, and widget headers.

Table 14-6	My Favorite CSS Colors
Color	*Value*
White	#FFFFFF or #FFF
Black	#000000 or #000
Grays	#CCCCCC or #CCC
	#DDDDDD or #DDD
	#333333 or #333 #E0E0E0

You can easily change the color of your font by changing the color property of the CSS selector you want to tweak. You can use hex codes to define the colors.

You can define the overall font color in your site by defining it in the body CSS selector like this:

```
body {
color: #333;
}
```

Font size

To tweak the size of your font, change the font-size property of the CSS selector you want to adjust. Font sizes are generally determined by units of measurement, as in these examples:

- **px:** Pixel measurement, or px; increasing or decreasing the number of pixels increases or decreases the font size (12px is larger than 10px).

- **pt:** Point measurement, or pt; as with pixels, increasing or decreasing the number of points affects the font size accordingly (12pt is larger than 10pt).

- **%:** Percentage measurement, or %; increasing or decreasing the percentage number affects the font size accordingly (50% is equivalent to 8 pixels; 100% is equivalent to 16 pixels).

In the default template CSS, the font size is defined in the body tag in pixels, like this:

```
font-size: 12px;
```

Putting it all together

Style the font for the overall body of your site by putting all three elements (font-family, color, and font-size) together in the <body> tag. Here's how they work together in the <body> tag of the default template CSS:

```
body {
font-size: 12px;
font-family: Georgia, "Bitstream Charter", serif;
color: #666;
}
```

Using borders in your design

CSS borders can add an interesting and unique flair to elements of your theme design. Table 14-7 illustrates common properties and CSS examples for borders in your theme design.

You can save lots of room by using the border shorthand in your CSS that defines the border size, style, and color all in one line, such as `border: 1px solid #CCCCCC`.

Table 14-7	Common Border Properties	
Border Properties	*Common Values*	*CSS Examples*
border-size	px, em	body {border-size: 1px;}
border-style	solid, dotted, dashed	body {border-style: solid}
border-color	Hexadecimal values	body {border-color: #CCCCCC}

Understanding Basic HTML Techniques to Use on Your Site

HTML can help you customize and organize your theme. To understand how HTML and CSS work together, think of it this way: If a website were a building, HTML would be the structure (the studs and foundation), and CSS would be the paint.

HTML contains the elements that CSS provides the styles for. All you have to do to apply a CSS style is use the right HTML element. Here is a very basic block of HTML that I can break down for this example:

```
<body>
<div id="content">
<h1>Headline Goes Here</h1>
<p>This is a sample sentence of body text. <blockquote>The journey of a thousand
          miles starts with the first step.</blockquote> I'm going to
          continue on this sentence and end it here. </p>
<p>Click <a href="http://lisasabin-wilson.com">here</a> to visit my website.</p>
</div>
</body>
```

All HTML elements must have opening and closing tags. Opening tags are contained in less-than (<) and greater-than (>) symbols. Closing tags are the same, except they're preceded by a forward slash (/).

For example:

```
<h1>Headline Goes Here</h1>
```

Note that the HTML elements must be properly nested. In line four of the previous example, a paragraph tag is opened (<p>). Later in that line, a block quote is opened (<blockquote>) and nested inside the paragraph tag. When editing this line, you can't end the paragraph (</p>) before you end the block quote (</blockquote>). Nested elements must close before the elements they're nested within close.

Finally, proper *tabbing,* or indenting, is important when writing HTML, mainly for readability so you can quickly scan through code to find what you're looking for. A good rule is that if you didn't close a tag in the line above, indent one tab over. This allows you to see where each element begins and ends. Tabbing can also be very helpful when diagnosing problems.

You'll use several very basic HTML markup practices over and over in web design. Earlier in this chapter, I discuss how to combine CSS styling with HTML markup to create different display styles (borders, fonts, and so on). The following sections provide you with commonly used HTML markup samples that are helpful as a reference for using HTML in your website code.

Inserting images

Many times, you'll want to insert an image in your website, whether within the body of a post or page, in the sidebar by using a widget, or within the template code itself. The HTML markup to insert an image looks like this:

```
<img src="/path/to/image-file.jpg" alt="Image File Name" />
```

I break down this code for you in easy snippets to help you understand what is at work here:

- **<img src=:** This is the HTML markup that tells the browser that the website is looking for an image file.

- **"/path/to/image-file.jpg":** This is the actual directory path where the web browser can find the image file. For example, if you upload an image to your web server in the /wp-content/uploads directory, the path for that image file would be /wp-content/uploads/image-file.jpg.

- **alt="Image File Name":** The alt tag is part of the HTML markup and provides a description for the image that search engines can pick up and recognize as keywords. The alt tag description will also appear as text on browsers that can't, for some reason, load the image file. For example, if the server load time is slow, the text description loads first to at least provide visitors with a description of what the image is.

- **/>:** This HTML markup tag closes the initial <img src=" tag, telling the web browser when the call to the image file is complete.

Inserting hyperlinks

Many times, you'll want to insert a link within the body of a website, commonly referred to as a *hyperlink*. This is a line of text that's anchored to a web address (URL) so that when visitors on your website click the text, it takes them to another website, or page, in their browser window. The HTML markup to insert a hyperlink looks like this:

```
<a href="http://wiley.com">Wiley</a>
```

To break down that markup, here's a simple explanation:

- **<a href=:** This is the HTML markup that tells the browser that the text within this tag should be hyperlinked to the web address provided in the next bullet point.

- **"http://wiley.com":** This is the URL that you want the text to be anchored to. The URL needs to be surrounded by quotes, which defines it as the intended anchor, or address.

- **">:** This markup closes the previously opened <a href= HTML tag.

- **Wiley:** In this example, this is the text that is linked, or anchored, by the URL. This text appears on your website and is clickable by your visitors.

- **</a>:** This HTML markup tag tells the web browser that the hyperlink is closed. Anything that exists between <a href="..."> and </a> will be hyperlinked, or clickable, through to the intended anchor, or web address.

Commonly, designers use URLs to link words to other websites or pages. However, you can also provide hyperlinks to PDF files (Adobe Acrobat), DOC files (Microsoft Word), or any other file type.

Inserting lists

You may need to provide a clean-looking format for lists that you publish on your website. With HTML markup, you can easily provide lists that are formatted differently, depending on your needs.

Ordered lists are numbered sequentially, such as a steps list of things to do, like this:

1. Write my book chapters.

2. Submit my book chapters to my publisher.

3. Panic a little when the book is released to the public.

4. Breathe a sigh of relief when reviews are overwhelmingly positive!

Ordered lists are easy to do in a program like Microsoft Word, or even in the WordPress post editor because you can use the What You See Is What You Get (WYSIWYG) editor to format the list for you. However, if you want to code an ordered list using HTML, it's a little different. My preceding steps list sample looks like this when using HTML markup:

```
<ol>
<li>Write my book chapters.</li>
<li>Submit my book chapters to my publisher.</li>
<li>Panic a little when the book is released to the public.</li>
<li>Breathe a sigh of relief when reviews are overwhelmingly positive!</li>
</ol>
```

The beginning `<ol>` tells a web browser to display this list as an ordered list, meaning that it will be ordered with numbers starting with the number 1. The entire list ends with the `</ol>` HTML tag, which tells the web browser that the ordered list is now complete.

Between `<ol>` and `</ol>` are list items designated as such by the HTML markup `<li>`. Each list item starts with `<li>` and ends with `</li>`, which tells the web browser to display the line of text as one list item.

If you fail to close any open HTML markup tags — for example, if you start an ordered list with `<ol>` but fail to include the closing `</ol>` at the end — it messes up the display on your website. The web browser considers anything beneath the initial `<ol>` to be part of the ordered list until it recognizes the closing tag `</ol>`.

Unordered lists are very similar to ordered lists, except instead of using numbers, they use bullet points to display the list, like this:

✐ Write my book chapters.

✐ Submit my book chapters to my publisher.

✐ Panic a little when the book is released to the public.

✐ Breathe a sigh of relief when reviews are overwhelmingly positive!

The HTML markup for an unordered list is just like the ordered list, except instead of using the `<ol>` tag, it uses the `<ul>` tag (*ul* stands for *unordered list*):

```
<ul>
<li>Write my book chapters.</li>
<li>Submit my book chapters to my publisher.</li>
<li>Panic a little when the book is released to the public.</li>
<li>Breathe a sigh of relief when reviews are overwhelmingly positive!</li>
</ul>
```

Both the ordered and unordered lists use the list item tags `<li>` and `</li>`. The only difference between the two lists is in the first opening and last closing tags. Ordered lists use `<ol>` and `</ol>`, whereas unordered lists use `<ul>` and `</ul>`.

15

Designing for WordPress as a CMS

s I note throughout this book, WordPress is not simply a blogging platform; it's also a solution for building your own website. The self-hosted version of WordPress, *WordPress.org,* is a powerful content management system that's flexible and extensible enough to run an entire website — with no blog at all, if you prefer.

A *content management system* (CMS) is a system used to create and maintain your entire site; it includes tools for publishing and editing, as well as for searching and retrieving information and content. A CMS lets you maintain your website with little or no HTML knowledge. You can create, modify, retrieve, and update your content without ever touching the code required to perform those tasks.

This chapter shows you a few ways that you can use the self-hosted WordPress.org software to power your entire website, with or without a blog. I cover various template configurations that you can use to create separate sections of your site. You also discover how to use the front page of your site as a static page or a *portal* — a page that contains snippets from other sections of your site, with links to those sections — which can include a link to an internal blog page, if you want a blog.

You can also add tools to your WordPress website that extend the basic functions of WordPress by adding elements such as an e-commerce store, photo galleries, social communities, and so on. Chapter 16 covers some of the tools you can add to WordPress to extend it to meet your needs, whereas this chapter shows you how to use internal, built-in features of WordPress to get started using it as a full-blown CMS tool.

Creating the Front Page of Your Website

For the most part, when you visit a blog powered by WordPress, the blog is on the main page. My personal blog (http://lisasabin-wilson.com), powered by WordPress (of course), shows my latest blog posts on the front page. This setup is typical of a site run by WordPress. See Figure 15-1.

But the front page of my business site (http://webdevstudios.com), also powered by WordPress, contains no blog; see Figure 15-2. This site doesn't display any blog posts; rather, it displays the contents of a *static page* — a page that's not dynamically updated chronologically like a blog — I created on the WordPress Dashboard. This static page serves as a portal to my design blog, my portfolio, and other sections of my site. The site includes a blog, but also serves as a full-blown business website, with all the sections I need to provide my clients with the information they want.

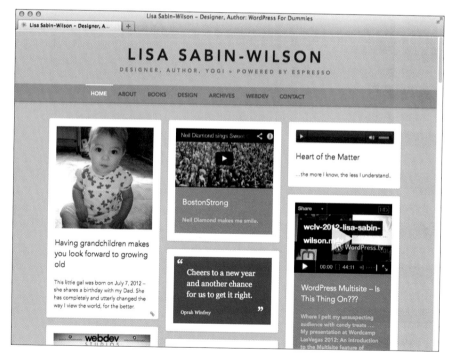

Figure 15-1: My personal blog, set up like a typical site powered by WordPress.

Figure 15-2: My business site, set up as a business website rather than a blog.

Both of my sites are powered by the self-hosted version of WordPress.org, so how can they differ so much in what they display on the front page? The answer lies in the templates on the WordPress Dashboard. (I discuss templates in detail in Part III of this book.)

You use static pages in WordPress to create content that you don't want to display as part of your blog but do want to display as part of your overall site (such as a bio page, a page of services, and so on).

Creating a front page is a three-step process:

1. Create a static page.
2. Designate that static page as the front page of your site.
3. Tweak the page to look like a website rather than a blog.

Using this method, you can create an unlimited number of static pages to build an entire website. You don't even need to have a blog on this site unless you want to include one.

Creating a static page

To have a static page appear on the front page of your site, you need to create that page. Follow these steps:

1. **From the Dashboard, choose Pages↪Add New.**

   The Add New Page screen opens where you can write a new page to your WordPress site, as shown in Figure 15-3.

2. **Type a title for the page toward the top.**

   For example, I want to create a Welcome page as the front page for my website, so I entered **Welcome to My Website** for the page title.

3. **Type the content of your page in the text box.**

   The content you include here is up to you. You can simply use text or a combination of text and images (see Chapter 16 for information on including images and photo galleries), and even a featured image if your theme is using that feature in WordPress (see Chapter 12).

Figure 15-3: Create the static page that you want to use as your front page.

4. In the Page Attributes section, set the options for this page, as needed:

- *Parent:* Leave this set to (No Parent) because this is the page you will use (in the next section) as the front page of your site. With other pages, you can set the page as a subpage, underneath a top-level, or *parent,* page to create a hierarchy of pages for your site navigation.

- *Template:* The Template option is set to Default Template. This setting tells WordPress that you want to use the default Page template (page.php in your theme template files) to format the page you're creating. The default template is the default setting for all pages you create. I discuss assigning a page to a different template in Chapter 12.

- *Order:* This is the order in which you'd like this page to appear in your navigation menu, if you are not using the built-in menu feature in WordPress (see Chapter 10) and are using the wp_list_pages() template tag (see Chapter 12).

5. (Optional) If you want to preview your page before publishing it, click the Preview button in the upper-right corner.

6. When you're satisfied with your page, click the Publish button.

The page is saved to your database and published to your WordPress site with its own individual URL (or *permalink,* as explained in Chapter 4). The URL for the static page consists of your website URL and the title of the page. For example, if you titled your page About Me, the URL of the page is http://yourdomain.com/about-me.

Assigning a static page as the front page

You need to tell WordPress that you want the static page you just created to serve as the front page of your site. To do so, follow these steps:

1. From the Dashboard, choose Settings⇨Reading.

The Reading Settings page appears.

2. In the Front Page Displays section, select the A Static Page radio button.

3. From the Front Page drop-down list, choose the static page that you want to serve as your front page.

In Figure 15-4, I choose to display the Welcome to My Website page from the preceding section. Don't worry about the rest of the options on the Reading Settings page because they don't pertain to configuring which page to use for the front page of your site.

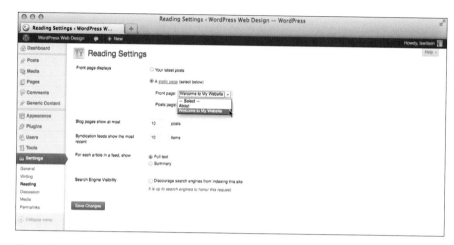

Figure 15-4: Choose which page to appear as the front page.

4. Click the Save Changes button at the bottom of page.

WordPress displays the page you selected in Step 3 as the front page of your site. Figure 15-5 shows my site displaying the page I created as my front page.

Figure 15-5: WordPress displays the page you selected as your front page.

Tweaking the page to look like a website rather than a blog

Using a static page as a front page allows you to get creative with the design and layout of your page. You can assign a page template (see "Creating Custom Page Templates to Achieve Different Layouts and Styles," later in this chapter) and/or use widgets to include different types of content and information, such as

- **Featured Images:** Chapter 12 covers how to add the built-in WordPress feature called Featured Images (or post thumbnails). You can create a page template that includes the titles and excerpts of your most recent blog posts (if you're using a blog) and display them in the body or sidebar with a featured image thumbnail. You use the WP_Query() class tag, covered in Chapter 12 and shown in the following code sample, which displays the four most recent posts from your blog:

```
<?php $the_query = new WP_Query('posts_per_page=4'); ?>
<?php while ($the_query->have_posts()) : $the_query->the_post(); ?>
<strong><a href="<?php the_permalink() ?>" rel="bookmark" title="Permanent
        Link to
<?php the_title_attribute(); ?>"><?php the_title(); ?></a></strong>
<?php if ( has_post_thumbnail() ) { the_post_thumbnail('thumbnail'); ?>
<?php the_excerpt(); ?>
<?php endwhile; ?>
```

- **Featured Content Slider:** Using a nifty plugin for WordPress called the Featured Content Slider (http://wordpress.org/extend/plugins/wp-featured-content-slider), you can include a slide show of your most recent posts (if you're using a blog) that contains featured images, excerpts of the text, and the title on your front page, which is a nice way to invite readers into your site to read the posts you've written. The Featured Content Slider provides you with an options page and widget to use on your front page. (See Chapter 12 for details about adding widget areas to your theme templates.)

- **Testimonials:** Many businesses like to include client testimonials on their websites, and one of the best places to display them is on your front page so that your visitors can immediately see quotes from your happy clients. You can display testimonials with a plugin for WordPress called IvyCat AJAX Testimonials (http://wordpress.org/plugins/ivycat-ajax-testimonials/); after you've installed this plugin (as described in Chapter 16), you can create testimonials and include them on your front page using a widget that the plugin provides. The plugin also allows you to create a full testimonials page to display all testimonials — be sure to read the plugin documentation to find out how.

- **Portfolio:** In the design field, you will most likely want to show off some of the work you've recently done for web design projects for yourself or your clients. On my business website at http://webdevstudios.com, we accomplish that through the use of WordPress custom post types, categories, featured images, and the WP_Query() template class. Create a category on your WordPress Dashboard (choose Posts⇨Categories) called *Portfolio* (or whatever you wish to call your body of work) and then create posts within the category, and be sure to assign featured images to the posts. (See Chapter 12 for more on adding support in your theme for featured images, including different image sizes.)

The featured images I use on my website are screenshots that represent the design work I've completed. I added a specific size for my images in the Theme Functions template called portfolio, and then using the WP_Query() template class, I inserted these lines of code in my home page template to display just the images (linked to the individual posts) in my portfolio:

```
<?php $the_query = new WP_Query('posts_per_page=3&category_name=portfolio);
        ?>
<?php while ($the_query->have_posts()) : $the_query->the_post(); ?>
<?php if (have_posts()) : while (have_posts()) : the_post(); ?>
<a href="<?php the_permalink() ?>" rel="bookmark" title="Permanent Link to
<?php the_title_attribute();?>">
<?php if ( has_post_thumbnail() ) { the_post_thumbnail('portfolio'); ?>
</a>
<?php endwhile; ?>
```

Adding a Blog to Your Website

If you want a blog on your site but don't want to display the blog on the front page, you can add one on your WordPress Dashboard.

Creating a blank page for the blog

To create a blog for your site, first you need to create a blank page:

1. **From the Dashboard, choose Pages⇨Add New.**

   The Add New Page screen appears (refer to Figure 15-3). This is the page where you can write a new post to your WordPress blog.

2. **Type a name for the page in the text box toward the top of the page.**

   For example, because this will be the main page for your blog, enter **Blog** for the name. This automatically sets the *page slug* to /blog. (See Chapter 4 for information on permalinks and slugs.)

3. **Leave the text box blank.**

You leave the text box blank here because you don't want to display any page content on your blog; rather, WordPress displays your blog posts using this page after you assign it as your blog (which you do in the steps in the next section).

4. **Click the Publish button.**

   The blank Blog page is saved to your database and published to your WordPress site.

   You have a blank page that redirects to `http://yourdomain.com/blog`.

Next, you need to assign the page you just created as your Blog page.

Assigning the new page as a blog

To designate your new, blank Blog page as a page for your blog posts, follow these steps:

1. **Choose Settings⇨Reading.**

   The Reading Settings page opens (refer to Figure 15-4).

2. **From the Posts Page drop-down list, choose the page you just created.**

   For example, select the Blog page as a posts page.

3. **In the Blog Pages Show at Most section, type the number of posts you want to display in the Posts text box.**

   This setting specifies the number of posts you want to appear on that page at any time. If you enter **5**, the Blog page shows the last five posts you've made to your blog. Enter the number of posts you would like to appear based on your preference.

4. **Click the Save Changes button.**

   The options you just set are saved, and your blog is now located at `http://yourdomain.com/blog` (where *yourdomain.com* is your actual domain name). Figure 15-6 shows the Blog page on my business site, `http://webdevstudios.com/blog`, which shows the most recent blog posts.

You can add a link to your blog in the navigation menu (as shown on my site in Figure 15-6) by adding it to your custom menu. To find out how to build your own custom menu, check out Chapter 10.

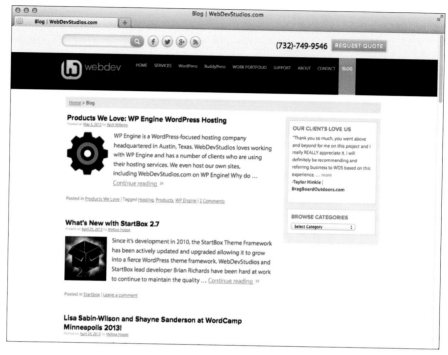

Figure 15-6: My blog at WebDevStudios with several posts displayed.

Creating Custom Page Templates to Achieve Different Layouts and Styles

In Chapter 12, I introduce you to using content-specific WordPress templates to apply different display views for content on your website. Using Page and Category templates, you can provide a different type of reader experience by defining the style with CSS and the features and functions with template tags.

You see this often on websites that offer more than simply a blog. Websites that sell products or services, or news websites that focus on articles, content, and advertising, use different page, or content, templates to achieve various layouts and styles all within the same website, using the tools WordPress gives them.

Viewing the default Page template (page.php)

Using my own business website as an example, you can see that the standard Page template (`page.php`) file displays regular static pages on my site in a two-column format. The content is on the left, and a sidebar is on the right of the About page at `http://webdevstudios.com/about`, as shown in Figure 15-7.

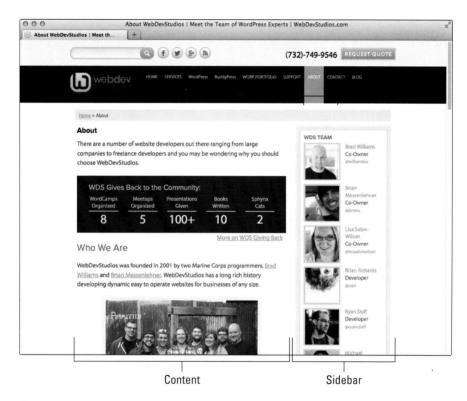

Figure 15-7: A standard two-column page layout.

The default Page template that creates the display in Figure 15-7 uses basic WordPress template tags to call in the header, content, sidebar, and footer files. The code within the template looks like Listing 15-1 in the `page.php` template file for my theme.

Listing 15-1:   Default Page Template (page.php)

```php
<?php get_header(); ?>
<div id="main">
<?php if (have_posts()) : while (have_posts()) : the_post(); ?>
<div id="post-<?php the_ID(); ?>" <?php post_class(); ?>>
<h3 class="title"><a href="<?php the_permalink() ?>" rel="bookmark"><?php the_
            title(); ?></a></h3>
<div class="entry">
<?php the_content(__('(more...)')); ?>
</div>
<?php endwhile; else: ?>
<p><?php _e('Sorry, no posts matched your criteria.'); ?></p>
<?php endif; ?>
</div>
</div>
<div id="side">
        <ul>
        <?php if ( !function_exists('dynamic_sidebar') || !dynamic_
            sidebar('Blog') ) : ?>
        <?php endif; ?>
        </ul>
<?php get_footer(); ?>
```

Creating a new category Page template

You can use the Page template (`page.php`) in Listing 15-1 to define the
layout and style for all the internal pages on your website, providing a standard and consistent style for your site visitors. However, if your website also
publishes a portfolio of work that you've done for clients, you probably want
that page to have a different style from the rest of the pages, mainly because
it presents images that represent your past work.

To accomplish this, create a Design Portfolio category on your site, and for
every entry you want to appear on the Portfolio page, create a post and assign
it to the Design Portfolio category. Figure 15-8 shows how my Portfolio page
appears in a web browser (`http://webdevstudios.com/work-portfolio`).
You can see that it's mainly made up of thumbnail images that are clickable
through to a full article providing a case study on the design project itself.

To accomplish this display, create a specific template for the Design Portfolio
category: `category-portfolio.php`. Every post you create that's assigned
to the Design Portfolio category appears in the format that you've defined in
the `category-design-portfolio.php` template in your theme folder.

If you want the Portfolio page to display a listing of images only, assign a featured image to each portfolio post, and then in the `category-portfolio.
php` template, do the following by using the code shown in Listing 15-2:

1. **Tell WordPress to display each post from the Design Portfolio category, but only display the featured image.**

2. **Link that featured image to the individual post page.**

The code to create the Design Portfolio display looks like Listing 15-2.

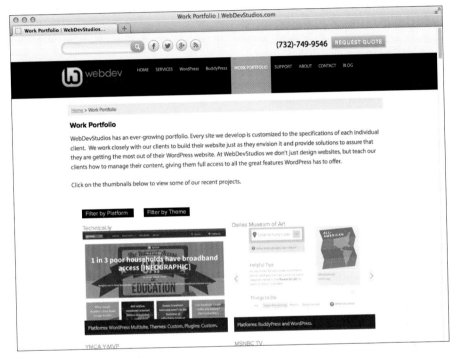

Figure 15-8: The Portfolio page layout at WebDevStudios.

Listing 15-2: Category Page Template (category-design-portfolio.php)

```php
<?php get_header(); ?>
<div id="main" class="fullwidth">
<?php if (have_posts()) : while (have_posts()) : the_post(); ?>
<div id="post-<?php the_ID(); ?>" <?php post_class(); ?>>
<div class="entry">
<a href="<?php the_permalink(); ?>"><?php the_post_thumbnail('thumbnail'); ?></a></div>
<?php endwhile; else: ?>
<p><?php _e('Sorry, no posts matched your criteria.'); ?></p>
<?php endif; ?>
</div>
</div>

<?php get_footer(); ?>
```

Comparing two Page templates

The differences between the default Page template (Listing 15-1) and the Category template (see Listing 15-2) are subtle and explained in Table 15-1.

Table 15-1 Differences between the Page and Category Templates		
Element	**In Page Template?**	**In Category Template?**
Call to the Header template `<?php get_header(); ?>`	Yes	Yes
Two-column layout	Yes. The `<div id="main">` styling is defined in CSS with a width: 600px.	No. The `<div id= "main" class= "fullwidth">` is defined in CSS with a width of 900px.
Call to the post/page title `<?php the_title(); ?>`	Yes	No
Call to the post/page content `<?php the_content(); ?>`	Yes	No
Call to the featured image `<?php the_post_ thumbnail(); ?>`	No	Yes
Call to the Sidebar template `<?php the_sidebar(); ?>`	Yes	No
Call to the Footer template `<?php the_footer(); ?>`	Yes	Yes

The differences between the standard, default page layout and the portfolio category page layout are but one example of the power behind the WordPress theme engine. The theme engine allows you to designate and define custom looks, layouts, and designs for different types of content. This feature helps you create unique websites for you and your clients and is the true power behind using WordPress as a CMS.

A lot of people still think of WordPress as simply a blogging platform where you can have and display a typical blog on your domain; however, with the example I just demonstrated, you can see how you can have a blog and so much more on your website with just a few simple tweaks and adjustments to the templates that power your website theme.

Creating Different Sidebar and Footer Templates for Your Pages

You can create separate Sidebar templates for different pages of your site by using a simple include statement. When you write an include statement, you're telling WordPress that you want it to include a specific file on a specific page.

The code that pulls the usual Sidebar template (sidebar.php) into all the other templates, such as the Main Index template (index.php), looks like this:

```
<?php get_sidebar(); ?>
```

What if you create a page and want to use a sidebar that has different information from what you have in the Sidebar template (sidebar.php)? Follow these steps:

1. **Create a new Sidebar template in a text editor, such as Notepad (Windows) or TextMate (Mac).**

2. **Save the file on your computer as sidebar-2.php.**

3. **Upload sidebar-page.php to your themes folder on your web server.**

   See Chapter 5 for more on transferring files with FTP.

   The new Sidebar template is listed in your theme files on the Edit Themes page. You can open this page by choosing Appearance⇨Editor on the Dashboard.

4. **To include the sidebar-page.php template in one of your Page templates, open the desired template on the Edit Themes page (Appearance⇨Editor) and then find this code:**

   ```
   <?php get_sidebar(); />
   ```

5. **Replace the preceding code with this include code:**

   ```
   <?php get_template_part('sidebar', 'page'); ?>
   ```

With the get_template_part(); function, you can include virtually any file in your WordPress templates. You can use this method to create Footer templates for pages on your site, for example. To do this, first create a new template with the filename footer-page.php and then locate the following code in your template:

```
<?php get_footer(); ?>
```

and replace the preceding code with this code:

```
<?php get_template_part('footer, 'page'); ?>
```

You can do multiple things with WordPress to extend it beyond the blog. This chapter gives you a few practical examples with the default Twenty Thirteen theme. The point is to show you how to use WordPress to create a fully functional website with a CMS platform — anything from the smallest personal site to a large business site. See Chapter 12 for a greater explanation of using template parts.

Creating Custom Styles for Sticky, Category, and Tag Posts

In Chapter 11, I discuss putting together a very basic WordPress theme, which includes a Main Index template using The Loop. You can use a custom tag to display custom styles for *sticky posts* (posts that stay at the top of your blog at all times), categories, and tags on your blog. That special tag looks like this:

```
<div <?php post_class() ?> id="post-<?php the_ID(); ?>">
```

The part of that template tag that is so cool is the `post_class()` section. This template tag tells WordPress to insert specific HTML markup in your template that allows you to use CSS to make custom styles for sticky posts, categories, and tags.

I mention at the very beginning of this book that I assume you already know how to use WordPress, which means you already know all about how to publish new posts to your blog, including the different options you can set for your blog posts, such as categories, tags, and publishing settings. One of the settings is the Stick This Post to the Front Page setting. In this section, I show you how to custom style those sticky posts — it's not as messy as it sounds!

For example, I've published a post with the following options set for it:

- ✔ Stick This Post to the Front Page
- ✔ Filed in a Category Called WordPress
- ✔ Tagged with News

By having the `post_class()` tag in your template, WordPress inserts HTML markup that allows you to use CSS to style sticky posts, or posts assigned to specific tags or categories, differently. WordPress inserted the following HTML markup for the post:

```
<div class="post sticky category-wordpress tag-news">
```

In Chapter 14, I talk about CSS selectors and HTML markup and how they work together to create style and format for your WordPress theme. You can go to your CSS file and define styles for the following CSS selectors:

- **.post:** Use this as the generic style for all posts on your blog. The CSS for this tag is

  ```
  .post {background: #ffffff; border: 1px solid silver; padding: 10px;}
  ```

  This style makes all posts have a white background with a thin silver border and 10 pixels of padding space between the post text and the border of the post.

- **.sticky:** The concept of sticking a post to your front page is to call attention to that post, so you may want to use different CSS styling to make it stand out from the rest of the posts on your blog:

  ```
  .sticky {background: #ffffff; border: 4px solid red; padding: 10px;}
  ```

  This creates a style for all sticky posts that consists of a white background, a thicker red border, and 10 pixels of padding space between the post text and border of the post.

- **.category-wordpress:** Say that you blog a lot about WordPress. Your readers may appreciate it if you give them a visual cue to which posts on your blog are about that topic. You can do that through CSS by telling WordPress to display a small WordPress icon on the top-right corner of all your posts in the WordPress category:

  ```
  .category-wordpress {background: url(wordpress-icon.jpg) top right
            no-repeat; height: 100px; width: 100px;}
  ```

  This code inserts a graphic — wordpress-icon.jpg — that's 100 pixels in height and 100 pixels in width at the top-right corner of every post you've assigned to the WordPress category on your blog.

- **.tag-news:** You can style all posts tagged with news the same way you've styled the categories:

  ```
  .tag-news {background: #f2f2f2; border: 1px solid black; padding: 10px;}
  ```

  This CSS styles all posts tagged with news with a light gray background and a thin black border with 10 pixels of padding between the post text and border of the post.

Using the post-class() tag, combined with CSS, to create dynamic styles for the posts on your blog is fun and easy!

16

Enhancing Your Website
with Plugins

In This Chapter

▶ Installing plugins on your WordPress website

▶ Exploring e-commerce options for WordPress

▶ Creating photo galleries and portfolios

▶ Providing web forms on your website

▶ Building networking and social communities

▶ Including popular social networks

*I*n the chapters leading up to this one, I demonstrate the features and functions that are built into the WordPress platform that you can use to create WordPress themes to provide an appealing visual layout and look for your WordPress website. However, several add-ons, or *plugins,* for WordPress provide solutions for specific needs, such as e-commerce (selling products), photo galleries and portfolios, web forms, social networking, and more.

Plugins exist for WordPress to provide solutions for needs that the majority of WordPress users don't have, so the good people at WordPress create them as optional, add-on plugins rather than make them part of the core WordPress package. That way, WordPress doesn't become a huge, unmanageable mess.

Several WordPress plugins are available to you for free from the WordPress Plugin Directory page at `http://wordpress.org/extend/plugins`, or you can search for and install plugins within the Dashboard. Other, more complex, plugins are available for a nominal cost from the developer; you pay a set price to download and use the plugin and to obtain support from the plugin author. In this chapter, I provide you with a mixture of free and commercial (paid) plugins that provide you with the solutions you need for different offerings on your website projects.

Installing WordPress Plugins via the Dashboard

This section walks you through the steps of searching for, downloading, installing, and activating free plugins in your WordPress Dashboard.

Finding free plugins

WordPress makes finding plugins on the Dashboard pretty easy. Choose Plugins⇨Add New to open the Install Plugins page, as shown in Figure 16-1. You have a number of selections, including the search box. Typing a term in this box and clicking the Search Plugins button searches WordPress for plugins that match the term.

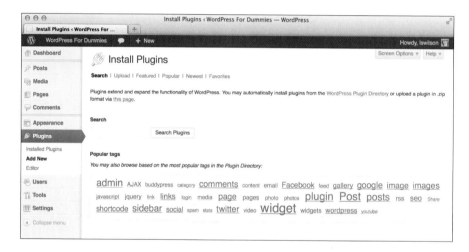

Figure 16-1: The Install Plugins page.

For example, I typed *All in One SEO* in the search box and then clicked the Search Plugins button. The Search Results tab, shown in Figure 16-2, appears.

At the top of the Install Plugins page, you find links for the following tabs:

- ✔ **Search:** On this tab, you can search for plugins within the repository. This view is the default (refer to Figure 16-1).

- ✔ **Search Results:** This tab appears after you have searched for a plugin using the search form. The tab displays the search results for your chosen keyword (see Figure 16-2).

- ✔ **Upload:** This tab provides you with a means to upload a plugin directly into WordPress.

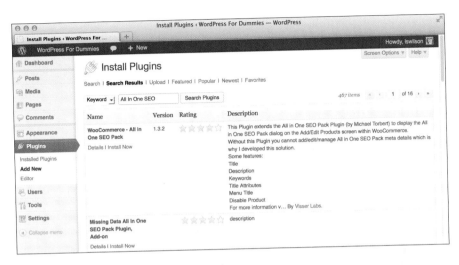

Figure 16-2: Plugins listed on the Install Plugins page.

✔ **Featured:** This tab displays a selection of plugins featured by WordPress as helpful plugins you may want to try.

✔ **Popular:** This tab shows the most popular plugins based on criteria selected by WordPress.

✔ **Newest:** This tab shows the most recently added plugins within the repository.

✔ **Favorites:** This tab shows the plugins you've favorited in the WordPress. org Plugins Directory.

Each of these tabs provides you with easy access to plugins that you may want to try without searching for them. Explore each of these tabs at your leisure; you may find some useful plugins this way.

At the bottom of the Install Plugins page is a selection of keywords (refer to Figure 16-1). When you click a keyword, WordPress displays all plugins tagged with that keyword. For example, clicking *gallery* shows all plugins tagged with that keyword, such as NextGen Gallery, a popular plugin. Use keywords to find popular plugins among WordPress users without searching by term or plugin name.

Installing and activating a plugin

After you find a plugin you like on the Dashboard, follow these steps to install it:

1. **On the Install Plugins page, click the Details link below the title of the plugin you want to install (refer to Figure 16-2).**

For this example, I clicked the Details link for the All in One SEO Pack plugin that I show you how to search for in the preceding section. The More Information dialog box, which provides a description of the plugin, appears with a number of tabs at the top, as shown in Figure 16-3.

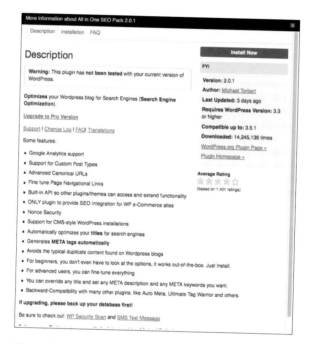

Figure 16-3: The More Information dialog box.

In Figure 16-3, you see the message `This plugin has not been tested with your current version of WordPress`, which is sometimes the case if the plugin author hasn't updated the plugin for the latest version of WordPress. You can choose to install it anyway and give it a try (and then uninstall it if you find that it doesn't work) — or try to contact the plugin author for information on whether the plugin works with the latest version.

2. **Click the Installation tab at the top of the dialog box to view the installation instructions.**

   Read the installation instructions before you proceed. Each plugin's installation and activation differ from the others.

3. **Click the Description tab and then click the Install Now button to install the plugin.**

The dialog box closes, and the Installing Plugin page appears, with a message stating whether your plugin was installed successfully, as shown in Figure 16-4.

4. Click the Activate Plugin link to activate the plugin on your website.

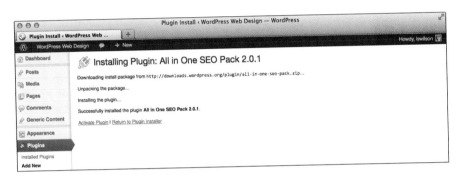

Figure 16-4: The Installing Plugin page.

If you see anything other than a message indicating success, follow the support instructions in the Plugin Information dialog box on the Description tab, including, possibly, the FAQ tab or Support link. Always note any error messages you see.

5. Choose Plugins⇨Plugins on the Dashboard to verify that the plugin installed successfully.

The plugin appears in the list on the Plugins page, as shown in Figure 16-5.

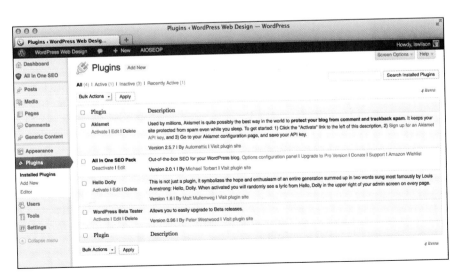

Figure 16-5: A list of installed plugins.

Installing Plugins Manually

Manually installing a plugin isn't as easy as the method I describe in the preceding section. However, you can use the preceding installation method only for free plugins from the Plugin Directory page within the Dashboard. Any commercial (or paid) plugins require that you install them manually via File Transfer Protocol, for example. (For more on FTP, see Chapter 5).

Follow these steps to install a plugin via FTP in your WordPress installation:

1. **Download the plugin from the source to your computer.**

   Commercial plugin developers provide you with links that you can click to download the plugin files — usually, in a Zip file.

   Throughout this chapter, I describe a number of commercial plugins that you may want to use on your site.

2. **After you download the plugin to your computer, if it's in a compressed Zip file, unzip it to access the uncompressed files.**

   If the file is zipped (compressed), use a free web application (such as WinZip, `www.winzip.com`) to unzip the plugin.

3. **Connect to your server using your preferred FTP application.**

   If you're not sure how to transfer files with FTP, see Chapter 5.

4. **Navigate to the `wp-content` folder within the WordPress installation for your website.**

5. **In the `wp-content` directory, find the `plugins` directory; upload your plugin to this location via FTP.**

   Congratulations — your plugin is installed, but you still need to activate it.

6. **Choose Plugins⇨Plugins on your Dashboard.**

   The Installing Plugin page appears.

7. **Click the Activate link that appears below the plugin's title.**

Some of the plugins I describe in this chapter are free ones that you can find on the Plugin Directory page, and others are commercial plugins that you have to download directly from the developers' websites. I indicate whether the plugin can be installed automatically within your Dashboard or needs to be installed manually through FTP.

Exploring E-Commerce Plugins to Use on Your Site

With a lot of businesses and individuals turning to the web to increase their profit margins or make a little money, e-commerce solutions have become a hot item in the WordPress world. WordPress already makes creating a website and publishing information easy — and some crafty and creative developers have designed easy-to-use plugins for WordPress that help people sell products on their websites.

Understanding what you can do with e-commerce plugins

E-commerce plugins add features to your WordPress installation that allow you to

- Create a dedicated store of product listings.
- Upload and display product images.
- Attach prices to each product.
- Provide inventory tracking.
- Include payment gateways, such as PayPal or Google Checkout, to make it easy for visitors to purchase items directly from your website.
- Configure sales tax and shipping rates.
- And more. . . .

Some examples of the types of products people use WordPress e-commerce plugins to sell are

- **Physical products:** Jewelry, clothing, or digital equipment
- **Downloadable products:** E-books or software, such as plugins
- **Memberships:** Clubs, societies, or members-only websites

Examining some recommended plugins

When I get a request from a client to build an e-commerce website using WordPress, I look at four plugins to provide the solution: Cart66, WooCommerce, WP e-Commerce, and Shopp. These four plugins all accomplish the task of building an e-commerce website, and each plugin differs in the way the store gets built. I don't have a preference of one over the other, and I usually stick with the platform I'm most comfortable with or the one I think may be easiest for my clients to use, depending on their skill levels.

Cart66

Cart66 (`http://cart66.com`) is an easy-to-use e-commerce solution that plugs into an existing WordPress theme with minimal tweaking required to get it to display correctly. You can sell physical or digital products, manage orders, sell subscriptions for members-only websites, and manage affiliates. This plugin isn't free; you must purchase and download it from the Cart66 website, and pricing starts at $89. The Cart66 plugin requires manual installation via FTP (see the section "Manually Installing Plugins," earlier in this chapter).

Figure 16-6 shows a jewelry website (http://halliefriedman.com) I created for a client with Cart66.

With Cart66, follow these steps to create a store:

1. **Install and activate the Cart66 plugin via FTP.**

2. **Configure the settings on the Cart66 Options page on your Dashboard (choose Cart66⟳Settings) for your preferred shipping, payment, and shop management.**

3. **Add products, including project images and prices, in the Products interface (choose Cart66⟳Products).**

4. **Create a new post or page in WordPress about your product.**

5. **Add the product info from the shop to your post by using the Add Product feature that Cart66 has added to the post editor.**

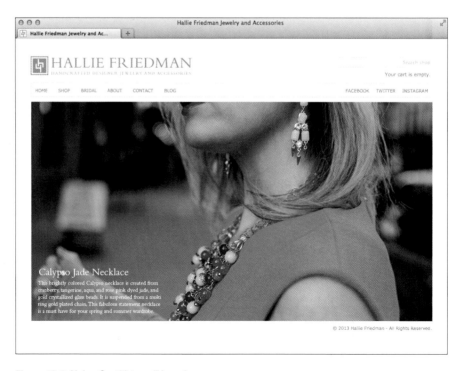

Figure 16-6: Using Cart66 to sell jewelry.

WooCommerce

The *WooCommerce* plugin (www.woothemes.com/woocommerce/) is a tool-kit for WordPress that helps you sell anything on your website. The primary WooCommerce plugin is free to download, and after you have it installed, you can browse a full selection of extensions to add specific features to the WooCommerce plugin, such as

- Accounting extensions
- Marketing extensions
- Payment gateway extensions
- Reporting extensions
- Shipping extensions

You can either download the WooCommerce plugin from the WooCommerce website or install it via the Plugins page on your WordPress Dashboard. The extensions, however, aren't free — they must be purchased and downloaded via the WooCommerce website.

This plugin works well with a *multisite setup* in WordPress (which allows multiple sites to be created in a single installation of WordPress) and with the BuddyPress social community plugin (which I cover later in this chapter). WooCommerce also makes it easy to spotlight different areas of your store, or individual products, with shop-specific widgets and short codes.

WP e-Commerce

The *WP e-Commerce* (www.instinct.co.nz/e-commerce) plugin is freely available on the Plugin Directory page at http://wordpress.org/extend/plugins/wp-e-commerce. You can use the free version to sell products, manage sales and inventory, and run a full shop on your website; however, *Instinct Entertainment,* the developers behind the plugin, also have commercial upgrades available for purchase in their shop at http://getshopped.org/extend/premium-upgrades. The upgrades address further needs, as described in the following list:

- **Gold Cart:** Extends the WP e-Commerce plugin by providing additional features, such as galleries, store searches, multiple image uploads, and additional payment gateway providers. Cost: $47.00.
- **Affiliate Plugin:** Helps manage affiliates for your product sales. Cost: $47.00.
- **DropShop:** Creates a beautiful drag-and-drop shopping interface where visitors can simply click and drag a product to the shopping cart for purchase. Cost: $117.00.

The WP e-Commerce plugin is a bit more challenging when integrating the shop and product pages into your existing WordPress theme, because it has its own set of templates that need to be configured and styled to coordinate well with your existing website design.

Figure 16-7 displays the dvDepot website (http://dvdepot.com), which sells DVD- and video-recording equipment via the WP e-Commerce plugin.

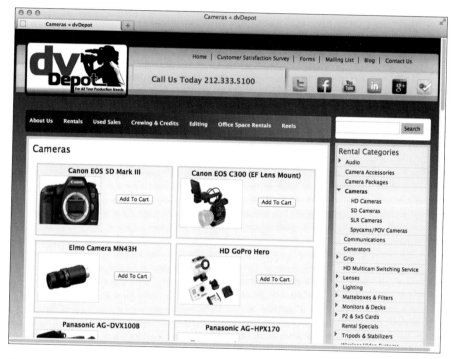

Figure 16-7: A site that uses the WP e-Commerce plugin.

Shopp

Shopp (http://shopplugin.net) adds a feature-rich online store to your WordPress website with the installation of its plugin. Shopp costs $55 for single-user access and $299 for developer access. Shopp also has several upgrades you can purchase for $25 each for various payment gateways, shipping add-ons, storage engine add-ons, and priority support credits.

The Shopp plugin website states that the plugin works out of the box with no theme adjustments necessary; however, in my experience, theme adjustments are required in most cases. Other features include

- Theme widgets for shop-related items, such as featured and random products and product categories
- Multiple product images

✔ Product categorization, allowing you to create multiple category levels for your products (as you'd do for your posts on a WordPress blog)

✔ Product searches

✔ And more . . .

Creating Photo Galleries or Portfolios

This section covers how to include photo galleries on your site, which are useful for anyone who needs to include a gallery or portfolio of visual design work, such as web designers and logo designers. I've even produced a few websites with galleries for bakeries whose owners want to display their cake decorations or chefs who want to display a photo gallery highlighting their yummy food creations!

You can display a photo gallery on your website in a couple ways. One way is to use the built-in gallery feature in WordPress. The other way is to use a robust photo gallery plugin that allows you to create albums with galleries, in case you need a more complex solution.

Inserting images into your page or post

Before you create a photo gallery with the built-in gallery feature in WordPress, you need to understand how to add images to a post or page you've created. Adding images to a post or page is pretty easy with the WordPress image uploader (via the Add an Image dialog box). You can add images in two ways: from a location on the web or from your computer.

Adding an image from a URL

Follow these steps to add an image to your page (or post) from a URL:

1. **From the Dashboard, choose Pages⇨Add New to add an image to your page. If you want to insert the image in a blog post, choose Posts⇨Add New.**

   The Add New Page page (or Add New Post page) appears.

2. **Click the Add Media button.**

   The Insert Media dialog box opens, enabling you to choose images from your hard drive or from a location on the web (see Figure 16-8).

3. **Click the Insert from URL link in the Insert Media dialog box.**

   The Insert from URL window opens.

Figure 16-8: The WordPress Insert Media dialog box.

4. Type the URL of the image in the text box.

Type the full URL, including the `http://` and `www.` portions of the address. You can find the URL of any image on the web by right-clicking (Windows) or Control-clicking (Mac) and then choosing Properties.

5. Type a title for the image in the Title text box, and then type a description of the image in the Alt Text text box.

The *alternative text* (or *ALT tags*) is what appears in a browser if, for some reason, the image doesn't load properly; it gives the visitor to your site a description of the image. Adding alternative text is also a good SEO (search engine optimization) practice because it gives the search engines, such as Google, additional descriptive text that helps them further categorize and define your site in their search engine listings and directories. (I discuss search engine optimization in more detail in Chapter 15.)

6. (Optional) Type the image caption in the Caption text box.

The words you type in the text box display as a caption below the image on your site. (WordPress automatically adds a class called `wp-caption` in the markup — you can use this class in the CSS to provide a style for the image captions on your site.)

7. **Choose an alignment option by selecting None, Left, Center, or Right.**

8. **Select the URL you want the image linked to.**

   Whatever option you choose determines where your readers go when they click the image you've uploaded:

   - *None:* Readers can't click the image.
   - *Image URL:* Readers can click through to the direct image itself.
   - *Custom URL:* Readers can click through to a URL you designate.

9. **Click the Insert into Page (or Insert into Post) button.**

   The HTML markup for the image is inserted into the body of your page or post.

Adding an image from your computer

To add an image from your own hard drive to your page or post, follow these steps:

1. **Follow Steps 1 and 2 in the preceding section.**

   The Insert Media dialog box appears (refer to Figure 16-8).

2. **In the Insert Media dialog box, click the Select Files button.**

   A dialog box opens from which you can select images from your hard drive.

3. **Select one or more images, and then click Open.**

   The images you select are uploaded from your computer to your web server. WordPress displays a progress bar during the upload and then displays the Image Options dialog box when the upload is finished.

4. **Edit the details of each image by clicking on the image thumbnail.**

   A box that contains several image options appears on the right side, as shown in Figure 16-9.

5. **Fill in the following information about each image:**

   - *Title:* Type a title for the image.
   - *Caption:* Type a caption (such as **This is a flower from my garden**) for the image.
   - *Alt Text:* Type the alternative text (as described in the preceding section) for the image.
   - *Description:* Type a description of the image.
   - *Alignment:* Choose None, Left, Center, or Right. (See Table 16-1, in the following section, for styling information regarding image alignment.)

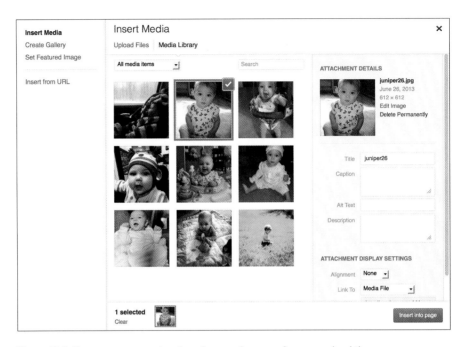

Figure 16-9: You can set several options for your images after you upload them.

- *Link To:* Type the URL you want the image linked to. Whatever option you choose determines where your readers go when they click the image you've uploaded: Click *None* to prevent the image from being clickable; *Media URL* to let readers click through to the direct image; *Attachment Page* to let readers click through to the post that the image appears in; and *Custom URL* to let them type their own URLs in the Custom URL text box.

- *Size:* Choose Thumbnail, Medium, Large, or Full Size.

WordPress automatically creates small- and medium-size versions of the images you upload through the built-in image uploader. A *thumbnail* is a smaller version of the original file. You can edit the size of the thumbnail by choosing Settings↪Media. In the Image Sizes section, designate the height and width of the small and medium thumbnail images generated by WordPress.

If you're uploading more than one image, skip the rest of the steps in this list and head to the "Inserting a photo gallery" section, later in this chapter.

6. **(Optional) Click the Edit Image link (to the right of the thumbnail of the image) to edit the appearance of each image.**

The Edit Media page appears, as shown in Figure 16-10.

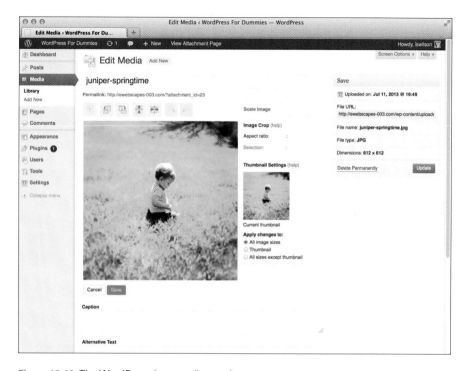

Figure 16-10: The WordPress image editor options.

These buttons are shown across the top of the image editor on the Edit Media page:

- *Crop:* Click this button to cut the image down to a smaller size.

- *Rotate Counter-Clockwise:* Click this button to rotate the image to the left.

- *Rotate Clockwise:* Click this button to rotate the image to the right.

- *Flip Vertically:* Click this button to flip the image upside down and back again.

- *Flip Horizontally:* Click this button to flip the image from right to left and back again.

- *Undo:* Click this button to undo any changes you've made.

- *Redo:* Click this button to redo image edits that you've undone.

- *Scale Image:* Click this button to open the drop-down menu that lets you set a specific width and height for the image.

7. **After you set the options for the image you've uploaded, click the Update button to save your changes.**

   You return to the Insert Media page.

8. **Click the Insert into Page button in the lower-right corner.**

In HTML view, you can see that WordPress has inserted the HTML code to display the image(s) on your page, as shown in Figure 16-11; you can continue editing your page, save it, or publish it.

To see the image and not the code, click the Visual tab that's just above the text box.

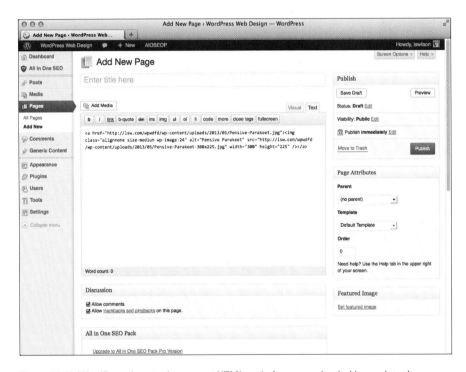

Figure 16-11: WordPress inserts the correct HTML code for your uploaded image into the page.

Adding image styles to your stylesheet

When you upload an image (as I describe in the previous sections of this chapter), you can set the alignment for the image as None, Left, Center, or Right. The WordPress theme you're using, however, may not have these alignment styles accounted for in its stylesheet. If you set the alignment to Left, for example, but the image on the page doesn't appear to be aligned, you may need to add a few styles to your theme's stylesheet.

I discuss themes and templates in great detail in Part III of this book. For the purposes of ensuring that you choose the correct alignment for your newly uploaded images, however, here's a quick-and-dirty method:

1. **From the Dashboard, choose Appearance⇨Editor.**

   The Edit Themes page opens. All the template files for your active theme are listed on the right side of the page.

2. **Click the Stylesheet template.**

   The Stylesheet (`style.css`) template opens in the text box in the center of the page.

3. **Add your desired styles to the stylesheet.**

   Table 16-1 shows the styles you can add to your stylesheet to ensure that image-alignment styling is present and accounted for in your theme. These styles are only examples of what you can do. Get creative with your styling. You can find more information in Chapter 14 about using Cascading Style Sheets (CSS) to add style to your theme.

Table 16-1	Styling Techniques for Image Alignment
Image Alignment	*Add This to Your Stylesheet (style.css)*
None	`img.alignnone {float:none; margin: 5px 0 5px 0;}`
Left	`img.alignleft {float:left; margin: 5px 10px 5px 0px;}`
Center	`img.aligncenter {display:block; float:none; margin: 5px auto;}`
Right	`img.alignright {float:right; margin: 5px 0 5px 10px;}`

Inserting a photo gallery

You can also use the WordPress Insert Media page to insert a full photo gallery into your pages (or posts). Follow these steps to insert a photo gallery into a page (or post):

1. **On the page (or post) in which you want to insert a gallery, upload your images by following the steps in the earlier section "Adding an image from a URL" or "Adding an image from your computer."**

2. **On the Add New Page (or Add New Post) page, click the Add Media button.**

   The Insert Media dialog box appears.

3. **Click the Create Gallery link on the left side of the Insert Media dialog box.**

   The Gallery tab appears only for posts or pages that have one or more images uploaded.

   This tab displays thumbnails of all the images you've uploaded for your page (or post). Figure 16-12 shows that I have six images uploaded and attached to the page.

Figure 16-12: The gallery of images within the Insert Media dialog box.

4. **Click the Create a New Gallery button.**

   This step opens the Edit Gallery page, where you can drag and drop the images to determine the order in which they should appear on your site.

5. **In the Gallery Settings section, set the display options for your gallery:**

   - *Link To:* Select Media File (the physical image file) or Attachment Page (a page that displays only the image itself).

   - *Random Order:* Select this option to make the images appear in random order.

   - *Columns:* Select how many columns of images you want to display in your gallery.

6. Click the Insert Gallery button at the bottom of the dialog box.

WordPress returns to the Add New Page (or Add New Post) page. You can see that WordPress has inserted into your page (or post) a piece of *short code* (a snippet of code that WordPress uses to execute certain functions, such as the gallery display) that looks like this:

```
[gallery]
```

Note: You have to switch to HTML view (click the HTML tab) to see this code.

Table 16-2 shows some gallery short codes that you can use to manually set the display settings for your photo gallery.

7. (Optional) In the Page (or Post) edit box in HTML view, you can change the order of appearance of the images in the gallery, as well as the markup (HTML tags or CSS selectors), by entering the following short code:

captiontag: Changes the markup that surrounds the image caption by altering the gallery short code. For example,

```
[gallery captiontag="div"]
```

places `<div></div>` tags around the image caption. (The `<div>` tag, which is considered a block-level element, creates a separate container for the content.)

To have the gallery appear on a line of its own, use the following code:

```
[gallery captiontag="p"]
```

This code places `<p class="gallery-caption"></p>` tags around the image caption. The default markup for the `captiontag` option is `dd`.

icontag: Defines the HTML markup around each individual thumbnail image in your gallery. Change the markup around the `icontag` (thumbnail icon) of the image by altering the gallery short code to look something like this:

```
[gallery icontag="p"]
```

This code places `<p class="gallery-icon"></p>` tags around each thumbnail icon. The default markup for `icontag` is `dt`.

itemtag: Defines the HTML markup around each item in your gallery. Change the markup around the `itemtag` (each item) in the gallery by altering the gallery short code to look something like this:

```
[gallery itemtag="span"]
```

This code places `<span class="gallery-item"></span>` tags around each item in the gallery. The default markup for the `itemtag` is `dl`.

orderby: Defines the order that the images display within your gallery. Change the order used to display the thumbnails in the gallery by altering the gallery short code to look something like this:

```
[gallery orderby="menu_order ASC"]
```

This code displays the thumbnails in ascending menu order. Another parameter you can use is `ID_order ASC`, which displays the thumbnails in ascending order according to their IDs.

8. **When you're finished, click the Preview button to preview your changes; when you're satisfied, click the Publish button to publish your page.**

Table 16-2 Gallery Short Code Examples

Gallery Short Code	Output
`[gallery columns="4" size="medium"]`	A four-column gallery containing medium-size images
`[gallery columns="10" id="215" size="thumbnail"]`	A ten-column gallery containing thumbnail images pulled from the blog post with the ID 215
`[gallery captiontag="p" icontag="span"]`	A three-column (default) gallery in which each image is surrounded by `<span></span>` tags and the image caption is surrounded by `<p></p>` tags

Follow these steps to edit the stylesheet for your theme to include the gallery styles in the CSS:

1. **From the Dashboard, choose Appearance➪Themes➪Editor and then open your CSS stylesheet.**

2. **Define the style of the `<span>` tags in your stylesheet.**

   The `<span>` tags create an inline element. An element contained within a `<span>` tag stays on the same line as the element before it; there's no line break. You need a little knowledge of CSS to alter the `<span>` tags. Here's an example of what you can add to the stylesheet (`style.css`) for your current theme to define the style of the `<span>` tags:

```
span.gallery-icon img {
padding: 3px;
background: white;
border: 1px solid black;
margin: 0 5px;
}
```

Placing this bit of CSS in the stylesheet (`style.css`) of your active theme automatically places a 1-pixel black border around each thumbnail, with 3 pixels of padding and a white background. The left and right margins are 5 pixels wide, creating nice spacing between images in the gallery. (See Chapter 14 for more on CSS.)

3. **Click the Update File button to save changes to your Stylesheet (`style.css`) template.**

Figure 16-13 shows a page with my photo gallery displayed, using the preceding steps and the CSS example in the default Twenty Thirteen theme. Here's the gallery short code that I used for the gallery shown in Figure 16-13:

```
[gallery icontag="span" size="thumbnail"]
```

Matt Mullenweg, a co-founder of the WordPress platform, created an extensive photo gallery by using the built-in gallery options in WordPress. Check out his fabulous photo gallery at `http://ma.tt/category/gallery`.

Some useful WordPress plugins work in tandem with the WordPress gallery feature. See the nearby sidebar, "WordPress gallery plugins."

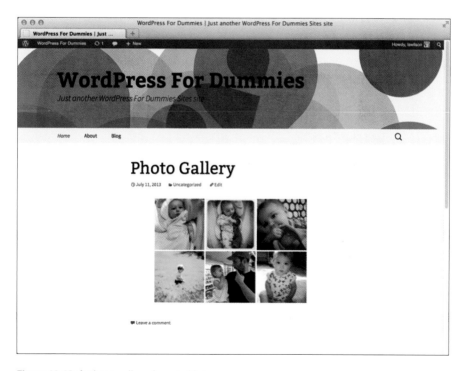

Figure 16-13: A photo gallery, inserted into my page.

WordPress gallery plugins

Here are a handful of helpful, free plugins that you can find on the WordPress Plugin Directory page and install automatically from within your Dashboard:

- ✔ **NextGEN Gallery:** This plugin creates sortable photo galleries and offers a display of random and recent thumbnail images in your sidebar through the use of widgets, and more. You can download it at `http://wordpress.org/extend/plugins/nextgen-gallery`.

- ✔ **Organizer:** Use this plugin to organize, rename, resize, and manage files in your image-upload folder. You can download it at `http://wordpress.org/extend/plugins/organizer`.

- ✔ **Random Image Widget:** This plugin lets you display a random image from your image-upload folder. You can download it at `http://wordpress.org/extend/plugins/random-image-widget`.

- ✔ **Mini-Slides:** Use this plugin to create inline slideshows from your uploaded images. You can download it at `http://wordpress.org/extend/plugins/mini-slides`.

Creating Web Forms for Your Site with Plugins

Some website owners need to provide a way for their visitors to contact them directly via e-mail. You don't want to publish your actual e-mail address on your website, because people run special programs — called *bots* or *spiders* — that travel around the Internet and collect published e-mail addresses. After these programs collect hundreds, thousands, or even millions of e-mail addresses, they create a database of user e-mail addresses and sell them to marketing companies. That's how a lot of people end up with gobs of spam in their inboxes!

If at all possible, never, ever publish your e-mail address directly on your website. Instead, use an easy form that your website visitors can fill out to e-mail you. Figure 16-14 shows an example of an e-mail contact form that I use on my personal website at `http://lisasabin-wilson.com/contact`.

Using this contact form on my website, visitors to my site can go to that page, fill out their information — including their names, e-mail addresses, subjects, and messages to me — and then click the Submit button. From there, their messages are delivered to my e-mail address. I can respond directly to messages while keeping all e-mail addresses private and away from the prying eyes of spam bots and spiders.

In the following sections, I describe some other types of forms you can create and recommend plugins you may want to use to create forms for your site.

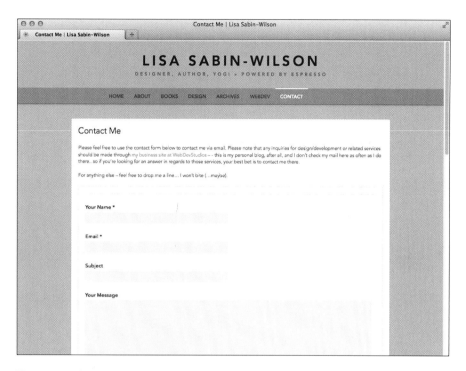

Figure 16-14: An e-mail contact form.

Exploring different types of forms you can use on your site

The e-mail contact form is a simple example of a form you can build and include on your WordPress website using the plugins that I list in the next section. However, you can build several other kinds of forms to help fulfill the individual needs of your website. Here are some examples of forms you can build and display on your website:

- ✔ **Order forms:** Collect the information you need from your customers by creating an order form with the necessary fields that they complete before sending the form to you. You can find an example of an order form I use on my business website at `http://webdevstudios.com/contact`. Potential clients who are interested in receiving project quotes from my company are asked to fill in different types of fields (such as their budget and site specifications) so that I can collect pertinent information about their needs.

- ✔ **Surveys:** Ask customers to review your product or services, or provide testimonials for your business.

✔ **Lead-generation forms:** Collect information on your readership and customer base. This form is the *opt-in* type (people fill it out only if they want to, so it's not considered spam), and it allows you to build a database of contacts to send updates and newsletters to.

Helpful plugins to create forms

I consider two plugins to be my go-to options when I need to create forms for my clients' websites: Contact Form 7 (available on the Plugin Directory page) and Gravity Forms (a commercial plugin).

Contact Form 7

The *Contact Form 7* plugin (`http://wordpress.org/extend/plugins/contact-form-7`) provides a quick-and-easy solution to include a simple e-mail contact form on your site. This plugin, freely available from the Plugin Directory page, can be installed from the Dashboard. To do so:

1. **Choose Plugins⇨Add New to go to the Install Plugins page in your Dashboard, and then type** Contact Form 7 **in the search box to find the plugin.**

2. **Follow the instructions in the section "Installing WordPress Plugins via the Dashboard," earlier in this chapter, to install and activate the plugin.**

   After the plugin is activated, the Contact menu item is added to the Dashboard menu.

3. **Click Contact to go to an option page where you can build the contact form and get the short code to add it to a page within your site.**

   Figure 16-15 shows you the Contact Form 7 page on the Dashboard, and you can find the short code to include in your page at the top:

   ```
   [contact-form 1 "Contact form 1"]
   ```

4. **Copy that short code, and then add it into any page where you want to display the contact form on your site.**

   You can even paste the code into a text widget to include the form in your sidebar.

Gravity Forms

Gravity Forms (`www.gravityforms.com`) is a commercially available plugin for WordPress that's much more robust than Contact Form 7 (described in the preceding section). If you need a more integrated solution with several tools to help you build different types of forms, get a more complex plugin like Gravity Forms. This plugin not only allows you to include a simple e-mail form but also provides additional features that make it a primary solution for many designers and developers.

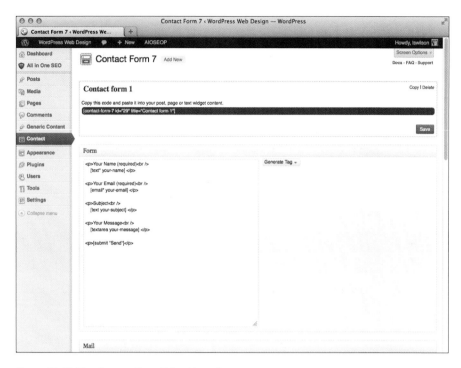

Figure 16-15: The Contact Form 7 Dashboard page.

This list describes some of the features of Gravity Forms:

- **An easy-to-use, click-and-add form builder** — no need to know, or even understand, any HTML, CSS, or PHP code. Figure 16-16 displays the Gravity Forms Editor page within my Dashboard (choose Forms⊅Edit Forms) on my personal site. The form fields are all ready for you to simply click and add to your new form — no HTML, PHP, or CSS required, because it's all done for you.

- **Multiple e-mail routing** that allows you to not only have the form results e-mailed to you but also designate multiple e-mail addresses that the form should be delivered to.

- **Conditional form fields** that allow you to build forms that are *intuitive*. You can show or hide a form field based on the value the user enters in previous fields within the form.

- **Form scheduling** that's helpful if you have a form you want to make available only during a certain, predefined period.

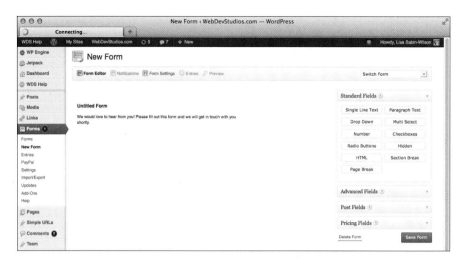

Figure 16-16: The Gravity Forms Editor page.

- ✔ **Form limits** that allow you to limit the number of times the form can be filled out before it's deactivated. This feature is helpful if you're running a time-sensitive contest, for example, where the first 25 people to fill out the form win a special prize. The form is then deactivated after it's been filled out by 25 people.

- ✔ **Dashboard management** that allows you to view and respond to the results of the form from a designated page within your WordPress Dashboard.

- ✔ **Easily embed a form within a page** (or post) on your website by using the Gravity Forms icon that's added to the Edit Page, and Edit Post, editors. Click the icon and choose the form you want to embed, and then WordPress enters the correct short code for the display of the form on your site.

- ✔ **Integration with** *MailChimp,* a popular provider for e-newsletters that many businesses and individuals use. Gravity Forms makes a MailChimp add-on available to allow your site visitors to easily subscribe to your e-newsletter when they fill out forms on your website.

Because Gravity Forms is a commercially available plugin, you download it from the Gravity Forms website and then manually install it on your WordPress site via FTP. (See the section "Manually Installing Plugins," earlier in this chapter.) You can purchase Gravity Forms from www.gravityforms. com; pricing starts at $39 for a single site license and increases to $199 for a developer license. The prices listed on the site are annual prices, so plan to pay the annual subscription to maintain your access to future upgrades and support from the Gravity Forms developers.

Building a Social Community with BuddyPress

The popularity of online social communities is undeniable. WordPress — the creator of the world's most popular blogging platform — is a great example of an online social community, allowing millions of users all over the globe to freely publish content on the Internet and invite others to join the discussion.

The *BuddyPress* plugin, introduced to the WordPress community in 2008, was the next logical step, enabling bloggers to expand their websites to include a social community for their visitors to participate in. BuddyPress can be installed and activated from within your WordPress Dashboard — just search for *BuddyPress* on the Install Plugins page (choose Plugins⇨Add New), and then install and activate it (see "Installing and activating a plugin," earlier in this chapter).

BuddyPress allows you to create a similar type of social community on your own WordPress-powered website, and it helps you take your existing website to the next level by allowing your visitors to become members. A BuddyPress social community gives its members a handful of core features that are easy to set up and allows them to immediately connect with other members of the community. Members can have extensive profiles that contain personal, biographical information that allows other members to find out more about them. Members share with other members any information they want, from personal information and news to website links, photos, videos, music, and more.

BuddyPress is an extensive suite of plugins that allows you to create the following features within your social community:

- **Extended member profiles:** Include shared personal information about each member of your community.
- **Member avatars:** Allow your members to upload unique, personal photos.
- **Member and site activity streams:** Provide a listing of member actions and activities throughout your community.
- **Activity wires:** Create a place where members can leave comments and messages for other members and groups in a public manner.
- **Member groups:** Let community members gather in groups based on topics and interests.
- **Member forums:** Let members create and participate in topic-related discussions with other members.
- **Blog tracking:** Provides a listing of blog activity throughout your community, including new blog posts and comments.
- **Searchable member, blog, and group directories:** Let you search member lists, group lists, and blogs to find specific information.
- **Member status updates:** Provide short but sweet updates about what members are doing now that they can share.

You may find that you don't want or need to use all the features that BuddyPress offers, and that's okay. You don't have to use them just because they exist. BuddyPress allows you to use only what you need — you can even delete extraneous features if you don't want to use them — enabling you to tailor your BuddyPress community to your liking.

If you want to take the interactivity on your website a few steps further, you can build a social community where visitors to your website can create a membership and become part of the content and conversation. In addition to leaving comments about articles, members can write their own articles, share more information, and participate in your site as a full contributor rather than just a visitor. Members can benefit from networking and connecting with other members within the community as well.

Here are a few examples of the types of communities I'm talking about, all built with the BuddyPress/WordPress platform:

- **Tasty Kitchen:** An active social community of members who like to cook, as shown in Figure 16-17 (`http://tastykitchen.com`)

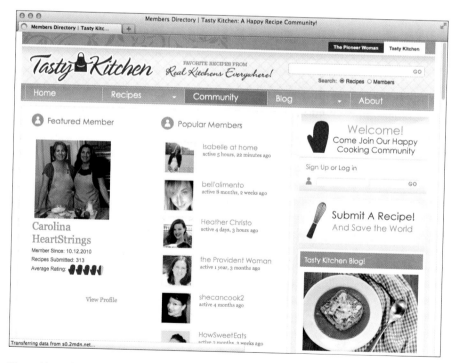

Figure 16-17: A WordPress site with a BuddyPress community.

- ✔ **GigaOM Pro:** A network of analysts providing technology-related research papers and notes (`http://pro.gigaom.com`)

- ✔ **TDI Truth & Dare:** By Volkswagen, a network of VW TDI drivers working to make a world-record mileage score (`http://tdi.vw.com`)

Whether your business is large or small, you can benefit from adding a social community component to your website by being able to invite your customers or prospects to participate in the discussion about their businesses.

If you're wondering whether the BuddyPress plugin is right for you, head over to the official BuddyPress Test Drive site at `http://testbp.org`. The site was put together by the BuddyPress developers for the sole purpose of giving people an opportunity to test-drive the features and components that are available in the BuddyPress plugin. Many times, when clients approach me and inquire about adding the BuddyPress plugin to their websites, I first send them to the BuddyPress Test Drive site to find out more about the plugin and to experience its features and components. After they've done all that, they can decide whether they want to use BuddyPress on their sites.

Using Plugins to Integrate Popular Social Networks with Your Blog

To continue the social community theme from the preceding section, this section introduces you to some great plugins that help you integrate your involvement in other social networks into your WordPress website. Having one website published on the Internet isn't enough: Many companies, individuals, celebrities, and news organizations are also involved in popular social networks, such as Twitter or Facebook, to increase their exposure and presence online.

I'll bet you have a profile page on at least one of these two social networks — am I right? There are several easy ways to integrate your social network membership into your WordPress website by using plugins that help your readers also connect with you on those networks. The two social networks I talk about in the following sections are the most popular: Twitter (`http://twitter.com`) and Facebook (`www.facebook.com`).

Integrating Twitter with Twitter Tools

An easy and effective way to integrate Twitter into your WordPress website is to connect your site to your Twitter account. That way, whenever you publish a new post on your website, the new post gets broadcasted to your

Twitter account to make it easy for your Twitter followers to click through and read it.

Twitter Tools, a plugin developed by Crowd Favorite, provides you with an easy interface to accomplish this task. Twitter Tools, freely available on the Plugin Directory page, can be installed and activated from your WordPress Dashboard (as I describe in the earlier section "Installing WordPress Plugins via the Dashboard").

After Twitter Tools is activated on your site, choose Settings⇨Twitter Tools from your Dashboard. The Twitter Tools Options page displays, and you can configure a few settings to get it connected to your Twitter account and working on your site.

Follow the directions on the Twitter Tools Options page to connect your WordPress website to your Twitter account, which involves registering your website on Twitter's application registration page. After you register your website with Twitter, you receive a Twitter consumer key, a consumer secret key, an access key, and an access token secret key to insert in the required fields on the Twitter Tools Options page.

After you complete the Twitter registration, the Twitter Tools Options page changes and provides you with a series of settings that you need to configure for your website. Here's what happens when you enable these settings:

- **Enable Option to Create a Tweet When You Publish a New Post on Your Blog:** Posts from your WordPress blog are published to your Twitter account.

- **Prefix for New Blog Posts on Twitter:** Set how your blog post titles are posted to your Twitter account. My blog post titles are prefixed with the text *New Post:* — you can configure it to say whatever you want.

- **Create a New Blog Post from Each of Your Tweets:** Your tweets are not only listed on your Twitter account but are also saved to your blog in the form of blog posts.

- **Create Tweets from Your Sidebar:** Your Twitter account is updated directly from your website.

Integrating Facebook with Wordbooker

Facebook is another social network where you interact with a group of friends and followers, so updating your Facebook Page with new posts from your blog is a great way to keep your Facebook friends up to date on the content you publish on your website.

Wordbooker, a nifty (and free!) plugin, provides you with an easy tool to publish posts from your blog to your Facebook profile page. Aside from sharing new blog posts on your Facebook profile, the Wordbooker plugin includes several other features to further integrate your website with your Facebook account; here are a few:

- **Facebook Like:** A Facebook Like button is inserted within every blog post on your site, allowing your readers to click it to publish on *their* Facebook Pages a blurb that they liked your post — bringing (you hope!) their friends to your website.

- **Include Faces:** For readers who like your post, their photos (or faces) display on your blog post to personalize it a bit for your readers.

- **Import Comments from Facebook:** When your blog post is published on your Facebook Page, your friends can leave comments on it in Facebook. Those comments are then imported into your post on your WordPress website — so that you have them visible in both places!

- **Push Comments to Facebook:** When people leave comments on the post on your website, those comments are then *pushed,* or published, into the comments area on your Facebook page.

- **Facebook Share:** A small button, visible within every post, allows visitors to your site to share your article on their Facebook Pages.

Part V
The Part of Tens

the
part of
tens

Discover ten great free themes that you can find in the WordPress Theme Directory and use on your website at www.dummies.com/extras/wordpress webdesign.

In this part . . .

- Discover ten fabulous WordPress plugins you can use to extend the features and functions of your WordPress website.

- Explore ten WordPress-powered sites and discover how they're effectively using WordPress as a content management system (CMS).

- Browse website examples that use techniques, features, functions, and plugins that you can read about throughout this book.

17

Ten Powerful Plugins for WordPress

In this chapter, I list ten of the most popular plugins available for your WordPress site. This list isn't exhaustive by any means; hundreds of excellent WordPress plugins can, and do, provide multiple ways to extend the functionality of your site. If these ten plugins aren't enough for you, you can find many more on the WordPress Plugin Directory page (http://wordpress.org/extend/plugins).

In Chapter 16, I explain how to install plugins, and I recommend some plugins you can use to extend the functionality and feature set of your site by creating e-commerce stores, photo galleries, social communities, and discussion forums. This chapter gives you ten plugins that should be present in almost every WordPress installation you do.

All in One SEO Pack

http://wordpress.org/extend/plugins/all-in-one-seo-pack

Almost every website owner is concerned about search engine optimization (SEO). Good SEO practices help the major search engines (Google, Yahoo!, and Bing) easily find and cache your site content in their search databases so that when people search using keywords, they can find your site in the search results. The All in One SEO Pack plugin helps you fine-tune your site to make that happen; it automatically creates optimized titles and generates HTML keywords for your individual posts and pages. If you're a beginner, this plugin works for you right out of the box with no advanced configuration. Woohoo! If you're an advanced user, you can fine-tune the All in One SEO settings to your liking.

BackupBuddy

```
http://ithemes.com/purchase/backupbuddy
```

Starting at $45 for the personal user and $197 for the entire development suite of plugins, the folks at PluginBuddy have hit a home run with BackupBuddy, which lets you back up your entire WordPress website in minutes.

With this plugin, you can also determine a schedule of automated backups of your site on a daily, weekly, monthly, and so on basis. You can store those backups on your web server, e-mail backups to a designated e-mail address, or store the backups in Amazon's Simple Storage Service, if you have an account there.

BackupBuddy backs up not only your WordPress data (posts, pages, comments, and so on) but also any theme and customized plugins you've installed (including all the settings for those plugins). It even saves and backs up all WordPress settings and any widgets that you're currently using. BackupBuddy also includes an import and migration script (`importbuddy.php`) that allows you to easily transfer an existing site to a new domain, or new host, within minutes.

This plugin is invaluable for designers and developers who work with clients to design websites with WordPress. In Chapter 8, I discuss how you can set up a development environment on your local computer to work on client sites.

WP-Print

```
http://wordpress.org/extend/plugins/wp-print
```

WP-Print is an easy-to-use plugin that provides a clean, printable version of your blog posts and pages. Unless your theme has a specialized stylesheet for printing, posts and pages print rather messily. WP-Print strips most of the style from your theme design (images and formatting, for example) and outputs a clean print of your article with black text on a white background.

You can configure these options for the plugin:

- **Print Text Link for Post:** This option configures a Print This Post link.
- **Print Text Link for Page:** This option configures a Print This Page link.

✔ **Print Icon:** Choose between two available icon designs: `print.gif` and `printer_fam fam fam.gif`. The icon you choose appears on your site.

✔ **Print Text Style Link:** This drop-down list presents settings for displaying the print link on your site.

✔ **Additional printing options:** You can specify whether comments, links, images, video, and disclaimer or copyright text prints.

WP-Print doesn't automatically appear on your site. You need to add a small snippet of code to your template in the area where you want the print link to appear with The Loop (see Chapter 11 for information about The Loop):

```php
<?php if(function_exists('wp_print')) { print_link(); } ?>
```

PluginBuddy Mobile

```
http://ithemes.com/purchase/mobile/
```

PluginBuddy Mobile is a premium WordPress plugin that starts at $45; however, it's worth every penny. This plugin adds a feature set and functionality to your website by creating a mobile-ready version that displays correctly in many major mobile web browsers, such as iPhone, BlackBerry, and Android devices.

PluginBuddy Mobile is easy to install and gives your website a professional mobile-ready theme within minutes. After you purchase and download the plugin, install it on your WordPress site (just like you would any WordPress plugin, as I discuss in Chapter 16). The primary features of PluginBuddy Mobile are:

✔ **Mobile Theme Style Manager:** Easily create and adjust your own mobile theme for the website you're building with WordPress.

✔ **Custom Header Uploader:** Include a header image that you designed to individualize your website's mobile theme.

✔ **Mobile Support for Multiple Platforms:** Assign different themes to different mobile platforms (iPhone, Blackberry, Android, and so on).

✔ **Mobile Starter Theme:** Three themes help get you started; you can use them as is or use the Mobile Theme Style Manager to customize them to suit your needs.

✔ **WordPress 3.0 Custom Navigation:** Supports the Custom Menu Navigation feature built in to WordPress (which I describe in detail in Chapter 10).

ShareThis

```
http://wordpress.org/extend/plugins/share-this
```

Every social media service has its own icon. People put these icons on their sites to let their visitors know that they can share the content with each social media service. This was a good concept when only a handful of services existed, but now there are dozens.

ShareThis allows visitors to share content through e-mail and popular social media services, such as Technorati, Delicious, and Digg. After you install the plugin, go to the Options page for ShareThis (choose Settings↷ShareThis) and set these options:

- ✔ **Enter the Widget Code:** Obtain the code from the ShareThis website (you can access this on the ShareThis website within your account); then enter the code into this text box.

- ✔ **Display the Link Only on Certain Pages of Your Site:** By default, the ShareThis link is added at the very end of your blog post and page. You can turn off this default option. To do so, choose No from the Automatically Add ShareThis to Your Posts and the Automatically Add ShareThis to Your Pages drop-down lists that appear on the ShareThis Options page. Then add the following ShareThis template tag to your template wherever you want it to display on your site (you can add it to any template in your WordPress theme):

```
<?php if (function_exists('sharethis_button')) { sharethis_button(); } ?>
```

This plugin requires the `wp-footer()` call in the footer (`footer.php`) of your template. If your theme doesn't include a `wp_footer()` call, you can add it easily by opening the `footer.php` template (see Chapter 11) and adding this bit of code:

```
<?php wp_footer(); ?>
```

Subscribe to Comments

```
http://wordpress.org/extend/plugins/subscribe-to-comments
```

The Subscribe to Comments plugin lets your visitors subscribe to individual posts you've made to your blog. They receive a notification via e-mail whenever someone leaves a new comment on the post. This feature goes a long way toward keeping your readers informed and making the discussions lively and active.

The plugin includes a full-featured Subscription Manager that your commenters can use to unsubscribe to certain posts, block all notifications, or even change their notification e-mail address.

WordPress.com Stats

```
http://wordpress.org/extend/plugins/stats
```

With the rise in popularity of the hosted WordPress.com service came a huge demand for the statistics that it provides in its Dashboard pages. Users of the self-hosted WordPress.org software drooled when they saw the stats available to WordPress.com users, and the cry for a similar stats plugin for WordPress.org went out across the blogosphere.

Andy Skelton answered that call with the release of the WordPress.com Stats plugin for WordPress.org users. This plugin collects all the important statistics, including the number of hits on the site per hour, day, or month; the most popular posts; the sources of the traffic on the site; and the links people click to leave the site.

You need a WordPress.com API key for this plugin to work. You can obtain an API key by creating an account on WordPress.com (`http://wordpress.com`); you get an API key in your Personal Profile there. Simply copy it and paste it into the API field under Plugins⇨WordPress.com after you activate the plugin. After you do that, a link called Blog Stats appears on the Dashboard menu, and you can click that link to view your site stats on your Dashboard.

WP Security Scan

```
http://wordpress.org/extend/plugins/wp-security-scan
```

This plugin is relatively simple to use; it scans your entire WordPress installation and looks for any security vulnerabilities that may exist and then suggests corrective actions that you can take to improve the overall security of your WordPress installation.

WP Super Cache

```
http://wordpress.org/extend/plugins/wp-super-cache
```

WP Super Cache creates static HTML files from your dynamic WordPress content. Why is this useful? On a high-traffic site, having cached versions of your posts and pages can speed up the load time of your website considerably. A *cached* version simply means that the content is converted to static HTML pages (as opposed to dynamically created content pulled from your database through a series of PHP commands) that are then stored on the server. This process eases the efforts the web server must take to display the content in your visitors' browsers.

WPMU Premium

```
http://premium.wpmudev.org
```

WPMU Premium isn't just one plugin; it's an entire collection of plugins that are geared toward and developed for users who take advantage of the multisite feature with WordPress, as well as the users who have developed a social community website by using the BuddyPress plugin for WordPress (covered in Chapter 16).

You can find all sorts of plugins to enhance your multisite and/or BuddyPress website. Here are just a few:

- **Membership plugins** that give you membership and affiliate capabilities on your network

- **Classified ad plugins** that allow you to grow a classified ads section

- **Chat plugins** that let you include interactive, real-time chat capabilities for your users to communicate with one another

- **Domain mapping plugins** that let you (and your community users) use your own domain on your network of sites

- **Anti-spam plugins** that prevent spam comments and spam sign-ups in your community

Access to the plugins at WPMU Premium isn't free. There is a nominal fee to join, and you can choose among annual membership packages from $35 to $79 per month, which gives you access to more than 100 plugins (and more than 150 themes) along with some stellar, world-class support.

18

Ten Well-Designed Sites That Use WordPress as a CMS

In This Chapter

▶ Seeing examples of how WordPress powers websites

▶ Discovering sites that use WordPress for more than just blogging

A tremendous number of well-designed WordPress sites are on the web. Picking only ten to highlight here was a near-impossible task for me. Sometimes, you can look at a website and not even know whether it's a blog or a site built with blogging software. Because users can extend the WordPress software to function as so much more than just a blog, people refer to WordPress as a content management system (CMS) rather than merely a blogging platform. (See Chapter 15 for more on WordPress as a CMS.)

In this chapter, I try to represent the types of websites built with the tools and techniques that I cover earlier in this book. So here you are: Ten sites that go beyond the blog.

IconDock

http://icondock.com

IconDock, created by the folks from N.Design Studio, is a perfect example of using WordPress as an online shop. IconDock has a fully functional and easy-to-navigate e-commerce shop where visitors can purchase high-quality icons and graphics. IconDock uses the WP e-Commerce plugin and the DropShop commercial add-on plugin to create the drag-and-drop shop feature for its products.

If you can take away one good idea from IconDock, it's the site's smart use of the WP e-Commerce plugin to power its online shop. You can install this plugin (www.instinct.co.nz/e-commerce) on any WordPress-powered website, and you immediately have a state-of-the-art e-commerce platform that allows you to host a full-featured shopping cart. Very professional! The possibilities of this plugin are endless. (See Chapter 16 for more on this plugin.)

Kate Rusby

www.katerusby.com

Kate Rusby (see Figure 18-1) is a folk musician whose website is powered by WordPress. The first thing that caught my eye is the pleasant, whimsical graphic design work that's been applied to her WordPress theme. Through stunning graphic work, creative CSS styling, and HTML markup, her website design is clean, professional, and very eye pleasing.

Figure 18-1: The Kate Rusby site.

Kate's website displays different types of content offerings on her website in a unique way that makes it easy for visitors to locate and consume. For examples, check out the following:

✔ **Audio recordings:** www.katerusby.com/recordings

✔ **Tour dates:** www.katerusby.com/tour-dates

✔ **Photo galleries:** www.katerusby.com/gallery

Katy Perry

www.katyperry.com/home

The website for recording artist Katy Perry uses WordPress to showcase her message, music, and content offerings in a nicely designed package.

A lot is going on with Katy Perry's website, but it's a clean design that's easy to navigate and includes some great features, such as

✔ The latest tweets from Katy's Twitter account

✔ A Breaking News section on the front page that pulls content from her internal blog

✔ Blog posts that integrate social media sharing tools for Facebook, Twitter, and so on

✔ Feeds on her front page from her online merchandise store, ticket sales, and tour dates

✔ A music section that contains her entire discography, including album images, embedded audio files, and Buy Now buttons that allow you to purchase songs from iTunes

✔ A photo gallery that contains feeds from Katy's Flickr account and integrates social media sharing for each photo

LIVESTRONG

http://livestrongblog.org

The official blog of the LIVESTRONG Foundation is a well-designed WordPress theme that places the blog content on the front page but also uses some interesting tools to provide additional content from some of the foundation's other websites. For example, in the right sidebar, you find great information and navigation links for its cancer support resource page on the web and its Team LIVESTRONG page about walks, runs, and triathlons to help raise awareness and money for cancer research.

In addition to integrating content from its several sites, the LIVESTRONG blog also participates in a lot of social media and integrates it nicely on its website via

- ✔ YouTube video sharing
- ✔ Twitter feeds
- ✔ Flickr photo sharing
- ✔ Facebook Connect
- ✔ Social media sharing tools

Mozilla Labs

```
http://mozillalabs.com
```

Mozilla Labs is an online hub where developers can network, collaborate, develop, experiment, research, and learn about building web applications. Built on the WordPress platform, Mozilla Labs takes advantage of custom category templates to create different types of content displays for each of the unique sections of its Projects page at `http://mozillalabs.com/projects`.

On the Projects page are more than 50 projects, both active and inactive, listed with well-designed icons and descriptions. Click a project, and you're taken to that project's page, which is either a static page or a category within WordPress. Each project page has a unique design that sets it apart from the rest of the pages within the site but is still branded with the Mozilla Labs look and feel.

In Chapters 12 and 15, I discuss content-specific templates that include static page and category templates.

MSNBC

```
http://tv.msnbc.com
```

The MSNBC website (see Figure 18-2) runs on the WordPress platform to present content for this online news network. MSNBC makes heavy use of the custom post types feature in WordPress (see Chapter 14) to organize the different television news shows presented.

Aside from the content aspects on MSNBC, the site also takes full advantage of built-in WordPress features, such as featured images to display photos for each news story, embedded videos with a dedicated video gallery, customized use of the WordPress navigation menu navigation feature, widgets, and social media sharing and integration.

Figure 18-2: The MSNBC website.

Time Healthland

```
http://healthland.time.com
```

The folks at *Time* must really, really like WordPress. Not only is the Healthland website fully powered by WordPress, but it's also one of the VIP WordPress customers that takes advantage of the VIP offerings from *Automattic* (`http://vip.wordpress.com/hosting`), the folks behind the WordPress.com service.

To go even further than that, the Time Healthland website is a child theme that uses the default Twenty Ten WordPress theme as the parent. (In Chapter 13, I show you how to create a child theme for the Twenty Thirteen theme.) The website was developed by the WordPress VIP consultants, WebDevStudios (see the section "WebDevStudios," later in this chapter).

Time Healthland is a great example of a WordPress-powered website that goes beyond the typical blog type layout by getting creative with

✔ **Post thumbnails:** Post thumbnails add a nice visual component to blog posts. (See Chapter 12 for more on this feature.)

✔ **Popular posts:** Listing the most popular blog posts (usually determined by the posts with the greatest number of views and/or comments) provides a nice navigation piece for new as well as returning visitors.

✔ **Posts by category:** Using the `query_posts()`; function (described in Chapter 12), this feature groups posts together nicely by topic.

✔ **Social media integration:** The site uses Twitter and Facebook integration through different tools and plugins, providing seamless sharing between website and social media.

WebDevStudios

http://webdevstudios.com

WebDevStudios is the website of the VIP WordPress consultants who designed and developed the Time Healthland and MSNBC sites (described earlier in this chapter), in addition to being the studio co-owned by yours truly. The WebDevStudios site is also a pretty stunning example (in my humble opinion) of what you can do with the Twenty Ten WordPress theme. (See Chapter 13 to find out how to create a child theme using Twenty Thirteen as the parent.)

Some of the features and design elements that really stick out as I browse through the website include

✔ **The navigation menu:** Just one look at its navigation menu isn't enough. Hover your mouse over some of the links to see the hard work that went into building a rich navigation experience for visitors. The menu is enormous, yet very clean, easy to read, and easy to navigate.

✔ **A featured content slide show:** At the top of the front page, underneath the logo and menu, WebDevStudios displays some of its more prominent content wrapped in a dynamic slide show via the WP Nivo Slider plugin, which you can find in the Plugin Directory at http://wordpress.org/extend/plugins/wp-nivo-slider. This slide show brings your most treasured content front and center to share with your visitors.

✔ **Social media integration:** WebDevStudios integrates its Twitter account prominently by posting its most recent tweets from the WebDevStudios Twitter page. Additionally, you can easily find WebDevStudios on other social networks, such as Facebook and Flickr, through the use of social media icons found firmly planted at the top middle section of every page of the website.

✔ **A static front page with internal blog:** One of the techniques I discuss in this book is using a static page as the front page of your website and including a blog as part of an internal section, rather than the main page. Check out WebDevStudios site for a solid example of this technique in practice.

WeGraphics

`http://wegraphics.net`

WeGraphics (see Figure 18-3) is an e-commerce shop, powered by WordPress and the Cart66 shopping cart plugin (described in Chapter 16), that sells digital or downloadable products. One visit to this website shows how WordPress and an e-commerce plugin, combined with a beautiful design and layout, can provide you with a pretty fantastic storefront online.

Figure 18-3: The WeGraphics site.

The navigation is very user-friendly, starting with easy-to-read product categories, with coordinating and designated icons to set the product selections apart. At WeGraphics, you can purchase one product at a time or purchase a membership subscription that allows you to download several products during a given timeframe.

Another reason why I include WeGraphics here is the high-quality graphic products it offers that benefit any budding web designer:

- Photoshop brushes
- Icon sets
- Texture files
- Vector graphics
- Theme designs

WordPress.org

`http://wordpress.org`

What else other than the official WordPress website? The site at `http://wordpress.org` is home to the WordPress software, itself. The front page is a static page with a custom page template that serves as a portal into the offerings of the rest of the site.

At WordPress.org, you will find

- **A gallery of websites in the Showcase:** The showcase at `http://wordpress.org/showcase` displays images of websites powered by WordPress.

- **Themes and Plugin directories:** You find a directory of all the themes and plugins available for the WordPress platform at `http://wordpress.org/extend/themes` and `http://wordpress.org/extend/plugins`.

- **Support forums:** The WordPress forums at (`http://wordpress.org/support/`) — powered by the bbPress plugin (`http://wordpress.org/extend/plugins/bbpress/`) — enable users to create their own discussion forums on their WordPress website.

- **Blog:** The blog at `http://wordpress.org/news` gives the latest updates and blog entries about the WordPress project.

- **WordPress software download:** The WordPress.org website houses the official WordPress code base that you can download and use on your own site to run your own fantastic, WordPress-powered website!

Index

About the Author

Lisa Sabin-Wilson has worked with the WordPress software since its inception in 2003 and has built her career around providing technical support, hosting, and design solutions for bloggers who use WordPress. She reaches thousands of people worldwide with her WordPress services, skills, and knowledge regarding the product. Lisa is also the author of the bestselling *WordPress For Dummies, BuddyPress For Dummies,* and *WordPress All-in-One For Dummies*.

Lisa operates a few blogs online, all of which are powered by WordPress. Her personal blog (`http://lisasabin-wilson.com`) has been online since February 2002; she and her partners, Brad Williams and Brian Messenlehner, at the custom WordPress design and development business at WebDevStudios (`http://webdevstudios.com`) provide custom development and design services.

When she can be persuaded away from her computer, where she is usually hard at work providing design solutions for her WordPress clients, she sometimes emerges for public speaking appearances on the topics of design, blogging, and WordPress. She has appeared at conferences such as the annual South By Southwest Interactive Conference, Blog World Expo, CMSExpo, and several WordCamp events across the country.

Lisa consults with bloggers both large and small. Bloggers come in many different flavors, from business to personal, from creative to technical, and all points in between. Lisa is connected to thousands of them worldwide and appreciates the opportunity to share her knowledge with *WordPress Web Design For Dummies.* She hopes you find great value in it, as well!

When not designing or consulting with her clients, you can usually find her at her favorite coffee shop sipping espresso, or on a mountaintop somewhere hitting the slopes with her family, or 100 feet beneath the ocean waters, scuba diving with her husband and swimming with the fishes.

You can find Lisa online at Twitter: `@LisaSabinWilson`.

Dedication

To the man who probably never thought he would ever have a tech book dedicated to him, my father, Donald Sabin. I have only ever wanted him to be proud of me, but so much more than that, I wanted him to be proud of himself for the man and father he was. By daily example, Dad taught me the lesson of unconditional love and the importance of family.

Author's Acknowledgments

To WordPress . . . and all that entails from the developers, designers, forum helpers, bug testers, educators, consultants, plugin makers, and theme bakers. Every single person involved in the WordPress community plays a vital role in making this whole thing work, and work well. Kudos to all of you!

Huge thanks to Amy Fandrei, Kim Darosett, and Amanda Graham from Wiley for their support, assistance, and guidance during the course of this project. Many thanks, as well, to my technical editor, Mitch Canter, and the other editors of the project who also worked hard to ensure its success.

To my family and close friends whom I may have neglected during the process of writing this book, thank you for not abandoning me — your support sustains me!

Finally, tremendous thanks to my husband, Chris, for his unending support and love and for having the patience of a saint during the course of writing this book!

Publisher's Acknowledgments

Acquisitions Editor: Amy Fandrei

Senior Project Editor: Kim Darosett

Copy Editor: Amanda Graham

Technical Editor: Mitch Canter

Editorial Assistant: Annie Sullivan

Sr. Editorial Assistant: Cherie Case

Cover images: Icons ©iStockphoto.com/ Aaltazar; laptop ©iStockphoto.com/ 4x-image; website screenshot courtesy of Lisa Sabin-Wilson